Right your RESUME

Fix or create your resume content so you stand out and impress the **Hiring Manager**

CHAR MESAN

Right your RESUME

First published in 2015
© 2015 Char Mesan

All rights reserved
No part of this publication may be reproduced, in whole or in part, in any form or by any means electronic or mechanical, including photocopying, recording, or by any information storage and retrieval system now known or hereafter invented, without written permission from the copyright holder. The Australian Copyright Act 1968 (the Act) allows a maximum of one chapter or 10 per cent of this book, whichever is the greater, to be photocopied by any educational institution for its educational purposes provided that the educational institution (or body that administers it) has given a remuneration notice to Copyright Agency Limited (CAL) under the Act.

Char Mesan Enterprises
Penrith NSW 2750
Australia
ABN 51 087 646 671

http://rightyourresume.blogspot.com.au

National Library of Australia
Cataloguing-in-Publication entry:
Mesan, Char
Right Your Resume

ISBN 13: 978-0-9942137-0-9

Notice of Liability
The author and publisher have made every attempt to provide the reader with accurate, timely, and useful information. The information presented is for reference purposes only. While every precaution has been taken in the preparation of this book, the author and publisher make no claims that using this information will guarantee the reader success and neither the author nor publisher shall have any liability to any person or entity with respect to any liability, loss, or damage caused or alleged to be caused directly or indirectly by the instructions contained in this book or by the computer software products described herein.

Book Interior:	Char Mesan
Cover Design:	Char Mesan
	Gareth Quinlivan
Proofreaders:	Samantha Lee
	Josephine Walker
	Ian Macpherson

10 9 8 7 6 5 4 3 2 1

Dedication

Cheers to picking up a pen; learning to write and type; discovering whims and passions; knowing strengths and abilities; keeping dreams close to one's heart; bravely leaping into decisive action; not foolishly succumbing to fears, doubts, criticisms or procrastination; enthusiastically learning new things, especially computer programs; gaining new experiences and brag-worthy moments; and, having exceptionally *awesome* family.

Acknowledgements

No book is possible without the assistance of other people, so I need to thank everyone who contributed either directly or indirectly to its creation. For I could not have completed this massive undertaking without all your help and support.

Thank you, family, friends and those who assisted – in particular Manwhore, Bubbygirl, Miss Independence, Daddikins and Motherdear. Your contributions, no matter how large or small, is immensely appreciated; as you helped turn crazy-wild Charmiesque ideas and plans into unbelievable, awesome reality.

Thank you to Samantha Lee and Josephine Walker for their proofreading assistance and editorial advice.

And great thanks must also go to Ian Macpherson for reviving and encouraging 'Figjam' moments.

Special mention and thanks to covercritics.com, specifically to those who provided me with such pleasant and insightful, well-considered feedback for the book cover: Nathan, Sirona, gp, AJ, Ron Miller, Axolotl, Bruce Fottler, Bonnie Farante, and Adrian. The cover is so much the better because of you.

To all jobseekers I have ever worked with in the past: without you, I may never have learned as much about resumes and jobsearch as I did, and this book might never have eventuated.

Thank you to every jobseeker who purchases this book and clients I am yet to meet: I hope you will find this book an invaluable resource that benefits you not only now but well into the future also. And, I hope your jobsearch success is to such an improved extent that you care to celebrate your pleasant surprises and hard-fought wins with me!

Oh, and my thanks to J.K. Rowling, because 'Help IS always given to those who ask for it, at Hogwarts" – *and* at home.

Right Your RESUME

Quote

"Do something today that your future self will thank you for."
@Inspire_Us

Preface

How would you feel if you clicked the APPLY button for a job you would most like to get and then have your phone ring less than fifteen minutes later. On the other end of the line, a hiring manager keen to invite you to come in for an interview?

You'd be shocked yet delighted, wouldn't you? Phone calls like that would lift your spirits and energy levels. You'd be left feeling that you are doing more things right than wrong within your jobsearch. And, because you would feel your jobsearch is going so well, you'd also gain a general sense of inner peace and experience less stress about any dire money and bill situations which may have been plaguing you for a while now.

The strong return on your extra-effort investment would naturally cause you to want to keep the high momentum going with every other job you apply to, in case this particular position isn't right for you. But no need to worry about all that right now, you have a job interview! If this *is* the position you are most keen on, at first you'd hardly be able to contain your excitement enough to undertake thorough preparations to see you nailing the interview – so you get the job. But, you have time to calm down and get your head together.

Only something really negative would take that beautiful smile off your face, wouldn't it!

The first time I received a phone call approximately fifteen minutes after I hit the APPLY button, a number of years ago sent me into that state of pleasant shock, for *days*.

I've since had this quick response occur more than once to now to consider getting such quick phone calls – especially those received on the same day as hitting the apply button – a resounding success. Especially when the call is received an hour, or few later.

And I still bask in the enjoyment of the whole experience. I'm just no longer shocked when it occurs.

I understand how rare, precious and enviable those quick invitations may seem to jobseekers who haven't had this happen to them. But, I'm not alone in having this type of jobsearch success as 'the normal' now, rather than as 'one-off' exceptions. I've learned of family, friends and former colleagues

Right Your RESUME

experiencing similar super-quick responses for applications they have sent off too, to know it doesn't just happen to me and them.

It can happen for you too. I have no hesitation is saying that.

Last week this wonderful situation occurred for one of my clients, who I had written her resume from scratch. Except this time my client received her call less than an hour after she had hit the APPLY button for a job in a capacity and industry that she had *never worked in* before.

That fast phone call was super-exciting for both of us.

I had honestly expected her to get invited to an interview. We had both felt her resume was a 'winner' as soon as we had a final draft. I simply hadn't imagined that her application would tip her over into the 'contact urgently' side quite so much as it did. In hindsight, I can see why it had done so. But at the time, we could only *hope* that might be the case.

If your application is just right – that is, if it ticks all the mental check boxes for the person making the culling decisions – you too can be the candidate that gets such a delightfully quick response.

And if you aren't yet experiencing them, don't be discouraged. Instead, see it as an indication that you need to make changes to your jobsearch materials, is all; whatever and however many changes that are required.

But even when calls inviting you to attend an interview don't happen quite so quickly as I've described, the very act in stepping your jobsearch tools up a notch – to get your resume doing more of what works and less of what doesn't – can greatly shift your jobsearch from frustration and lack of results, to heading in the right direction and achieving a faster successful outcome for yourself.

This book aims to try to help you reach getting a moment or two (or more!) to feel like *you've* just won the jobsearch lottery – so you too can experience those highs and pleasantness. But, you'll need to be super-keen to impress and excite a hiring manager.

If you aren't prepared to put in some quality time into writing or righting your resume content, then you may as well stop reading this book right now. That's right; you can stop and put the book back. Maybe even return it for a refund. Because, if you aren't ready to learn (and use) good communication techniques in your resume then this book isn't the right one for you. And therefore is simply a waste of both your time and money to buy or read this book.

If you are super-keen to learn what you need to do, then first read on and second **take action** to right your resume content from what you learn herein. I aim to teach you what to do and how to do it, and will endeavour to assist you make important content decisions along the way.

If you follow through to take the needed action and implement the advice and suggestions given – because not everyone that reads quality advice will follow through on it – this book will push you to tap into the minds of the hiring managers for the type of work you seek to gain. And it will urge you to use the wording and placement of content so that it convinces that hiring manager to view you as *potentially suitable*, regardless what that type or level of work you seek is. Enough for them to become greatly impressed by your application, excited and motivated to learn more about you as a person and as a potential candidate.

So impressed and keen to learn more about you that they just have to pick up the phone and call you to arrange a good time to meet *immediately;* scared that the best applicant they've received will apply to other jobs and be snapped up by a rival company if *they* don't take action NOW.

Char Mesan

Right Your RESUME

About the author

Hello and thank you for purchasing *Right Your Resume: Fix or Create your Resume Content so you Stand Out and Impress the Hiring Manager.*

For readers who do not know anything about me, have not read my blog articles or seen my posts and updates in any of the Jobsearch Facebook Groups I regularly participate in, hello, my name is Char Mesan. I live in the outer western suburbs of Sydney, Australia in the Nepean / Blue Mountains region and work as an independent resume writer and jobsearch trainer. I enjoy helping people gain suitable, meaningful work – whether that help is my creating resumes from scratch, assessing existing ones to see what can be righted to improve results, or else providing personalised jobsearch or computer advice and coaching.

I have a number of formal qualifications in employment, business, administration, customer service and computers (Certificate III to Diploma's – seven in total, plus eligibility to apply for Recognition of Prior Learning for two more certificates), which when combined with my professional history in word processing, communication, administration, writing, self employment and various job roles within the Employment Service industry (including jobsearch trainer, employment consultant case manager, marketer, post placement support and office coordinator) enables me to successfully write and assess resumes and cover letters for a living. And provide you with quality, specific, effective professional resume and jobsearch advice.

To be honest, I don't know how many resumes I have worked on over the past ten years, but it must be in the high hundreds – maybe even low thousands by now. Unfortunately I never counted them. Whatever the actual number though, clients have consistently provided feedback that they like and are 'delighted' with the resume I wrote or repaired, and always express gratitude 'for the invaluable advice' I've given them.

Of the clients I've assisted that genuinely wanted to work and to find it quickly (those not being fussy or at all choosy about roles and offers, for whatever reason), they generally gained work within three months from me handing the completed resume over to them. (Though, I am no longer surprised by how picky and choosy some clients are, even those who are supposedly 'desperate' for a position, compared to what I used to be when I first started out in this line of work).

Right Your RESUME

It is my eighteen months plus experience as the dreaded Hiring Manager, culling bulk numbers of applications down to a small shortlist, which should be of greatest interest and will benefit readers the most. Because I've worked from both the application making *and* the hiring decision sides.

You see, in one of my former employment services roles, the agency I worked for had a dedicated fax-printer machine set up to receive applications from the multiple different job vacancies we were concurrently filling. That fax printer machine was arguably the busiest and most over-worked team member in our entire office, as we went through about two reams of paper per weekday just receiving resumes and cover letters. One after the other, with barely a break in between.

Our Sales team members were the staff that met with employers to obtain job vacancies from across all industries, and if our agency didn't have a suitable unemployed person on our rather sizeable case load, then the Sales team put up a job advertisement on a free online job board so our agency could still try to fill the vacancy with an unemployed persons perhaps assigned to one of our competitors' caseloads. We might be able to talk such jobseekers into transferring to our agency (or we couldn't place them in the role otherwise), and if they were happy to do so (not all were), the whole situation became a winning one: for the employer, the jobseeker and our agency.

My role in all this was to perform the initial cull of the large piles of resumes for each of the vacancies and get that pile down from the hundreds received to just three (or less) suitable candidates; and then pass only whichever resumes were deemed worthy of further review to the Site Manager. At any given time, our agency usually had about fifteen vacancies externally advertised all going at once. So I not only had to work out which job each candidate was applying for, I also had to review the resume and any cover letters or fax cover sheets to then decide which applications would progress to further consideration by the management team, or not.

Once I had rejected the majority of applications, the agency site manager, and oftentimes the sales rep team members, then reviewed and further considered whichever resumes I had passed on – if I had indeed passed any on. (Sometimes, through necessity, I rejected every application received, to the praise and thanks of the others!) We valued only introducing the Best-of-the-Best applicants to our employers – so those employers would use our agency again next time they needed staff. If an application didn't show the person as being **high quality** and if they didn't fit the brief, I rejected the application **immediately** and without **any** hesitations. If I didn't do it, the management team would have rejected it anyway.

Right Your RESUME

Once I had handed over the best candidate's applications (if there were any decent ones), the manager and sales team then made the subsequent hiring decisions during our daily Sales team meetings, such as deciding whether to call that person in for an interview, or dismiss their application for additional reasons. Usually, the jobseekers that passed those more scrutinising reviews were then handed to the sales team member managing the vacancy to run the remainder of the hiring process. The Sales Rep then invited the person to attend our office for a preliminary interview with them, and if the person passed that preliminary interview, the Rep then arranged for the applicant to meet with their employer and perhaps coached them on how to answer questions during the employer interview.

If the person was from another agency, they were advised about the employment opportunity being exclusive to clients assigned to our agency, and generally transfer paperwork was only completed after the employer wanted to offer them the role.

Before the Sales Reps took suitable candidates out to meet with the employer at an agreed date and time, the Sales Reps often handed the applicants resume back to me with request I improve the content and presentation, and so that our agency had an electronic version.

In short, I might not have decided who was ultimately offered the job, but as all applications were initially assessed by me, I directly decided which candidates were (and weren't) interviewed, making me the person jobseekers had to impress and convince first and foremost; as well as being the person that improved the content, wording and presentation of resumes, to minimise employers rejecting those candidates who were presented to them.

Although I'm no longer in that particular job, I've continued to apply the skills, knowledge and experiences gained from this role in each position I've held since. And I know I have directly contributed towards many jobseekers gaining jobs because of my unique skill set.

When I first started in that role I imagined, like you might, that the culling task would be rather difficult because of the high responsibility in regards to deciding people's futures. But it turned out to be one of the easiest parts of the role instead – because jobseekers made it so *easy* for me to reject their application! Hardly any application ever stood out to impress me. And if I wasn't impressed (and I'm a fairly easy-going person), neither would my manager, the sales team members, or the employer be.

By the time I reached one month in the role, I had developed the skill to be able to take one glance at the application and know if the person would be

Right Your RESUME

suitable or not. The words didn't even have time to come into focus, I already knew.

Now, I am right handed, and a fairly neat worker. The culling task was only one of my *many* responsibilities within that role. I was usually so busy with everything else (especially the Accounts and getting invoices paid on time, and managing the cash we held on site with which to purchase employment related products and services for qualifying jobseekers who couldn't afford to buy the product or service their own self), that I often did the sorting and culling of resumes in batches. I often left the task for Friday's if I could, because that was my quietest day and the team generally tried to make Thursday the advertisement's closing date, so that everything was finalised and ready the following Monday for their to proceed to the next stage.

As an organised person, who frequently had to switch tasks mid-task to complete something more urgent, I'm naturally inclined to keep everything I still need to do in neat piles off to my right (where it is easier for me to retrieve when needed) and to file everything that is not important or is to be stored away or binned off to my left (so it is out of the way until I could do so).

Because of this, when I reviewed resumes most candidates ended up in a pile off to my left – *my rejection pile* – and the handful that I wanted to take a closer, second look at or immediately thought the manager and sales team would be most interested in, I automatically put onto a pile created off to my right (which also happened to be the most convenient spot in that role for staff to come and pick things up from my desk when I was busy on the phone (which I almost always was)).

Actually, it was my doing that – placing 'right' resumes in the right pile – that helped me title this book.

I want **you** to write a resume that is right in the view of the hiring manager so that it is placed in the right hand pile (the 'still in contention' one, whether the particular hiring manager creates their piles to the left, right, middle or anywhere else). And, if you have a resume that has been failing you, then you can right (as in, correct) it, so you change your results around towards increased success and less rejection.

My goal in writing this book was to mostly help mainstream jobseekers who struggle with **what to write**; that is, school leavers looking to gain their first job, long term unemployed who may or may not have barriers to overcome, parents and carers returning to the paid workforce after a number of years being at home caring for the kids or other loved one, or for a person with a disability, health condition or injury needing an employer to overlook their disability-barrier.

Because these are the jobseekers who I know *need* my assistance most. But, I aim to keep the advice as relevant and appropriate to all jobseekers, industries and position levels as I can make it so as not to exclude anyone that needs resume writing help.

So that is a little bit about me, and why I feel I have the right skills, knowledge, experience – and even expertise – to help you with getting your resume right.

Now, let's start on fixing or creating your resume content so you stand out to make a ***good*** impression!

Right Your RESUME

Right Your RESUME

Table of CONTENTS

Acknowledgements	v
Preface	vi
About the Author	x
Part 1 – Before we start righting	1 - 40
01. Before you start	3
02. Note for non-Australian readers	5
03. Special terminology used	7
04. There are jobs out there	11
05. Quality over quantity	12
06. Keep the position firmly in mind	15
07. Don't fix what isn't broken	16
08. Kill your darlings	17
09. Think 'position specific' if you don't get 'targeted'	18
10. No more one-size-fits-all resumes, please	20
11. Standing out from the crowd	22
12. A brief overview of recruitment	24
13. The different types of resumes	27
14. Resume length	33
15. The prime resume real estate area	37

Righting or Writing your Resume – Sections

Part 2 – Personal Details	41 - 80
16. Personal Details section	45
17. Name	49
18. Contact details	54
19. Optional details	64
20. What personal details to exclude	68
Part 3 – Summarised Information sections	81 - 182
21. Summarised information (overview)	83
22. Career Objective	86
23. Career Snapshot	94
24. Skills Summary	99
25. Personal Attributes	105

Right Your RESUME

Table of CONTENTS (continued)

26. Area of Expertise — 112
27. Licences, Tickets and Checks — 115
28. Training, Education and Qualifications — 122
29. Tools of the trade — 136
30. Computers, technology and social media savviness — 139
31. Hobbies and personal interests — 144
32. Achievements and Awards — 150
33. Referees and References — 157

Part 4 – Employment and Development History — 183 - 246
34. Employment and Development History — 185

Part 5 - Finetuning Your Resume — 247 - 266
35. Consistency — 249
36. Tense — 249
37. Wording — 250
38. Positivity — 251
39. Numbers — 251
40. Priority of information — 252
41. Get your spelling, punctuation and grammar right, and proofread before sending out! — 253
42. Photos, pictures and other such fancinesses — 261
43. Leave out the labels — 263
44. Saving your resume — 264

Part 6 - Appendix — 267 - 274
Action Words — 268
Thank You — 271
Connect with Char — 272
Leave a Review — 274
Bonus information — 274

Before we start righting

Part 1.

Right Your RESUME

Quote

"When you know, and you are aware that you know, confidence can replace fear."
Unknown

Part 1
Before We Start RIGHTING

01 Before we start

Whether you are currently unemployed, or employed and looking to change jobs or gain a second one, the chances are you are going to need a resume.

I've found that most jobseekers already have a resume (and know what they are). But, in the absence of knowing how to create a good one, they use samples or templates they find, which often aren't very effective in progressing the jobseekers applications forward within the hiring process; because templates don't teach you how to write the content. They only help you present what you've written. And, if what you've written isn't top-notch, then your entire application becomes less effective than it could be. .

Poor resumes – the ones I received the most of – frequently used bland, uninspired language, and unintentionally emitted a message that the person applying is '*average, ordinary,* and *nothing special.*' The focus was all about the candidate – what they've done in the past and what they want and need in the future. And there was little to nothing specific to the job applied to, the employer or key details the decision makers are looking for.

When it comes to jobsearching, I think you'll agree that you don't ever want to be viewed as average, ordinary, and nothing special – the opposite to what you hope to achieve when you send off an application – because that is the fastest track to Rejectionville.

Quality resumes on the other hand, are the ones that get the hiring manager paying increasingly closer attention while the person reviews the resume. They cause the reader to mentally picture the applicant within the role and to like what they imagine to then urgently pick up the phone to get the person in for an interview. The application achieves a positive response because the applicant has put greater focus on the wants and needs of the job and the business. In other words, although the details contained in the resume come from the person, that person's focus is on the employer and role and leaves out what they – person behind the resume – is after.

Candidates with quality resumes stand out in a good, non-gimmicky way because they are rare (well, for some types of jobs any way). They set themselves apart from their competition as a person 'above-average, extraordinary, and indeed special' because they successfully demonstrate their suitability on paper, against a stack doing the very opposite.

Right Your RESUME

I'm sure many a jobseeker will be able to successfully argue that they have secured a job previously without the use of a resume, and I agree this does happen. But in Australia this is *rare*. Even when the employer or recruiting agency is internet savvy, most employers seeking staff still advertise in some way – whether that is in the more traditional newspapers or online job boards, or their using modern approaches like tweeting about it, and posting the opportunity to their Facebook page, website and other online accounts. The instructions usually state, even when a vacancy is found from within the hidden job market, *'email your resume to...'*

In parts 2, 3 and 4 of this book, we will discuss the format (the types of resumes) and the wording (what to say and how to say it) of resume content. But we will not deal as much with the final stage of presenting the content (the design and styling of elements) because that information is too lengthy to fit inside this book and will therefore need a book of its own (which I may write in the future).

For now, there are a few 'big picture' things I feel you **need** to know before we dive into the nitty-gritty 'smaller picture' aspects to righting or writing the content.

Part 1
Before We Start RIGHTING

02 Note for non-Australian readers

1.

This book uses **Australian English** spelling, grammar and punctuation (except when typographic errors and authorial weaknesses have been overlooked during the editorial stages – hopefully of which there are minimal, thanks to my wonderful team). The book follows guidelines recommended in Style Manual, Sixth edition and uses the Macquarie dictionary spellings. As such, if you detect errors, please take our conventional differences into consideration before providing feedback regarding what may first look like misspelled words and incorrect use of grammar and punctuation when compared against your own countries conventions.

If a detected mistake is genuine though, I encourage and welcome you to please provide feedback so that we can enter corrections for future editions.

2.

I have tried to make the advice and suggestions contained herein as universally relevant and appropriate as possible while remaining true to what I know works in and readily applies to creating a resume that is effective within the *Australian* job market. Because that is where I have gained and use my experience, but understand readers may reside elsewhere throughout the world. (A big shout out, 'Hello! And thanks for purchasing!')

Therefore, jobseekers living or applying for positions in *other countries* may need to undertake additional jobsearch and resume writing research to best enable them to decide whether to follow some or all of the advice in this book ***as is*** or to just use the advice as a ***starting point*** and to make relevant adjustments where necessary when it varies for your country.

Though, I cannot imagine that the content will differ too vastly, as employers everywhere need to be provided with essential details to help them determine your suitability. And from what I can tell, Australian resume writing is similar to that for American, English and Canadian jobseekers. We just don't need industry accreditation to become a resume writer, career coach or jobsearch mentor (even though we seem to be heading that way for the future).

Right Your RESUME

However, don't just idly take the ideas and advice given herein and apply it to your resume without first researching your own country's expectations and preferences. And, in the absence of finding out rules applicable to your country, do use common sense to decide whether you should or shouldn't include a certain detail.

As I advise each of my clients: **test** and **tweak** your resume often.

If you don't get the results you are after in proportion to the amount of effort you are putting in within a reasonable period of time, then you must re-examine your resume and other application materials or you won't break through whatever is holding you back.

I encourage all jobseekers to review their resume **every three months**, at a minimum, regardless who wrote their resume.

Part 1
Before We Start RIGHTING

03 Special terminology used

I have two favourite phrasing that I use all the time when I'm speaking with job seeking clients which I would like to explain before we get into righting or writing your resume (because I'm sure to use that same wording throughout the remainder of this book so it would be best if you understand my meanings).

Those two personal favourites are:

1. Potential Suitability, and
2. Hiring Manager.

Potential suitability

If I haven"t used the term already, you will soon see that I write '**potential suitability**' rather than straight up suitability. This is because, no matter how interested and qualified and suitable to the role we may think ourselves to be, until you have successfully convinced the employer of this – so that they believe in your suitability also – you remain only *potentially* suitable to the position. In other words, until they offer you the job, you are only *potentially* the right person for them, not *the* right person for them.

I'll back this up with a little bit of evidence to validate my belief.

> Say you are a forklift driver, and have the necessary skills, experience, interest and capability for that type of job. Now, let's say you find an advertisement for a Forklift Driver vacancy in Perth, Western Australia, and you live just five minutes down the road. *Would you say you are suitable for the job?* Yes? Good.
>
> But what about if you live in Sydney, New South Wales (which, for those not familiar with Australia is on the other side of the country – roughly fours by plane)? *Would that vacancy still be suitable?* Most probably not. You might have all the requirements and capabilities to ultimately cause the employer to want to hire you; except, if you aren't interested in relocating then that vacancy is no longer suitable, is it?
>
> Therefore, for the brief moment before **you** made a decision, you were *potentially suitable* for that vacancy. You may have applied and might

Right Your RESUME

have been successful too, had you not just eliminated your own self from applying based solely on the employment's location.

Now, what about if our forklift driver found a vacancy for a Beauty Therapist role only fifteen minutes away from where he lives, and he has no interest or relevant skills for that type of job? *Would you say our forklift driver is suitable for this job?* Clearly not.

It should be evident from this brief glance at jobsearching that during the application phase jobseekers get the opportunity to discern whether an individual job vacancy is suitable to their interests and needs or not. When the position looks potentially suitable in their view, they can choose to apply. When the position doesn't look suitable or doesn't meet their needs, they can decide to **not** apply.

Hiring managers make suitability decisions too. Not just because they **want** to, but because they **need** to too.

Once applications have closed, the employer then gains the opportunity to discern whether each individual candidate that applied is potentially suitable to their needs or not.

When a applicant looks possibly suitable for the role, the hiring manager can decide to keep that person's application 'alive' and continue progressing them on through the hiring process every time the person passes the current stage being dealt with. At any point, when the person doesn't, or no longer, looks suitable in the employers view, the hiring manager gets to decide to eliminate that particular person's application from progressing further. Slowly but surely reducing the number of alive applications down from which to choose from.

That Perth Forklift Driver employer may require someone with *High Reach* forklift driving experience, and our jobseeker might only have experience and licensing for Low Reach. *Is this forklift driver still suitable now that we see things from what is required by the employer and the vacancy?* Not completely. The applicant still has closely related skills and experiences, so whether the employer will consider this applicant further will be based on the business' requirements and the quality of all other applications received.

The more applications that better match the ***employers needs***, the greater chance this forklift driver's application will be rejected during one of the culling rounds. But the more the other applicants don't have strong skills and experiences, the increasing chance the employer might keep this person's application in contention as a 'maybe'. If no other suitable person applies, the employer might decide to interview this 'not fully suited to the role' forklift

Part 1
Before We Start RIGHTING

driver, because he does already have experience and therefore it wouldn't take too much time or cost to upgrade his licence level to get him up to meeting their requirements.

So that is why I prefer to use the words *potentially suitable* for all candidates still in contention, because to me every applicant is potentially suitable right up until that exact moment when the hiring manager reaches a final decision, for each and every person that applied. Sometimes that final decision occurs quickly from a cursory first glance over; other times it only occurs once the applicant has been thoroughly assessed and considered.

Hiring manager

Next, you will also notice that I also prefer to use the term '**Hiring Manager**' rather than citing 'employer' or 'recruiter' or even 'human resources manager'.

This is because most applications are culled during a *first* round of readthroughs, and the person performing those readthroughs and culling decisions may very well not be the 'employer', a 'recruiter' or have a 'human resources manager' position title.

I've used the term Hiring Manager throughout this book because, to me, the term pinpoints the person who makes the culling decisions better (though not necessarily the final hiring decision). And it allows for multiple decision makers within the process too.

That hiring manager, who reads your resume first during one of possibly many culling rounds – who *you must impress* right while they are comparing each of the bulk of the other applicants along with your own with a view of rejecting the majority – could be a business owner, the HR Manager in a small or large company, a recruitment consultant, a panel of internal or external staff, or a person from any other position assigned this particular reviewing and sorting task as part of their everyday duties. Like when I did the first round readthroughs while working in the role of Office Receptionist / Admin Assistant.

(Really? The Receptionist rejected my application? Yes. Not all hiring managers are Executives or 'The Boss'. And just because they aren't 'The Boss' or the C.E.O doesn't mean that you should dismiss attempting to impress them.)

Inevitably, the person with the **final say** about who is hired is also a Hiring Manager. And they probably *are* 'the Boss' or will be someone in a higher

Right Your RESUME

position; but nevertheless, your application will probably have been reviewed by a handful of other people well before that one individual gets to make their final decision.

So, you really have to focus on impressing **as many people within the organisation as you can**, not just one particular person or level, so they *all* view you as a possible fit for their role.

Part 1
Before We Start RIGHTING

04 There ARE jobs out there

I want to take a moment also to dispel a commonly believed generalisation that there are '*No jobs out there*'.

In one of the Facebook jobsearch groups for which I am a member, every day members (these can be Admin (mostly), jobseekers, recruitment agencies or employers) post details of local job opportunities. They post anywhere from 10 to 30 or so vacancies in a single day, often in batches uploaded by the same person. With multiple people uploading opportunities.

And yet, with surprising regularity, some of the job seeking members publicly complain that there are 'no jobs'.

Umm, that is NOT correct.

There are *plenty* of jobs being advertised. They just need to notice them to see that this is true. The vacancies may not all be the type of work the member is particularly interested in, but there *are* job opportunities even during economic down periods.

And, 10 to 30 vacancies a day is self-evidently not 'no jobs'.

It is just the person happening to not be interested in the roles that are being posted, or not getting calls from those they have applied to – probably because their application tools are lacking in quality or their negative attitude is coming through.

So, I want to take a moment to encourage all jobseekers to step away from such **scarcity** and **negative thinking**. And really, how many jobs do they need there to be before they no longer think there are no jobs out there?

If you think you must apply to 10 jobs, 20, 30 a week to give yourself the best possible chance of gaining success, you are wrong. You actually may need to narrow down how many you apply for (quantity) to **up your level of quality** for your applications.

Right Your RESUME

05 Quality over quantity

I've had 'highly picky' clients who applied to only one job a fortnight (or less) and still gained interviews for *each* application submitted.

It is a common jobsearch mistake – fuelled perhaps by social security and job network providers setting specific numbers of jobs benefit-recipients must apply for in order to keep receiving government financial assistance. I understand that these agencies have to set numbers and expectations, otherwise some jobseekers simply won't apply for jobs they are suitable for, holding out for something bigger and better (or because they just don't want to work at all and would avoid jobsearching completely if not compelled to comply under threat of having their payments cut off if they don't).

But, it is too easy to compete on the number of applications sent and how horrible our situation is.

"I applied for ten jobs last week, and never heard back from any of them."

"Ten? I applied for twenty, and didn't get even one response! How is anyone supposed to live on dole payments, for any great length of time?"

"I know. I've got bills mounting up, and my jobsearch sucks!"

"I'm doing it worse than you."

(Why are we competing on how **badly** we are doing?)

What we should be competing on is **quality** and **getting positive results**:

"I spent three hours working on that Penrith application."

"Three? It took me five hours to tweak my resume and write the cover letter for the Blue Mountains job I applied for to make sure I addressed all of the employers needs. How quickly did the Penrith employer take to contact you, to invite you in for an interview?"

"Oh, I was pretty chuffed. They contacted me two hours after I hit the apply button."

"Wow, really? I'm so jealous. The employer took two days to contact me. For

Part 1
Before We Start RIGHTING

a moment there I thought I must have overlooked something essential and important!"

"Oh no, you poor thing. That must have been a highly anxious wait."

"I know, right. It was terrible! I breathed a huge sigh of relief when they finally called. Apparently the hiring manager took a week's leave, and had a huge stack of applications to go through when they got back. But, the feedback he gave me was that my application was by far the best he had received, so that was a relief."

"Well, at least they called you in the end and saw how much effort you put in. Good luck in your interview."

"Yeah, you too."

Oh how I would really love to hear or read a real conversation like that! (But, I shan't hold my breath.)

The one thing that I would dearly hope you take away from having completed reading this book will be an increased intention to focus less on **how many** applications you will make in favour of submitting **better quality** applications. Sure, you are going to gain more success if you are a Forklift Driver and apply for ten Forklift Driver positions than if you applied only for one – if you submit ten *quality* applications.

But you can send out ten crappy resumes and it isn't going to improve your chances all that much compared to sending off one crappy resume. Actually, sending off crappy resumes is the best and fastest way of guaranteeing more 'no' responses and painful rejection notifications that eat away at your self esteem, as *ten* employers are not impressed and consider your application inferior rather than just the one.

From my observations over the last ten years, too many jobseekers sacrifice quality in favour of quantity, getting it the wrong way round. And then wonder why they aren't successful, why the Hiring Managers aren't contacting them, and get disheartened when the response they do get, if they get one at all, is a negative one.

If you, reader, send out poor quality applications, change that bad habit NOW.

Right Your RESUME

Apply using quality written applications. And if quality means sending off less, then sacrifice the quantity and don't beat yourself up about it – you'll be happy once your phone starts ringing. And who knows, maybe, just maybe, one day I will get to hear or read a real conversation of two jobseekers discussing the time and effort they put into each application.

Oh, and it *is* okay to have interest in multiple types of jobs – so long as you have a quality resume for (and specific to) each of those different job types.

Part 1
Before We Start RIGHTING

06 Keep the position firmly in mind

You have to know what position you are applying for to get the most 'mileage' out of your resume.

Keeping the position sought firmly in mind allows you to think about and pre-research what skills, knowledge and experiences are required. Which then allows you to think about your own background, so you can then work out what skills, experiences and abilities you have that match the needs and wants of the job.

For every single piece of information that you want to include in your resume, you need to metaphorically hold it up and examine it in a scrutinising and close-up fashion, from a couple of different angles.

When you first see the likelihood that a specific detail *might* make a good match for the type of work you intend applying for, you can then re-examine it to consider that detail from the hiring manager's perspective. If you conclude the detail will be of high interest to them, after you've carefully weighed up any possible negatives and can determined just how important or not the details might be, then you are more likely to be travelling on the right path towards impressing hiring managers than the wrong one.

As you work on your resume, remember that it is not all about you. Your goal is to create a document that is *YOUniquely* focused on the employer and job. So keep the job firmly in mind as you right or write your resume.

07 Don't fix what isn't broken

Now, it would be irresponsible of me if I didn't say this:

If you are sending off your resume and **are** already frequently getting invitations to attend job interviews, then you probably do not need to undertake a major overhaul revision of your resume. The odd tweak here and there to refine and tailor it to each position applied to is perfectly acceptable, and indeed encouraged. But doing a major rework, which is what this book is about, is not necessary.

If you are getting invites to attend interviews but aren't being offered the job, then what you *really* need to be addressing is your ***interview skills*** instead. Because you are already getting the first stage right, and now just need to work on the next stage (which you can't always really do fully *until* you're getting the first stage right).

Part 1
Before We Start RIGHTING

08 Kill your darlings

In the writing world, advice often provided to new writers is for them to 'Kill Your Darlings'. What this means is that the writer should never become so attached to their own words, articles, manuscripts, scenes and ideas that it causes them to not be able to cut words, sentences and scenes – even whole chapters – when necessary, for the betterment of the whole works.

And that is fabulous advice for jobseekers too. Never be so attached to including a particular skill, experience or some other element that you can't see that it is not needed for the type of work applied for, to chop it or leave it out, immediately.

The way to resolve that is to target your resume to the type of work sought. And if you are confused how to do that, it might help to think **position specific.**

09 Think 'Position specific' if you don't get 'targeted'

I have seen resume writers, recruiters, career coaches, jobsearch trainers and other employment-related professionals frequently tout the important advice '**tailor your resume**' for years; and yet, jobseekers still don't seem to understand what tailoring a resume entails.

To help overcome any difficulties you may have with that phrase, it might be helpful to understand that your goal is to make your resume '**position specific**' instead.

I've found '*tailored*' is often interpreted to mean *tweak* your resume for each application you send; some jobseekers don't have the patience (or know-how) to make such small changes to each application; others do this already. And although I encourage tweaking your resume for each application as *good* jobsearch practice (because it can give you an edge over your competitors), tweaking your resume isn't absolutely necessary *if* the resume is already position specific to begin with.

So when I give you the advice that '*you must tailor your resume*', what I mean is that you need to 'build a resume that is not only YOUnique but is also specific to the particular type of work that you want to gain'.

That is, if you want a job as:

- a forklift driver, you must create a resume that specifically demonstrates your potential suitability *as a forklift driver*.
- a fast food cook, then you must create a resume that specifically demonstrates your skills, experiences, interests and capabilities etc., *as a fast food cook*.
- either a forklift driver *or* a fast food cook, because you would be happy to take whichever job first comes along and you have the skills and experiences that will help you gain either, then you must **write two (2) resumes**, not one (1) – with each resume singularly-specific to the particular type of work, i.e. forklift driver or fast food, not a single resume sent off to both types of work.

Part 1
Before We Start RIGHTING

I'll spell it out like all those who have done so before me: Generic, one-size-fits-all resumes **do not work**. So don't create or use one.

If you are serious about getting a job, then you must tailor your resume so that it is position specific. And the best time to achieve that is while you are building it, and to not be too precious about keeping in details that don't suit the work sought targeted.

Right Your RESUME

10 No more one-size-fits-all resumes, please

I've had a handful of jobseeker clients argue they are being 'smarter' than other jobseekers because they've created a one-size-fits-all resume, on the (misguided) belief that it will save them time and effort. But I think those jobseekers' reasoning is faulty, and that they are just lazily cutting corners (which speaks volumes about their jobsearch and workplace behaviours and attitudes).

When you do the Math, jobseekers who put in greater time and effort into writing the resume and applications they send generally find work much sooner than those who adopt that horrible knock-through-it-as-quickly-as-I-can approach. So, although these first jobseekers spend more time at the beginning of the jobsearch process and a little bit longer on each application, the overall result they get is *worth* that extra effort because they gain employment quickly, thus reducing how long their jobsearch takes.

For example

It might take a jobseeker committed to sending quality applications five hours to create their resume, and they might spend 2 hours a day every day of the week to send off a handful of applications (and let's say they send off two (2) quality applications per day, which is one per hour). If this jobseeker successfully gained work within three (3) months (a *realistic time frame* for such quality applications), this person would have:

- **spent 187 hours jobsearching** (5 hrs + 14 hrs p.w x 13 weeks = 187 hours), and

- **sent off 182 applications** (2 x 7 x 13 = 182)

Whereas the jobseekers who cut corners to give themselves more immediate *free time* who doesn't put in the time and effort to craft quality applications (taking a hit-or-miss approach), don't get the phones, don't get the interviews, and so over time they send off double, triple – sometimes even more than that – applications; thus putting in significantly *more* time and effort in the long run than those 'dumb schmucks' they derisively sneered at and who they claim 'foolishly do it the hard way, in *my* humble opinion'.

But, they haven't done the Math.

Part 1
Before We Start RIGHTING

For example

It might take this jobseeker only one hour to knock up a basic resume, and they might spend an hour a day applying to new job opportunities they find (and let's say they have sent off (5) applications per day., because they naturally apply for more because they don't put much time into any of them). If they successfully gain work nine (9) months later (an *optimistically quick* time-frame for such a poor quality applications), as 13 weeks (3 months) x 3 (to make 9 months) = 39 weeks, they would have:

- **spent 274 hours jobsearching** (1 + 7 hrs p.w. x 39 weeks = 274 hours) and

- **sent off 1,365 applications** (5 x 7 days x 39 weeks = 1,365).

Hmmm, who did that jobseeker earlier say was the 'foolish dumb schmuck doing it the hard way'?

I don't know about you, but 187 hours 182 applications and job within 3 months sounds *way more appealing* to me than 274 hours 1,365 applications and nine months of doing it financially tough!

So please. No more One-Size-Fits-All Resumes. Ever.

11 Standing out from the crowd

I have found – and I'm sure most employers and recruiting agencies would agree – some types of jobs are, for whatever reason, simply more popular and appealing than others.

This job popularity can present a problem to jobseekers looking to get their foot in the door for those types of roles – especially first-timers, as higher numbers of people are looking to do the same thing; and resultantly employers of the type of work receive much higher numbers of applications to consider. And with the extra toughness from this increased competition comes a rise in the advice and practice of jobseekers seeking to make their application **stand out from the crowd**.

With high numbers interested in and applying for their vacancies, and with hiring manager's only interested in interviewing the best-of-the-best, it is important that candidates do follow that advice if they want to stand any change of remaining in contention for the job.

BUT, a strong word of caution applies here: Standing out from the crowd **doesn't** mean '*do something gimmicky!*'

The only good way to stand out from the crowd is for your resume (and cover letter) to demonstrate to employers that you have the necessary skills, experiences and capabilities to do the job. And that you possess the right attitudes, behaviours and performance levels to **do the job well**, so that the employer can see that you are a good match and will therefore want to learn more about you; enough for them to take action to contact you.

Standing out involves making the details *relevant* and *of great interest* to the employer, and presenting the details using quality wording and an appealing presentation. No jobseeker ever needs to resort to doing something gimmicky, like use scented paper, or attach a sachet of coffee to a printout of their resume so that the hiring manager can kick back to read their resume: not when so many other jobseekers apply for the same vacancy using a poor quality resumes, cover letters, and use such trickery. If the resume doesn't make the hiring manager interested, the gimmicks aren't going to change their mind. It just makes jobsearching unnecessarily more costly for cash-strapped jobseeker!

Part 1
Before We Start RIGHTING

Employers will have an **essential** and **desirable** criteria for each vacancy they advertise. That is, there will be things that they expect the ideal candidate will definitely have and there will be things where it would simply be just nice for that person to have also.

The more you match employers essential and desirable criteria, the stronger your application will be. Equally, the reverse is true: the less you match, the weaker your application will be. And that is why it is important to fully understand the type of work you wish to gain – so you can demonstrate your potential suitability.

12 A brief overview of recruitment

Okay, you've understand all the reasons why it is important to write or right a good quality resume, but you still don't know much about them. If that is you, then read on.

For those of you still not fully familiar with resumes and applying for work, a resume is simply *a document which sets out pertinent employment, skill and ability related information about the person as a worker for the type of work the person intends applying for*, so that the person can market themselves to potential employers with vacancies.

In that sentence using italicised text above, most jobseekers understanding of what a resume is stops at the word 'worker', which overlooks the most critical part of successful job seeking. 'For the type of work the person intends applying for' is key, and the secret to fast jobsearch success.

Although the word 'resume' derives from the French language, in Australia we do not use diacritic marks when writing it; though other countries may still use acute accents for the last or both letters 'e' so the word looks like 'résumé' or 'resumé'.

Without or without the use of diacritic marks, most jobseekers will need to have a resume in order to find a job.

The basic recruitment process

As you may already know, jobseekers find potentially suitable vacancies either by accessing the **open** or **hidden** job markets.

The **open job market** is any vacancy that the employer has advertised, whether that advertisement is found in a newspaper, in an online job board listing, on the employer (or recruiters) website, or as a post on one of the company's social media platforms.

The **hidden job market** is where the vacancy has not been advertised, and the jobseeker applies from having networked or undertaken cold-canvassing to have discovered the vacancy, or is approached by the company (head-hunted).

When you apply to a job vacancy that the employer has listed on an online

Part 1
Before We Start RIGHTING

job board (such as seek.com.au – or for my international friends, monster.com – or something similar) you will most likely use both a resume and a cover letter. Together, the two documents must provide sufficient information to enable the employer (or a recruiter) to make preliminary decisions as either viewing you as either potentially suitable (which results in your being placed on their shortlist) or unsuitable (in which case your application will unfortunately be rejected).

Although different employers and recruitment agencies can follow vastly different recruitment processes, they generally follow a similar recruitment process pattern, of:

- Advertising the vacancy
- Assessing the applications received and culling the volume down to a shortlist of potentially suitable candidates
- Contacting shortlisted candidates to ask them pre-qualifying questions or to invite the person in for a face-to-face interview
- Interviewing a handful of preferred candidates, and
- Later deciding which candidate is successful and offering that person the job.

Some employers and recruiters use additional steps to those basic steps listed above, such as doing multiple rounds of phone interviews, each time culling the short list down in size before finally reaching sufficiently low numbers to send out interview invitations. Yet other employers and recruiters might interview via video teleconferencing instead of requiring candidates to attend their business premises.

Regardless whether specific employers and recruiters have additional steps or not, the general nuts and bolts of the recruitment process usually follow that basic process as its core, and the process can be broken down to five distinct stages:

- Receiving Applications
- Short-listing candidates
- Interviewing most suitable candidates
- Deciding between applicants, and then the
- Hiring and Commencing of the successful person

How many applicants interviewed is determined by the individual employer or recruitment agency. Some will only interview two to three candidates on a one-to-one or a panel-to-one basis, others might interview up to ten candidates using those bases, and yet others might carry out preliminary group interview stages before they reach going for one-to-one.

Part 1
Before We Start RIGHTING

13 The different types of resumes

Resumes can come in lots of styles, layouts and variations. But at the heart of personal style preferences underlie three distinct resume structural formats, which have been around for at least thirty years and which you should use to build a resume from scratch or to fix an existing; as these structural types indicate what sections and particulars are included and excluded along with where the focus of the resume lays and how much weight the focus should be given.

The main problem I've observed is that a significant number of jobseekers who create a resume for their own self, to save money, aren't aware of the different types of resumes – nor what is expected for each type, despite so much information abundantly available, so can end up with a resume that on the surface *looks* like a particular resume type, but it just doesn't work like it is supposed to.

The goals of your resume is to firstly enable the hiring manager to see your potential suitability to their vacancy, and secondly to prompt them into taking appropriate action (to contact you to discuss your application and potential suitability further). Fail to market yourself properly, and you'll fail to gain your sales opportunity, where you can attempt to convince the hiring manager to hire you over other candidates they might be considering.

So the first **decision** that you will need to make (when you are ready to start writing or righting your resume) is which **Style** of resume you will use for *your* resume.

You have probably heard or read somewhere that there are three (3) different types of resume – and that is true.

Those resume styles (or formats) are:

1. Functional
2. Chronological, and
3. Combination (sometimes called 'Hybrid')

Right Your RESUME

As each resume style has it own particular and unique style, look, focus and features, let's now go through each of them in turn so you can make the right decision as to which one to use.

Functional

Functional resumes focus on the person's skills, qualifications, abilities and competencies for the type of work being applied for, and place little to no focus on the person's work history.

The strength of using a functional resume format is that it focuses on the type of work sought (or is supposed to), rather than what has been done in the past.

Because functional resumes do not provide in-depth information about former job roles, resumes using this format are usually condensed to appearing on just one page.

The weaknesses in using the functional resume format are that the information can look cluttered and ugly on the page (which impacts upon a hiring manager wanting to read the resume), and because workplace activities and achievements are not 'fleshed out', hiring managers might not be able to see the person's value compared to applicants that have provided more in-depth information, as the information can seem 'shallow' or incomplete, and if not written correctly, the focus isn't on the future and the type of work sought like it is supposed to be. All of which can result in the person not being invited to attend an interview because the hiring manager hasn't developed enough interest in the person to feel compelled to call them.

Chronological

Chronological resumes focus on the person's work history, the activities performed and achievements gained within the role (skill statements); and lists the employment details and accompanying skill statements in reverse date order. That is, the person's most recent work history is fully detailed and then positioned as the first listing in the employment history section of the resume, and then progresses backwards towards the first position held so that the time line of events is listed the opposite to how they occurred, i.e. from last to first (instead of first to last).

Part 1
Before We Start RIGHTING

The strength of using a chronological format is that it demonstrates strong work background, achievements, range of tasks and skills performed in the past job and shows the overarching career progression.

Because chronological resumes provide in-depth information about former job roles, resumes using this format often become multiple page documents.

The weaknesses in using the chronological resume format are that the resume can become too long and detailed, they can reveal employment gaps, and can inadvertently focus on what has been done in the past rather than where the person wants to go in the future. And because of this, the hiring manager can quite easily make a decision about the candidate's suitability without needing to meet or speak to them.

Combination

Combination resumes are a hybrid of chronological and functional resumes, so that the focus is balanced more equally across a person's skills, qualifications, abilities, competencies, work history, activities and achievements.

The strengths of using a combination format resume is that it better matches providing the information in a manner which hiring managers are hoping to see and because this structure shows the strengths of the chronological and functional resumes, hiring managers are better able to assess candidates to determine their potential suitability and make appropriate preliminary culling decisions, as the picture they gain is clearer and more fully fleshed out.

Because combinations resumes provide the in-depth information about former job roles like the chronological resume does, resumes using this combination format also usually become multiple page documents, which can become too long and reveal employment gaps (though the focus is now appropriately future oriented), and the hiring manager can quite easily make a decision about the candidate's suitability without needing to meet or speak to them.

The table below shows the differences within the three types of resumes.

Right Your RESUME

Chronological	Functional	Combination
Time to create: Longer to write	***Time to create:*** Quick and easy to write	***Time to create:*** Longer to write
Ideal length: 2 – 4 pages	***Ideal length:*** 1 page	***Ideal length:*** 2 – 6 pages
History: Up to 10 years, detailed listing	***History:*** All positions, briefly listed	***History:*** Up to 10 years, detailed listing
Skills: Briefly listed, relevant to job and the past	***Skills:*** Detailed listing, relevant to the job	***Skills:*** Detailed listing, relevant to the job and the past
Strength: Career progression Achievements Range of tasks	***Strength:*** Skill Development Work sought / employer wants	***Strength:*** Career progression Skill Development Achievements Work sought / employer wants
Weaknesses: Employment Gaps Focus on past Can be too long	***Weaknesses:*** Cluttered details Inconsistent presentation Insufficient details	***Weaknesses:*** Employment Gaps Can be too long

Part 1
Before We Start RIGHTING

Mostly used by jobseekers with:	Mostly used by jobseekers with:	Mostly used by jobseekers with:
Strong, consistent work history	Longer terms of unemployment	Strong, consistent work history
Strong performance and high achievement	Small range of duties and responsibilities	Strong performance and high achievement
Wide range of duties and responsibilities	Problematic history	Wide range of duties and responsibilities
	Job-hopping	Seeking to gain competitive edge over those that use Functional or Chronological Formats
	School leavers	
	Career Changers	
	Returning to Work parents and carers	
	Migrant jobseekers with little or no history in their new country	
Favoured by:	*Favoured by:*	*Favoured by:*
Most industries	Hospitality industry	Most industries and hiring manager's (especially those that do the first readthroughs)
	Employers requesting a 1-page	

Which sections are included in the different types of resumes?

The sections that are commonly included in chronological, functional and combination resumes are mostly the same; the difference lies mostly in the brevity or completeness of the details included for each section. See table 2 below:

Right Your RESUME

Chronological	Functional	Combination
Personal Details	Personal Details	Personal Details
Career Objective	Career Objective	Career Objective
Brief Skills Summary	Detailed Skills Summary	Detailed Skills Summary
Detailed Work History	Brief Work History	Detailed Work History
Education & Training	Education & Training	Education & Training
Qualifications & Licensing	Qualifications & Licensing	Qualifications & Licensing
Activities & Achievements	Abilities & Competencies	Activities & Achievements
		Abilities & Competencies

Which type of resume should I use?

As you can see from the table, the Combination resume provides the greatest scope to demonstrate potential suitability for a role compared to Functional and Chronological resumes that go in-depth for part of the resume and brief in other parts due to its in-depth details across all parts.

I have found that the Chronological and Combination style resumes are the ones that are more effective in the Australian labour market with the resumes I write for jobseekers. This is most likely because they provide the hiring manager with enough of the 'meat' hiring manager's need to help make their decisions (and go from being bored by a resume to becoming highly interested in the person for a role).

Functional and Chronological resumes have their place though, so you will need to decide early on which type of resume you intend creating. As this will influence how much detail you go into in each of the specific sections.

Part 1
Before We Start RIGHTING

14 Resume length

I am frequently asked how long a resume should be. And, I have frustrated many a jobseeker by not stating an outright definitive answer. Broadly, depending on your country of origin's preferences and practices, a resume can be as little as one page, or as multi-page documents (no more than six pages).

The most important point is that resumes are **not** meant to list your full employment or personal history. (That is the purpose of a Career Portfolio (if you create one)).

In Australia, resumes that use the *combination* style are generally 2, 3 or 4 pages in length. For Americans, I've read conflicting information (in equal ratio) that the preference is for resume to be *one-page only* versus arguments adamantly declaring *'don't listen to that advice'*, and then agree with my viewpoint that a resume should be **only as long as it needs to be** to best showcase your ability to do the job being applied for.

For some jobseekers, say, people seeking basic entry-level work who have little history, then the ideal resume length might be one or two pages. But, for another jobseeker, with a lot more history and skills behind them and going for a higher level position, a resume that is less than 4 pages might do that person a disservice if they try to condense it down. I don't believe any resume needs to end up longer than six pages though.

It really boils down to a couple of things:

- What skills and experiences you have
- The type of work you are seeking
- What is required within the role
- What the employers for that industry consider normal, and then
- Including only sufficient details to enable the hiring manager to see your suitability to keep your application in contention, and
- Excluding any additional information that would enable them to make elimination decisions without their ever meeting or speaking with you.

Right Your RESUME

An old resume of mine – before I became a resume writer – was six pages, and had been getting me invitations to attend interviews consistently for more than eight months. I was lucky in that at that time I could afford to be highly selective about job offers, and turned each job offer down for various personal reasons – mostly that the terms and conditions of the employment didn't suit the needs of my family, which wasn't known to me when I applied and interviewed.

When I enrolled in one of the qualifications I completed, the training company requested students' resumes so the company could **reverse-market** us to suitable job opportunities for us, to time our commencement in a job as close to our course completion as possible, as part of their services.

I handed over my six page resume that I knew 'worked'. The trainer took one look at the length of my resume and said, 'This is too long. We'll cut this right back and update it for you.' A few days later, I received their email with my new 2-page resume attached. When I looked at the resume, I didn't like it but kept my opinion to myself. It had been heartlessly bludgeoned, and in my view, it no longer showcased my most important skills, abilities and experiences for the type of work I wanted to gain, because those key details had been axed along with my professional growth and notable achievements. But, the person who 'fixed' my resume was (supposedly) an industry professional who 'knew their stuff', so I let them market me with it, and used it myself when I found vacancies I was interested in.

And, despite the training company marketing me to potential employers, I did not get a single phone call or invitation to attend a job interview for jobs that I had been used to getting interviews for.

What I noticed instead was that as the lack of results continued, the reverse marketer started putting my name forward for 'lesser' roles. Roles that were far below my skill and pay expectation level; and roles that I was not interested in going back to doing at all! Who wants to take backward career steps when they don't have to?

Three months later I finished the fast-track course, and gladly went back to doing my own jobsearch, and immediately ditched their two-page resume to once again use my old 'unacceptable' six-pager, updated with my new qualification.

What I had realised as I was about to apply for a job, was that without all those crucial details that I had so carefully and deliberately originally put in to make sure my application stood out, the training company had cut out, and in the process (ignorantly) made me just look like an average, entry-level candidate with ordinary, nothing special qualities – a struggling, hopeful

Part 1
Before We Start RIGHTING

jobseeker instead of the fully qualified and experienced potentially suitable candidate that I was.

And I knew, if I didn't convince the person culling applications that I had what it takes, my application would be rejected. And I'd keep on failing and not getting results.

So, at that last moment, I changed back to using my old resume instead of the training company one. And, low and behold, from that very first application, I started getting the phone calls and invitations to attend interviews again.

The moral here is although my resume was indeed on the long side, it was *necessary* for the type of work I had been applying to at that time. None of the details in the six page resume were more than four years old, and *every* small detail was completely relevant to the industry and that type of work. When I had built that resume, even though I didn't know much about resumes (though I was fast learning!) I had packed it with details I suspected employers would be most interested in. A few years later, once I had started writing resumes and knew better, I was able to tighten that resume down to just four pages, but it also made me realise that the person who updated my resume didn't know a thing about resumes or how to generate potential employer interest.

So, that is why I say, your resume needs to be as long as it needs to be, without being excessively wordy, going into any unnecessary detail or doing anything that allows the hiring manager to make a 'no' decision.

The instructional chapters within the rest of this book will assume you will create a **Combination Resume** because it combines both the *functional* and *chronological* resume styles into one, which works best. If you intend creating or fixing up a Functional or Chronological resume you can skip over the chapters discussing sections where you don't need to go into in as much detail.

For example, if you choose to create a functional resume, you can read-through the chapters relating to the Work History section, but rather than spending any great amount of time in following the instructions contained in those chapters, you would simply create a list of the different roles you have previously held to spend your greater time working on the details needed to suit the functional style.

And vice versa.

If you will create a chronological resume, when you reach the instructions that relate best to functional (and combination) styles, you can skip over the

Right Your RESUME

instructions that are irrelevant for use in the chronological style.

But one last thing before we get to those instructions, one last thing I feel it is important for you to know before we start writing or righting your resume. Where you position your sections and details in your resume is important. So, I need to tell you about what I call 'the prime resume real estate' zone.

Part 1
Before We Start RIGHTING

15 The prime resume real estate area

About ten years ago once I was actively informally studying how to create nicer looking and better formatted word documents (not just for resumes), I stumbled across an online resource (which I didn't bookmark and no longer remember the name of the website) where the article-writer instructed readers to test out a practical **reading exercise** in support of the author's point being made. The exercise involved my going off to find and pick up a printed A4 sized document page that was filled with text and then return to read the rest of the instructions once you had your printed page in hand.

Curious about what the results of this simple exercise would be, I decided to try it out, and with no 'cheating' on my part to read ahead. Once I had a found a suitable printout – which just happened to be a discarded draft page of a resume that I had recently been working on for a client – I returned to the article and was instructed to glance down and take notice of where I was *holding* the page.

I took mental note then returned to the instructions, keeping the page in my hand as is.

The writer predicted that I would be holding my sheet of paper roughly at about the two-thirds of the way down mark with my right hand – if I was right handed (or with my left if I was left handed) – in a way that saw my thumbs stick out slightly into the middle of the page, which would prevent the last third of text being legible to me, unless I shifted my grip.

The author of the article was correct.

I was indeed holding the sheet of paper in this exact manner, so I was keen to read the 'punchline' of what this little exercise all meant!

And the writer's point was quite clear (I still remember it even all these years later – good things have the great habit of just sticking with you like that, don't they? Even when I don't remember the source). The area **above** my hold mark, where possible, was the position where *the most important details needed to be*.

Ahh yes, okay. That sounded reasonable enough.

$\mathcal{R}$ight Your RESUME

I checked the resume I had created (and final version already handed back to the client), and sure enough it seemed like I had placed the most important details in that top area. Pleased that I had got it right even though I hadn't known it while I was creating it, I made a mental note to remember this for all future documents I wrote or typed up – particularly resumes where I felt this really applied.

Not long after having read that article, maybe a week or two, I was fortunate to gain another client wanting their resume to be typed up.

This client was a real estate salesperson looking to change company's because he was experiencing problems with being paid correctly. The client provided me with copies of two or three different previous resume versions – 'none of which ever got [him] results', he advised. He explained did much better when he met employers in person, but this time he didn't want his current boss to find out he was looking to change, so needed a resume to send out in response to advertisements and cold calls made from home.

He requested that I 'work out what needs to be put into the new resume' – meaning I shouldn't duplicate any information; just re-arrange and piece together the rest of the details so that it was logically presented and looked like a typical resume. He handed me his documents in typed form rather than handwriting exactly what he wanted (like most clients did) because, he advised, 'most people find my handwriting too messy and hard to read'. (He *had* tried to handwrite out what he wanted me to type up, but had given up because he didn't have the confidence that I would work out what he had written – heck, there were some words he had written that even he couldn't work out what the word was now himself!)

Later, after he had left, as I settled down to make a start on completing the job, I happened to look down and noticed that once again I was holding the multiple pages in the same position from that article I had read – and was impressed that it 'worked' even when holding more than one page. But, during that glance at the topmost page of his resume, I noticed something else.

Apart from seeing my client's name and personal details typed in *massive* size (I'd say a font sized at 72 pt or more), there were **no other details** in that physical space.

That article, I recalled, had clearly stated that the top two-thirds of the page – that is, the area above my protruding thumbs – was where the most important details need to be. The article was meant for students writing essays, but I saw it as even more important for *resumes*.

Part 1
Before We Start RIGHTING

Was the clients *name* the single most important detail? Or, was their better details that could occupy that space?

Now, at that point in time I had **no** experience in hiring, recruitment or employment. Heck I wasn't even a real resume writer yet. This was only my third or fourth resume ever that I was typing up – and even then, I wasn't *writing* the resume. All I was doing was creating the electronic file from handwritten notes as part of my small, part time *typing* business.

But I instinctively knew that any Real Estate Agency principal (employer) would surely want to know more than just an applicant's name. They would have to *expect* to see some information related to the job which would enable them to see this highly experienced and strong performing real estate salesperson as potentially suitable for them.

Each of the former resumes he had given me had nothing in that 'most important' space except his name and personal details. Taking up almost half a page! All those fantastic, *impressive*, 'meaty', 'essential particulars' that future employers would want to read only started below my thumb line. *Was this the reason his resumes didn't get him results?*

Except, the original sentence 'the position where the most important details need to be' wasn't the wording that sprung into my mind while I had his resumes in my hand. Instead, I thought, 'this real estate agent is wasting his opportunity to sell his skills and abilities within the *prime resume real estate zone*'.

That physical space in a document had suddenly metamorphosed into being more specific to this client and his employment as a real estate agent. And from that moment onwards, regardless of the type of work sought, whenever I handled a person's resume, I mentally called that top two-third portion, '**the Prime Resume Real Estate**' – or 'the PRRE', for short.

When the client came to collect his resume and USB and noticed how small I had made his name, he instructed me to resize those details as the only changes he wanted me to make. But, with my newfound knowledge (and confidence) I advised him that I didn't think it was in his best interest to waste the prime resume real estate in favour of only showcasing his name and contact details. I discussed that instead I believed he needed to ensure that only the information a real estate agency **principal** would want and expect to see would work best; and my belief that his name taking up more than half a page made his resume too much about him, and too little about what an employer would like to know about his skills and capabilities for the job.

Right Your RESUME

I was taken aback when he responded with 'you're right', though he struggled with having his name and contact details remain so tiny by comparison to what it had been, saying something along the lines of 'I've always had a dominant personality – like good real estate agents should have. But I do need to tone myself back for applications or a licensee will view me as a threat rather than an asset and good fit.'

We compromised in the end. I made his name 24 point instead of 18. And he got invitations to attend interviews from the very first application, and soon moved on to a different agency.

So, there you have it. There is an area on a printed resume page that is prime resume real estate. Just as the real estate industry expects to see quality houses in prime real estate areas, so too must jobseekers include quality details that interest and excite a hiring manager when they view the prime resume real estate area.

But not all resumes ARE printed out, are they? Some hiring managers only open the document electronic file to do their initial read-through, whether through personal reading preference or as a print cost-cutting measure.

The **prime resume real estate** for an *electronically viewed* resume therefore, is actually less than that of a printed document.

Why *less* you ask, horrified?

Because, when you open Microsoft Word (which is what most businesses use, even if you personally don't) on a typical computer screen, the viewing area is only about **half an A4 printed page** length when viewed at normal size (the standard page size in Australia). The File menu, Ribbon and Tabs take up a fair bit of the actual screen real estate – unless you switch across to full screen view mode, which not every reader does (and even then it only shows roughly two-thirds of an A4 page, when using a wide-screen).

A hiring manager is able to gain an accurate *feel* for what the rest of the resume will be like just from that viewable half page worth, because our brain's visual processing power is so significantly faster than our text reading ability.

In the resume writing sections coming up in this book, I will specify which sections and section details belong inside the Prime Resume Real Estate (PRRE) area.

Now I think it is time to start on righting or writing your resume!

Personal details section

Part 2

Right Your RESUME

Quote

"Do the best you can until you know better; then when you know better, do better."
@Inspire_US

Part 2
Personal DETAILS

Note

When I first started out writing this book, I had hoped to simply just break the details (which go into the Personal Details section) down into three distinct groups: a *'yes, you should include'*, a *'no, you shouldn't include'* and an *'optional, because it depends on…'* separation.

However, while writing I found that by strictly adhering to that formula, instead of the anticipated well-laid out advise, what I was ended up with was that a specific topic had become 'scattered' around the chapters too much. This was because a single detail might have a *'yes, you should include'* aspect while simultaneously having a *'no, you shouldn't include'* or *'optional, because it depends on…'* aspect to it too. And so, that one detail was ending up being discussed under each grouping, making the topics feel disjointed and prolonged.

I mention this because you might end up surprised by how long the discussion on a single element can get, over one – what you might think is an insignificant – tiny element! Also, because in other parts of this book, I'll revert back to this plan of using distinct groups.

But for now, as you need to set the expectation (and impressiveness) high when the hiring manager picks up (or opens) your resume, and then maintain it throughout the rest of the document, I would rather you fully understood each of my reasons about a single element before you can make an educated decision.

Right Your RESUME

Quote

"Everything you've ever wanted is on the other side of fear."
George Addair

Part 2
Personal DETAILS

16 Personal details

It doesn't matter which country you live in, somewhere in your resume you will *need* to provide the recruiter or potential employer with some basic personal information about yourself. This is so the hiring manager knows *who* has applied and *how* they can contact the person (if they want to).

Three common mistakes

When I was the person who made the first-round culling decision, I came across three mistakes too frequently. These were resumes:

- That did not have any contact information
- With some of the crucial details missing
- That included far more personal information than was absolutely necessary.

Each of these mistakes destroys the effectiveness of the jobseeker's application.

And unfortunately, more oftentimes than not, it justifiably sets the expectation level for the rest of the resume to low and a waste of the hiring manager's time in reading it.

What is the hiring manager looking for?

Within the **Personal Details** section, the information the hiring manager is first looking for, while sorting through hundreds of applications, is simple:

- what is this candidate's name, and
- will I be able to contact them if I am interested in them for the position?

The hiring manager isn't going to pay too close attention to the name and contact number at this early skim-reading stage, except to mentally tick off that these details are present.

After the first read-through though, for those handful of candidates having just successfully demonstrated their potential suitability to the role, the hiring

Right Your RESUME

manager is going to turn back to the first page to recheck out the personal details.

The hiring manager may be ready to contact potentially suitable candidates straight away, or may just be checking that the contact details are present for when they are ready to contact later on. Most hiring managers, if they notify applicant that they have been unsuccessful, will do this later, once interviews have been arranged.

My job was just to cull the large pile down to *three (or less) people* from the hundreds received, and then pass those few resumes over to my Manager for secondary reviews. The manager, and or the Sales Reps, then reviewed whichever resumes I had handed over and then made the decision whether to call those applicants in for an interview or not.

Our agency didn't contact unsuccessful applicants to advise they had been unsuccessful either. Our Fax-Printer was too busy spitting out applications for the other jobs we had advertised and *1.* not all applicants provided their contact number (or an email address either), and *2.* we simply did not have the time to reply to any of them (especially me). There was a also certain expectation on our company's part that by having required jobseekers to *fax* their application to us they should not expect a personal reply, except if they were to be interviewed.

Include or exclude this section?

Let's be clear so there is no mistake: a personal details section is ***essential*** to every jobseekers resume, and therefore the section ***must be included*** somewhere in your resume document.

> ✓ **Include**
> * Exclude
> * Optional, or It Depends...

Part 2
Personal DETAILS

Positioning

The best place to position your Personal Details section in your resume is somewhere both *expected* by and *easy to find* for the hiring manager: and that is, on the first page (of a multi-page document); up the top, as the first detail listed.

You can align your personal details to the left margin, right margin or centre it, as a personal preference in layout and presentation style. And, you can add your personal details in the Header for *subsequent* pages. But for the initial skim read, your key personal details need to be the first thing present and accounted for.

What details to include

We have now established that a Personal Details section must be included, no 'ifs', 'buts' or 'maybe's'. Now, let's cover each of the individual considerations (those tinier elements) that could go into this section, and then look at what you should and shouldn't include when we view this section from the hiring manager's perspective.

(Though, I remind you that the hiring manager *won't* be concerned about these details until AFTER they have read your resume and are seriously interested in you for the job.)

The finer details

Although the *section* is a must, not all 'finer details' need to or should be included though; actually, including some type of personal details is not only unnecessary but can cause a hiring manager to:

- Use the information provided to discriminate against you (oftentimes without your knowledge), or
- Make a 'no decision' without ever speaking to you first.

Those unnecessary details (when ill-consideredly included) can also cause unscrupulous people to misuse the information provided, without your awareness or consent, against:

- Your own self, or
- The businesses and referees you mention within your resume.

Right Your RESUME

The two essentials

The two essential elements that must be included are:

- the **person's name** and
- a **means of contact**.

All other personal details will fall into either the *optional* or *exclude* categories.

Part 2
Personal DETAILS

17 Name

Now don't laugh, but I have received resumes for the positions we were managing that did not contain this one crucial piece of specific detail. Why, I will never understand.

The candidate either had to have made a significant oversight in not providing this 'the most important detail of all' (in which case the hiring manager could justifiably assume that the person could very well miss carrying out crucial steps or overlook important details within the job role too) or the person was perhaps deliberately sabotaging their application. (Perhaps because the person is being required to apply for a set number of jobs each week by their social security or job network provider, which prompted them to send their application but be defiant in their doing so; in which case the person clearly isn't serious about obtaining this job role, enabling the hiring manager to reasonably and immediately reject the said application in order to spend quality time in finding the applicants who do want the job).

Although you are not up to creating your electronic document just yet, make a mental note to remember to include your name, first thing, when you are ready to make it. Put it on your 'before I send my resume out' revision self-check list.

Positioning

Your name needs to be on your resume – no ifs, buts' or maybes, like the Personal Details section as a whole! And in the case of the applicant's name, not just included as the document filename or placed only within the Header or Footer area.

Your name needs to appear in the *body copy* part of the document too, as the headlining detail for your Personal Details section, on the first page.

The reason for this is that computer scanning technology that many of big name companies and recruitment agencies use might not pick up the Header and Footer details, and they won't analyse the file name to 'put two and two together' for you. Therefore, you have to specify it within the body copy for the words to be correctly detected.

However, the applicant doesn't necessarily need to include their *full* name. The only parts of an applicants name that is absolutely necessary is the person's:

Right Your RESUME

- *first* (or given) name, and
- *surname.*

That's all.

Now for details to exclude

The personal details that can be excluded are:

Middle names and maiden surnames

Middle name(s) and *maiden surnames* should **not** be included in your resume.

Firstly, employers don't *need* to know a candidate's full birth name during the application process. They might need to gain those details if the person is offered the job to enable them to maintain accurate employee records, for taxation and accounting purposes; but we aren't up to that stage yet, are we? So let's not get ahead of ourselves within the hiring process.

Next, a resume, because of its very nature in providing detailed information about a person, exposes jobseekers to increased **risks of identity theft**. Therefore, withholding non-essential details is of paramount importance.

Risk of identity theft

These days, with increasing amounts of scammers and identity thieves cropping up for almost everything we do, you *must* to protect yourself against potential abuse of your personal information (and not just while job searching either) in any way you legitimately can. If you want to avoid the pain and hassle of having to sort out the financial havoc scammers can inflict upon you, that is.

Fake job advertisements abound and, most times you don't know who you are sending your resume off to or that the recipient will stick to strictly using the information for the purpose with which it was given and as you intended. I read recently that scammers can learn a lot about a person quite easily, and that some scam-artists will go to great lengths to obtain the last of a missing few crucial details with which to then proceed with their plan to rob you of your money or steal your identity. And that they give up though on the people who make it too hard for them. It makes sense.

Part 2
Personal DETAILS

You will make yourself less of a target to those would-be scammers and identity thieves *if* you only provide the barest of essential information about yourself in your resumes and applications (and not just for job applications!).

Don't make it easy for dishonest people like this by ignorantly sending out your resume with lots of excess personal details. You need to become increasingly stingy about giving out your personal details. I'm encouraging you to become highly selective about what personal details you do, and don't, reveal.

It is (mostly) safe to assume that you can submit an application to a government department that contains additional personal details, like your residential address, when asked for it. But for all other job advertisements, the need for your scepticism and caution is warranted.

Honest businesses and hiring managers will understand why you've cut back to just the basics compared to 'the good old days' where all details were automatically and lavishly provided.

My recommendation is to **think of your own safety first** (- though, your *personal details* are the ***only*** details that I am saying 'think of yourself over the employer', okay). Question every small personal detail and ask, "*Is this detail absolutely necessary (at this stage)?*" and "*Could this detail be misused?*" If the answer is 'no, it is not' and 'yes, it could be' then choose to exclude.

Now, I've covered as much of the additional personal details as I can think of within this section below, but if you happen to find something that is not covered, then you are probably safe to exclude it, or to err on the side of exclude, than to include the detail.

What if I don't go by my official first or last name?

No problem; apply using the first and last name you do go by. Or, apply using your official first and last name.

For example

A woman I know uses her official middle name and surname because she doesn't like her first name.

For this discussion, let's say her registered name is Mary Louise Jobseeker. All her friends know her as, 'Louise'. Louise's birth certificate, driver's licence and her formal education certificates all use her official registered name, 'Mary Louise Jobseeker'.

Louise could apply for jobs as Louise Jobseeker; if she gets the job, the employer is probably going to request a copy of those documents, and will soon learn that she goes by a **preferred name** rather than her official one. The employer may ask her *why* (if they are interested); so Louise could have a simple explanation ready for if she is asked, such as, "Oh, because there were too many Mary's within my family", or "I actually prefer Louise."

Or,

Louise could apply using her official first and last name. And if she got the job could tell the people she works with that she would rather they call her by her preferred name, like her family and friends do.

The important point to remember here is that you aren't trying to be fraudulent or misleading (unlike scammers and thieves). And it shouldn't be viewed as such. You are simply keeping your resume details to a minimum to prevent (or lower the likelihood of) unwanted actions by others from happening, and to present your information neatly.

Special considerations

If you are a foreigner with a long name that does not indicate whether you are male or female or it can be difficult for natives to pronounce with ease, then you may like to use a **nickname** or clarify the information. For example, if your name is Paolo which roughly translates to Paul in other languages, you could list your name as Paolo and add a clarifying name in brackets – e.g. Paolo (Paul).

This can help hiring managers to know what to call you if they are interested enough to phone you. Your name may be obvious and pronounceable within your own culture that you are male or female, and I don't mean any disrespect in saying this, but to those outside of that, your gender might not be so obvious, and name not so easily pronounceable. I say this because people mispronounce my name and surname all the time.

(For the record: Char is pronounced 'Shar' like 'shhhh ar' (but most people pronounce it 'char' like when saying 'charcoal' or 'chair'). And with my surname, it is pronounced 'Me San', as in 'me' and 'san'. I have to laugh when people mispronounce it, with great frequency, as 'Messen' or 'Mess An', because it sounds like they have a drawling accent and are saying I am 'messin' around or somethin'.)

Part 2
Personal DETAILS

Emphasis tips

Hiring Managers with a lot of years experience can often tell a lot about a job candidate and their personality just from how large a font the person lists their name on their resume.

Over-confident and attention seeking personality types tend to go with making their names **BIG AND NOTICEABLE.** (I once received an application where the first half of the first page was just the candidate's name – in 100 point or larger font size!) Whereas many school leavers, returning to work parents, long term unemployed and other people who aren't as confidence in their abilities for the type of work being applied for, or are 'meeker' within their personalities, tend to use a font size that is the same size as the rest of the body text in their document (or is only fractionally bigger); so that their name just 'blends on in' and is barely noticeable.

Although I agree with the principle of enlarging the text of the person's name so that it stands out and is easier to spot, you never want to over-emphasise any single element within your resume. And same goes for your listing your name.

I advise not to go any larger than **double the body text font size** for your name. This means if your body text is Size 12 (which it should be if you are using a professional font style and size), than your name should be no larger than Size 24 pt.

For Example

Size 12   Your Name

Size 24   ## Your Name

See how the larger text stands out from the smaller text, but not so much that it commands *prolonged* attention or wastes valuable prime resume real estate.

18 Contact details

When the hiring manager skim reads your resume for the first time, the only thing they will be interested in (if they are going to be interested upfront) is your name.

If you progress through the rounds of their application culling to make it onto the short list of candidates, then the hiring manager is going to need a way of contacting you to invite you to an interview.

Most hiring managers I worked with preferred **phoning** the person. As it was an opportunity for them to ask the person a few questions before settling on whether to invite the person in for a job interview or not. (Many a potential candidate inadvertently ruins their chance during this phone call, by answering in an unprofessional manner or by how and what they say while answering questions; which changes the hiring manager's mind during the call – so keep this in mind when you speak to them).

A number of jobseeker clients (when I was an Employment Consultant) reported of hearing back from a few larger employers **directly by email**. Those employers deliberately bypassed phoning the potential candidate to instead invite the candidate to attend an interview via email and provided the accompanying interview particulars within that email.

I think I know why those company's did that.

My guess is: so they could gauge how serious that jobseeker is.

Jobseeker's who check their email accounts regularly are going to discover they have been successful in gaining the interview, in sufficient time to attend. Whereas those candidates who don't check their emails, or who do so infrequently, often only discover they had been successful in their application after they have missed the interview date. Thus missing out on the opportunity to progress forward in the hiring process.

Because I've noticed that these big name employers didn't give any candidates a second chance or alternative interview time; it was a case of either you show up at the one opportunity we give you, or keep on looking elsewhere. A tough stance perhaps; but if you ever have been involved in recruiting, you would sympathise with the employer. Jobseekers run late and don't turn up for interviews all the time. They don't try to contact the employer to let them

Part 2
Personal DETAILS

know about the situation either. Yet jobseekers complain when they don't hear back from the applications they apply to.

So, you must include a way for employers to contact you. And you have a choice in providing an email address, a telephone number or both.

You won't know which method the employer or recruiter prefers, so my advice is to include both your email address *and* a contact number – but only one of each when you have multiple email addresses or contact numbers.

Email addresses

If you choose to provide your email address – and I encourage you to do so – then you need to check your email account every weekday.

The impression your email address can have upon the hiring manager matters too. You want to avoid anything that can create a negative impression or cause them to make a no decision.

Although the choice is fully up to you, it can be a good idea to have a separate email account that you use exclusively for jobsearching purposes. To allow you to keep your jobsearch related emails away from your personal. If you can manage your emails in just one account, then that is perfectly fine, if your email address is professional. (With scammers and identity thieves posting fake job advertisements, having separated email addresses will contribute to keeping your private emails away from their gaining access).

The best structure to have as an email address is:

yourname@provider.extension

The extension can be .com, or, more likely for an Australian email address, .com.au or whatever is relevant for the country you live in. It doesn't matter what the extension is so long as you list the proper extension so emails don't bounce back. Undeliverable emails are a sure-fire way for your application to end up on the rejection pile despite a hiring manager's interest.

If you don't have an email account, or your existing one isn't suitable for use during jobsearch, then you should create a suitable email account. You can always close it down or stop using it once you have found your ideal job. The best way to get one is to use a free email provider.

Right Your RESUME

Your name is already taken

When I was an Employment Consultant and the client didn't have an email address (usually because they didn't have a computer at home or didn't know how to get an email account), I helped them create a free account. I chose web based email providers, like Gmail, Yahoo, and Hotmail etc (so the client could access it from any computer with an internet connection, or from their smart phones). I consistently found that unless the client's name was somehow unique or unusual, most of the time their name was already taken.

Google, Yahoo etc. do automatically provide suggestions for alternatives addresses that you could use, but most of the time these were not suitable for use during jobsearch either.

So, don't just use one of the options that are available, willy-nilly. It is not necessary (see my Pro Tip below).

If you cannot get yourname@provider.extension, before you select an alternative (and please check your existing email account too, if that is what you are going to use), you need to make sure:

Age revealing

Any numbers you use don't that lead the employer to guess your age

Reason: to prevent age discrimination.

Example: yourname1977@provider.com or yourname24@provider.com.

See how you can take the current year and minus the birth year to work out the person is 37 years of age (i.e. 2014 − 1977 = 37), and if you minus your age from the current year we can work the year you were born (i.e. 2014 − 24 = 1990), or a close estimation if the person has had a birthday or two since they created the account.

In the first example, if the employer wants someone younger, say, only in their 20's, this calculation can be used to make a 'no' decision – even though you have the skills and would be capable in the role. In the second example, if they are looking for someone older, then knowing or working out the person's age can help eliminate them too.

Scammers and identity thieves will be most grateful that they now have a

Part 2
Personal DETAILS

crucial piece of your personal information, your year of birth – now all they need to do is work out your day and month too and they are possibly a step closer to their goal of being able to take action damaging to you.

Pro tip

I had my clients use their name followed by a full stop and then the initials 'js' before the '@' symbol (the 'js' stands for 'Job Search') e.g. yourname.js@provider.com and consistently found the email address available because no one else was doing something similar.

Typing ease

Your email address isn't difficult for the hiring manager to type in.

Reason: to make life easier *for hiring manager*

Example: Don't use too many full stops (periods), underscores or include excessively fanciful use of fonts, e.g. n.A.M E@*PrOV idER*.com as these are difficult to type.

Pro tip

You need to make it easy for all levels of typing ability to enable the person to type your email address quickly. The reader should not have to spend *any* time figuring out the email address. Nor have to use excessive hand motions switching between upper and lower case; so a plain, standard text type email address is necessary.

In the above example, the space between the 'M' and the 'E' and again with the 'V' and the 'i' is ambiguous, they could be either blank spaces or underscores ('_'), which the hyperlink underlining the address covers up. Having to work this out slows the hiring manager down in their attempt to contact you. It can cause them to notice that you haven't made it easy for them to contact you (a negative that could go against you). If they try again and get it wrong a second time, they are more likely to simply give up making any further attempts, and thus transfer your application to their rejection pile (or list), as they are highly unlikely to spend time trying different combinations until they strike it right. All because you made it (and they found it) too hard, and or concluded that you didn't supply a valid email address.

Right Your RESUME

Pro tip

If you have a really long or difficult first or last name, you can reduce your email address to a shorter combination. For example, you might just use your initial with a longer surname (i.e. jsupercalafragalistic@provider.com). Or your first name with the initial of your surname (i.e. josephs@provider.com. Or even your first name with a shortened version of your surname (i.e. josephsuper@provider.com), to help keep the email address concise and easy to type. And, to keep the detail fully relevant and associative towards you.

Professionality

Your email address doesn't hint at your private personality, attitude or personal beliefs

Reason: to prevent a 'no' decision from assumption of your not fitting in with the image or culture of the business.

Example: sexymumma@provider.com or f*ckAsbott@provider.com.

If you want to have those types of email addresses, that is fully your choice. But, leave them as your *personal* email addresses, not your professional, job seeking one.

Hiring manager's will notice the above style email addresses. When the address portrays the person in a way that is contrary to the businesses ideals or beliefs, then the misalignment could cause the hiring manager to eliminate the otherwise perfectly suited person.

Hyperlinks

In Microsoft Word when you press the space bar after typing in an email address, the autocorrect feature automatically corrects the text to a hyperlink (unless you have this feature disabled) so that in your document you get <u>yourname@provider.com</u> instead of yourname@provider.com.

That seemingly innocuous hyperlink allows a reader of an electronic document to go straight to that email or web address by its opening up the appropriate default browser when you click on it. That is, an email program when it an email address that is clicked on (Outlook (on PC's) or Mail (on Mac's)) or a web browser when it is a web address (such as Internet Explorer, Firefox, Chrome, Safari or whatever you have set as your default browser).

Part 2
Personal DETAILS

At the same time as hyper-linking the text, the font colour is also changed to the standardised default 'hyperlink blue'; so that when looking at the resume on screen, the blue hyperlink text stands out against the rest of the text (usually in black). You don't want the hyperlink to be emphasised.

When you print out the resume (if printed in greyscale, which most businesses use, rather than colour), that supposedly innocuous blue text suddenly isn't as harmless as you first thought; because it appears faded in comparison to the rest of the text. You don't want the hyperlink to be de-emphasised either.

The choice is yours, but I remove the hyperlinks from the resumes I create. I personally think a resume looks better without active hyperlinks.

The reason for that is I find most recruiters don't use the hyperlink to open up a blank email so that the address is already filled in. They would rather use a form rejection (or form invitation to attend interview) letter template instead, which they can then just personalize with the finer details in the body copy. For this reason, why hyperlink the text then?

Deactivating the hyperlink better allows the hiring manager to 'highlight, copy and paste' the email address with greater ease (because they aren't competing against the hyperlink trying to force the user to use a specific default program – that they might not want to use). Deactivating the hyperlink immediately permits the text to remain consistent in style and presentation throughout the entire resume (which is what can make all the difference between a good resume and a superior-quality one).

Contact number

Most employers will prefer to contact by phone so they can speak with you first.

As mentioned earlier, perhaps they have a few qualifying questions they want or need you to answer before they are permitted or want to invite you in for an interview. Maybe they just want the convenience of being able to pick up the phone and make a call rather than have to compose an (lengthy, time consuming) email.

In our modern times, you might find otherwise but I find that employers prefer contacting people directly on their **mobile phone number** rather than a **landline number** when they want to speak with an individual. (To a landline number when it is a business and when the specific person they need to speak with isn't known).

Right Your RESUME

Even as little as ten years ago, people didn't have mobile phones like they do so commonly in today's society. When mobile phones first came out, calls were expensive. But as more people adopted the technology, better service plans and wider usage brought the costs down. And now, calling someone on their mobile phone can, in fact, actually be cheaper than calling someone on a landline number (at least here in Australia). Plus, we have the bonus of convenience; people carry their mobile phones around with them wherever they go. The chances of immediately reaching them are higher than when trying to contact someone on their landline number because of that portability.

Hiring managers only really need one phone number with which to call you on. So my advice is even if you have both a landline number and a mobile phone, to list just one phone number. Make that your mobile number (preferred) over your landline number. Otherwise you are sledge-hammering the hiring manager with unnecessary extra details and taking away from valuable and visually appealing 'white space' on your resume document.

Now, although these next few pieces of advice have nothing to do with writing your resume content, while I am on the related topic of you providing your contact number, it is still worth mentioning a couple of jobsearching 'musts' that many jobseekers get wrong. So you don't make the same silly, fully avoidable mistakes.

Answering your phone

How you answer calls matters!

Firstly, if you are available, answer all calls. Even (though some might say, especially!) unknown numbers (blocked, private and or unfamiliar numbers) as it could very well be a potential employer trying to speak with you.

Next, answer in a *professional* manner.

Answer with a polite and informative, "Hello, [Your Name] speaking," or something similar, in a light, welcoming tone.

Whatever you do, do not – I repeat, do not – answer your phone with just a grunting, "Hello?" or worse, "Who's this?"

Imagine you are an employer wanting to invite someone to an interview and they answer like that… your immediate impression is a negative one, isn't it?

Part 2
Personal DETAILS

Remember, you need to make a good impression throughout the entire job search process, not just on your resume. Back up your superb-quality resume. Use good personal behaviours and actions during jobsearch too. Or what is the point in getting your resume up to quality?

If you genuinely miss a call, or can't answer because, say, you are driving, return the call. As soon as possible. Employers aren't going to keep chasing you unless they were super-impressed, and you keep returning each other's calls. In which case they know you are keen and act professionally so they will persist until they get a hold of you – if the process isn't too drawn out. No effort to return their call means they will give up and move on to someone easier to reach, and more professional in behaviour.

Voice mail

If you have voice mail, before you begin sending out applications, make sure you update your voice mail message so that it is professional also. Yes, I know it is a personal item and you will have family and friends calling you too; but, if a hiring manager is interested in you enough to try phoning you, you don't want to undo the good impression you have carefully created by having an inappropriate voice mail message.

Same goes for landline answering machines, if you have to provide your landline number. Make your greeting message professional.

Think about the impression you can cause and how quickly the situation can change you from being a candidate they want to know more about, to 'Nah, not for us.'

Style conventions

Each country has a style convention for how to list phone numbers. In Australia, we use standard business letter communication guidelines and the convention is to list a landline number with the area code number followed by the telephone number in the following style:

    02 9600 3010

Which is: two digits space four digits space four digits.

The convention for listing mobile telephone number for local listings is:

    0410 600 900

Right Your RESUME

Which is: four digits space three digits space three digits

The convention for listing mobile telephone numbers for international dialling is:

    +61 410 600 900

Which is: +61 (Australia's international country code) space [note, the 0 is dropped] three digits space three digits space three digits

Just because you tell people your number using a sequence that is easier for you to remember doesn't equate to that is how it should be listed on your resume.

For example, say your number is: 0411 119 922. It would be easier for many people to tell others that there number is:

    O (zero) four pause eleven pause eleven pause ninety nine pause twenty two.

    04 11 11 99 22

Which is: two digits space two digits space two digits space two digits space two digits

But you would not be using standard business formatting if you listed your number in that (non-conventional) style. I know this might seem like a trivial detail, but as a jobseeker you would be inadvertently demonstrating your ignorance of how to provide such a detail within standard business communications.

A resume, although often has slightly modified rules, is still a standard business communication tool.

That might be fine if you are applying for a job as a labourer and will never need to use a computer and or use written communication skills within your job; but remember, the hiring manager probably does use written communications skills and follows conventions, so it can be jarring for them to see such a detail listed in an alternative way.

If you were applying for a job as a receptionist or office assistant then you would actually be negatively demonstrating that you do not possess the necessary skills with which to maintain the business branding, image and communication standards.

Part 2
Personal DETAILS

You might not care about such small details, but the employer certainly might. And that misalignment could cost you getting the job.

Positioning

Again, this is entirely up to you, but I think listing the person's name, followed by their email address (on the next line), followed by their contact number (on the next line) looks the best on-screen and on paper, and is easiest for hiring managers to dial your phone number.

You might disagree, so if you want to swap the email and contact number around, go right ahead.

For example

Your Name
yourname@provider.com
0410 600 900

Or

Your Name
0410 600 900
yourname@provider.com

19 Optional details

So far we have covered the essential information that must be *included* in a resume: your name and contact details.

Before we move on to talk about the extensive list of details that you should *exclude*, we will first look at an *optional item*: **social media profiles**.

Social media profiles

More and more recruiting agencies and employers are checking social media profiles and the online presence of candidates they are considering for their vacancies. And are even doing online searches to find suitable candidates in the first place (sometimes to avoid having to advertise their vacancy).

How you behave online and offline has the power to help or hinder your jobsearch because employers perform this 'background checking'. (There has been a lot of and frequent criticism from jobseekers in all of the different job seeking groups I am a member of about their doing this).

Employers and recruiters are going to do this regardless of how you feel about it and agree or not. Remember my discussion earlier about you as a product? From a hiring perspective, they are just being thorough and covering themselves from all bases in their desire to ensure the person they hire has provided the business with a somewhat honest and accurate view of who they are as a person (rather than a greatly distorted or dishonest one that too many provide). And are thus, checking that the person seems like a right fit before they make a costly mistake hiring a clearly wrong person.

So YOU want what they find to *support* your jobsearch efforts, not end up prolonging your unemployment or a need to remain in your current role longer than you want to remain in it.

If you have social media accounts, then you may decide to add clickable links, or icons, so that the hiring manager reaches your account not someone with a similar name to yours; to ensure they don't develop a *negative impression* about you because they are erroneously seeing the profiles and images of someone completely different. But you also want to make sure that when they reach the right profile, they aren't going to find out things you would prefer they didn't see. For example, your 'rant' posts, or your photos. Especially ones that are of a 'provocative'. nature

Part 2
Personal DETAILS

If you decide to provide hiring managers with your social media links, then before you start sending off applications, carry out a web search and check each of your account profiles *thoroughly*, to ensure that the impression employers will come away with match the image you are trying to create; because they *will* visit the links that you provide. (Note: you may need to ask a family or friend to check your profile for you because you will be able to see everything in your profile, and what you need to find out is what a prospective employer without full access will see).

You will need to weigh up the pros and cons of providing social media links in your resume for your own self; and weigh up the potential consequences of your doing so.

So, let's say you decide you want to include them…

Hyperlinks or icons?

If you decide to aid the hiring manager to visit the right profile, then you need to decide upon whether to use a hyperlink or an icon they can easily click on in your resume.

Plain resumes are best for jobseekers who are applying for non-creative based roles, and therefore using plain text that is hyperlinked is preferable.

But, these days, more and more roles involve or use high levels of creativity, like blogging, marketing and graphic design (to name but a few). Jobseekers applying for these types of high-creativity roles, generally can better demonstrate their skill level by applying using a **designer resume** rather than a plain one. These jobseekers use graphics, colour and other such designer elements to demonstrate their skills and ability level; so the use of social media icons would fit right in, and would therefore be better to use than a boring hyperlink.

Not only are these jobseekers more likely to have multiple social media accounts, they are likely to already have some nice social media icons on their computer too.

Clickable icons for that jobseeker may give their resume that slight competitive edge over candidates that have submitted a plain resume.

For example, compare the difference in looks achieved by using a plain, professional style compared to a designer style:

$\mathcal{R}$ight Your RESUME

Plain style

Your Name
yourname@provider.com
0410 600 900
Facebook: www.facebook.com/yourname
Twitter: @yourhandle

Designer style

Your name
yourname@provider.com
0410 600 900

If you use icons like this, then you will need to hyperlink them to your accounts to make them clickable.

(If you hover your cursor over the icons in the electronic version of this book it will bring up the URL and provide you with the instructions to use the Control button while clicking on the icon to go to that link).

I reiterate, you need to send out a resume that is best suited to the type of work you are applying for. And, once decided on appropriateness of listing your social media profiles, and which way you will go (hyperlink or icon), then you need to stick with that decision and apply graphical elements consistently.

What I'm encouraging here is not to provide a hyperlink for one social media account and then use an icon for another if you include social media details on your resume. And, don't make any one particular icon larger than the others.

$\mathcal{H}$yperlinks

If you decide to use a hyperlink, then you may want to consider changing the hyperlink colour to black so that it can blend in with the rest of the document. (And, if this is the case then you can leave your email address hyperlinked too, to maintain consistency of all similar items.)

Part 2
Personal DETAILS

Icons

If you are going to use icons, make sure you use nice ones that are consistent in style (perhaps created by the same designer, or come from the same style pack).

Don't make the icons too large; your goal is not to emphasis your social media profiles, it is to simply make it convenient for the hiring manager to access them (it could save them time). I recommend that you make the icons no larger than the text size of your name.

Also, think about the order that you place the icons in. Try to balance the colours, and if necessary, shapes. For example, Facebook and Tumblr icons are a similar blue, whereas the Google Plus icon is red. It would look better if it went 'blue, red, blue' instead of 'blue, blue, red'.

Note

I haven't included social media icons in any of the resumes I have created for clients, yet. There hasn't been a need, or it hasn't been appropriate. If I, personally, were to apply for work requiring me to submit my resume in the future (because I would most likely apply for work that still involved my helping jobseekers) and I have a blog aimed at helping jobseekers, I would consider putting icons in my resume. If I thought it was appropriate and that it would give me an edge within the particular application. I would make my decision to include or exclude on an application-by-application basis though.

Although I would normally not encourage jobseekers to include graphics in their resume; including social media buttons that are not obtrusive or overly prominent could give your resume a slight lift and could even give you that small competitive edge.

I encourage you to weigh up the pros and cons carefully before making the decision to include or exclude, based on the type of work you are seeking and whether that type of employer would need or want to check out your online presence and social media profile(s).

20 What personal details to exclude

So far, we have covered the personal details that we must include (name and contact details) and optional social media profile links.

Now, we will discuss the personal details that you can **exclude** from your resume. Excluding could be because the detail might cause a hiring manager to make a 'no' decision, discriminate against you without your knowledge, or to protect yourself from scammers, online hackers and potential identity thieves.

Full residential address

Too many jobseekers provide their full residential address on their resume; yet where a person lives is not an essential detail during the **application stage** of the hiring process.

Of course, an employer may be required to obtain this detail if they offer you the position in order for them to keep their personnel files up to date and accurate. But this can be where you ruin a scammer's day by withholding the information about where you live. If they have to go looking for this type of detail then they will be more inclined to forget about you and move on to a much easier target when you leave out this unnecessary detail.

If you have good reason to want an employer to get an indication of where you live (perhaps you want them to know you live locally), then include the name of your **suburb** and leave it at that. But, particularly if you live in an area that has a bad reputation, you can protect yourself from being discriminated against based on the suburb you live in by leaving this detail out completely.

If you are applying for a position, you may need to provide your address, if you are sending with a cover letter and by mail. Most applications are made online using an online form, though.

If you **trust** the advertiser, perhaps it is a big name company and their online form asks for the detail, then include it as part of your application (or you might not progress). But, when you are using a job board, like Seek.com.au, you are not asked to provide your residential address when applying for

Part 2
Personal DETAILS

a specific vacancy and although you can attach a pre-written cover letter, I suggest using the 'write one in the space provided' option so that your cover letter becomes the body copy of the email that is sent to the employer. This way you won't feel obliged to include your address.

Age and date of birth

Job applicants can help make their suitability to a vacancy be based solely on their skills and abilities, and lessen being rejected or discriminated against based on their age when they keep their resume 'clean' of age revealing details. Again, you can ruin a scammer's day too, by making it too hard for them to obtain the sensitive information they need in order to do their damage to you.

It is important to understand, though, that a person's age can be revealed by both **direct disclosure** or inadvertent, **indirect disclosure**.

Directly disclosing your age occurs when you state:

- How old you are, or
- Provide your date or year of birth

either, by listing the detail in your personal details section or elsewhere in your resume or application.

Indirectly disclosing your age occurs when you provide details within your resume (or application) that enables the reader to make an accurate 'guesstimate' or out rightly calculate it, such as:

- School leavers providing particulars that show they have recently left school
- Older workers who list full employment history and or education history dating back to their school days more than ten years ago, which enables hiring managers to calculate the person's age group, or make a fairly accurate assumption.
- Jobseekers who use their age or birth year as part of their email address.

An employer is likely to have a strong mental image of what their ideal candidate will be like when they advertise a vacancy. For some employers, that ideal candidate will be young and keen, with a drive to learn new things and take bold risks; for other employers that ideal candidate will be someone

Right Your RESUME

older, more experienced and perceived as more reliable. However, just because an employer has an ideal image or preference in mind doesn't mean that they aren't willing to hire a candidate who fits outside of that.

An employer can't discriminate against a candidate based on age *during the application stage* if the candidate's resume doesn't disclose their age directly or indirectly. Of course, they will still be able to discriminate against the candidate based on their age during or following the interview stage though – and no one has control over that.

But ideally, by the time the applicant comes face to face with the employer, the employer is already keen based on them from their having demonstrated they possess the required skills, attributes and experiences. And won't then allow their personal preference for age to stop them from hiring you if you are the best and most suitable person for the job when you fall outside of it.

You can't control whether an employer will discriminate against you based on age after having met with them in person, but you can prevent them from dismissing your application based on age during the application stage if you pay careful attention to the details you provide throughout your entire resume not just the Personal Details section. To assess whether your age can be guessed or determined from details provided.

There are different ways in which you can accidentally reveal age so when we reach them in later within this book, I will bring them to your attention.

Marital status

Many, many, many years ago, when I was a teenager embarking on obtaining my first job, it was standard to include personal details like marital status on your resume. But, I'm old (my children tell me this all the time), and that was, like I said, many, many, many years ago.

Times have changed. It is no longer a normal practice. It changed many, many years ago. Yet occasionally I still assess a resume from young and older clients which includes their marital status. (Because darn pathetic resume templates are still in abundance!)

Who cares if you are married or not? What **relevance** does this have on your ability to do a job?

It is not only inappropriate to include details of your marital status in your resume, it is illegal (in Australia at the very least) to be even asked by a potential employer if you are married or for them to use this fact as basis

Part 2
Personal DETAILS

for their decision for you gaining the position or not. So don't proffer this unnecessary information, which can easily be used to discriminate against you.

(Also, scammers will love to learn that you are married. If they can't get access to your identity or bank accounts, maybe they can access your partners?)

Once you are in the job and are a colleague, of course fellow staff members may become curious to know you on a closer, personal level. Your marital status will of course help the office matchmaker to know whether to set you up on a date because we all love a good office romance. Or protect you from being hit on by Joe over in Accounts because that guy hits on everyone!

But you aren't working there yet. Save all these type of juicy personal details for when you start.

All joking aside, unless it is a requirement for you to disclose your marital status within your applications in the country you live in (not Australia), if you go against the grain to include personal details like your marital status, it is actually a strong indication to hiring manager's that you are carrying out your jobsearch very much from a *'me'* perspective instead of from a professional, employment oriented one. And as such you need to adjust your thinking immediately, or you will experience difficulties within your jobsearch.

Parental status

Although it is not illegal (in Australia) for an employer to ask you if you have children, it is still not information that you should be too forthcoming about either. Unless you are asked directly during a job interview.

Employers can justifiably develop valid concerns about candidates who have children / don't have children.

Both having them and not having them can be a double-edged sword.

Women can become pregnant and go off on maternity leave, costing the employer money. Parents (males and females!) may need to take time off at inconvenient times because their child gets sick or injured; they may not have anyone else who can babysit while the kids are on school holidays; the employee could run late for work and miss crucial meetings or be otherwise unreliable or unproductive at times, simply because they are going to put their children first – again, costing the employer money.

As a jobseeker, you want to be judged solely on your merits to do the job,

Right Your RESUME

not on your personal situation; you don't want to be rejected because the employer views your parental or non-parental status as being too much of a risk.

Don't give them details like these that can cause them concerns or assist them to make a 'no' decision without meeting you.

This information may be repetitive, but I have compelling reasons for having to spell it out, and repeat myself. I still assess resumes containing these details frequently.

Your resume is a tool to help you **market** yourself to potentially suitable employers; you want and need them to view you as nothing but a complete professional suitable and capable for the job.

So again, if you have included details about your parental status, such as providing details of how many children you have or what their names are, then you are approaching jobsearch and developing your marketing tools from the wrong mindset – that of the '*me*' perspective instead of the 'YOUnique, as a professional' one.

Sexual preference and gender

Just as earlier I didn't care if you are married or not, I do not care whether you are straight, gay, swing both ways, or even whether you have sex or not. You are not applying for a dating service or a sexual encounter; you are applying to be considered for a job.

And as such, this is another of your personal details where it is illegal, in Australia and possibly every western country that has anti-discrimination laws, for an employer to use a person's sexual preference or gender as criteria to not employ them. It is not just illegal for them to ask whether you are gay or straight, it is just plain *rude* of anyone who does ask.

You can't prevent employers from working out that you are male or female. Either because your name gives it away on paper, or they can tell when you attend the job interview. Your gender should not stop you from applying for the type of work you want to do, even if that industry or job type is traditionally the type of job performed by the opposite sex. If it is the type of work you want to do, and you have the skills, then go for it!

Part 2
Personal DETAILS

People can have very strong judgments about another person's sexual preferences. Send out the clear but silent message that *intimate* details like this are *'none of their* [insert an expletive of your choice here, if you like] *business*!

Religious preference and ethnicity

Religion can be a touchy subject for some people who hold strong opinions too, especially when their belief or viewpoint differs vastly to another's. One only needs to watch the nightly news and read historical records to see that disagreements over religious practices, ideals and cultural practices have formed the basis of causing many wars throughout world history, and many a dispute within local communities and families.

When it comes to jobsearching, once again I need to say it: you are applying for a job, not (or should not be) initiating a religious discussion or debate. A person's religious beliefs or their ethnic differences – in a jobsearch context – is nobody else's business. Without good reason to mention them, the detail should not be included on your resume, as it can lead to a jobseeker being discriminated against without their awareness.

The only times that I feel you could break this rule is if by mentioning this detail it may **increase** your chance of success towards gaining an interview or being considered for the job. For example, where a church group advertises a vacancy and you practice that religion and support that religion's beliefs; because it demonstrates that you are aligned well with the church group's aims. Or where a person of a certain ethnic background would make the most suitable person (such as an ambassador, or interpreter role).

Again, it is illegal for employers to use a person's religious beliefs and ethnic background as the basis to not employ that person – whether it is because the employer doesn't want to hire a person from a particular faith or ethnicity, or because an employer doesn't hire an otherwise fully suitable person because they do not practice a particular faith or aren't from a particular ethnicity.

Political preference

Politics is another subject that can bring out strong views and beliefs in people, and probably accounts for the other half of the wars, riots and disputes that have broken out throughout history.

But once again, although politics can significantly affect the lives of individuals, the operations of a business and the safety, policies and comfort level for a country and its citizens, when it comes to applying for a job, there is little to justify including your political preference (or opinion) on your resume. Except perhaps for those who will be applying for a job within a political office.

Disability, injuries and health Conditions

Disabilities, injuries and health conditions can impact upon the type of work we are able to do or how many hours we can sustain doing it for.

But do you need to tell employers that you have a disability, injury or health condition? Not in your resume.

Having a disability, injury or health condition does not automatically mean that a person cannot do the job. Fully or in part. Yet, having spent five years in Disability Employment Services, many of these jobseekers struggle to overcome this barrier to employment because 'cannot do the job' is an assumption people often make.

Jobseekers with disabilities, injuries and health conditions are often told by their doctor(s) and have this reiterated by their family, friends and their own selves that they can't do certain things. But this doesn't make the jobseeker *unemployable*. So why then make it even harder on oneself to gain the job by prematurely raising the issue and thus allowing an employer to develop concerns about their capability to perform the role, before the employer gets a chance to see their suitability?

Every strength we have can also be a weakness, depending on the situation. This is true for **all** jobseekers, not just those with disabilities, injuries and health conditions. The trick for jobseekers is to find and market their positives, and only address their weaknesses and negatives **if asked**.

If your disability, injury or health condition is observable, and you think it could go against you, then you might want to address it during a job interview. But don't raise matters that can cause concerns yourself.

Think about how your condition can be viewed as a positive, and have strong, compelling reasons prepared for why your condition won't cost the employer time or money, and won't negatively impact upon your ability to do the job well, and discuss those.

Part 2
Personal DETAILS

Disability diversity policies

The only time it might, perhaps, be suitable for you to mention your disability, injury or health condition in your resume or cover letter is if the company you are applying to has a **'diversity'** policy. Usually, these companies are big name employers, that have made a commitment with the government stating they will hire a certain percentage of employees as people with disabilities, injuries or health conditions.

With these applications it could actually be to your advantage to mention that you have a low-level disability, injury or health condition so that if the company isn't at its diverse percentage, they might be forced by their diversity agreement to hire a person with a disability over a person who doesn't have one, until such time as they meet the agreed percentage rate. (But, before doing this, you should do a bit of research and seek further advice from a relevant government department or disability organisation to satisfy yourself that doing so would be appropriate for your particular circumstances.)

In Australia, people with disabilities, injuries and or health conditions that may need **workplace modifications** can access specialised help or government funding so they don't miss out on jobs that they would otherwise be suited to. That assistance might be the purchasing of specialised equipment to assist a visually impaired person to view a computer screen, or a relocatable raised platform to assist a short statured person be visible behind a service counter.

Other countries may have programs like this run by their governments or community service organisations too. If you have a disability, injury or health condition, regardless of which country you live in, be sure to look into that type of support and assistance if you feel you need it.

Case Study

A colleague of mine (when I worked for one of the Disability Employment Service providers) used their own disability as her strength in carrying out her Employment Consultant role. She reinforced the *'you are capable of getting a job'* message to clients with less severe injuries or health conditions than what she suffered and to confront them when the person used their condition as an excuse when they didn't want to work. (Most conditions do not prevent people from working).

Her catchphrase, which she said loudly and frequently to job-evaders, was a bluntly stated: 'So, you have an injury [or health condition]... lar-dee-dah. So do I, and I've got a job. What other excuse have you got?'

This harsh but honest view greatly contributed to her getting placement results compared to other consultants. Clients took one look at how severely her injury impacted upon her ability to walk, and saw that she was [usually] worse off than their own self.

I know her challenging those clients **negative beliefs** impressed our employer, who occasionally took her off working with clients with disabilities to instead work with mainstream job-evader clients from time to time. Because our employer saw (and capitalised upon) the advantage of her position as a person with a noticeable disability (and her personality that had no qualms in) telling a fully-abled person that their excuse for not getting a job was just that, an excuse.

Case Study 2

You might be surprised at just how willing some employers are towards helping a person with a disability when the person does genuinely want to work, but perhaps cannot work at full capacity, too. They are more bountiful than most jobseekers believe exist.

Over the period where I filled the role as Post Placement Support Officer for a disability exclusive Employment Service provider (they did not also deliver mainstream job services), each and every employer we dealt with knowingly and willingly hired our clients. Those employers often phoned us when they needed further staff too. My role was to help keep both our jobseeker and employer client happy within their employer employee relationship, and assist resolution of problems if they occurred within the first six months of employment.

When issues arose – which happens whether the person has disabilities, injuries, health conditions or not – I stepped in to mediate and work towards bringing the parties to resolution. I can tell you now, most times the problem could be resolved quite easily.

If I had to go and purchase a back brace so my disability client didn't exacerbate their back condition, I went out and purchased a back brace. If I had to negotiate with the employer to reduce the range of tasks, or workload, I met with the employer to discuss the problem, offer solutions and negotiate a win-win situation for both.

When the employee took a bit longer in their training to reach the required level of competence, I went in and learned how to do the job and then personally taught the jobseeker how to do their new job – so that it wasn't costing the employer more than they expected to pay to have the person get up to speed. And so the employer wasn't getting upset by the

Part 2
Personal DETAILS

prolonged learning need.

If you have a disability, injury or health condition that negatively impacts upon your ability to work, then you should investigate, especially if you are in receipt of social security type payments, if you can be assigned to a specialist disability job network. Rather than tough it out as a mainstream jobseeker, as you will benefit from this additional type of support.

But, the main reasons jobseekers fell out of employment had little to do with jobseekers having a disability, injury or health condition. The problems were more to do with poor attitudes and behaviour, or disputes over pay, conditions and rostering with far more jobseekers doing the wrong thing by employers than employers doing the wrong thing by jobseekers.

Case Study 3

A cousin of mine has a disabled left arm; in that his arm is paralysed but he has partial use of his left hand. Back when this cousin was a teenager and reached the good old age in being able to convert his learner permit into a driver's licence, the government department worker took one look at his non-functioning arm and handed him an application form to apply for a disabled person licence – which would restrict him to only being permitted to drive an Automatic vehicle.

(The rule was that (because Australia drives on the left-hand side of the road), the person must be able to use their left arm and hand with which to change gears. For safety reasons, drivers with disabilities couldn't say, use their right arm and hand to carry out that operation because they need that hand to control the steering.)

Some would say, 'fair enough' and leave it at that.

But the trouble was, my cousin's disability prevented him from being able to operate the automatic gear's T-bar to change gears. He didn't have the strength of movement within his fingers to lift that crossbar in an upward motion so that the shift could move forward or back. And for the side button variety, he didn't have the strength of movement to push that button in either. In other words, the mechanics which enable a shift to be moved, he couldn't operate.

He did, however, have the full use and movement of his left shoulder and, had over his sixteen years nine months of life, learned to use his shoulder in combination with locking up his elbow to move his arm, and was thus able to simply open and close his hand to grab a hold of things while growing up.

And, before this cousin had even obtained a learner's permit the year before, he and his parents had identified that this absolute 'born car-enthusiast since an early age' would actually need to learn to drive a manual vehicle, or investigate the possibility of operating a modified vehicle.

Learning to drive just proved that that best type of vehicle for him to operate was indeed a manual right hand drive vehicle (so no moving to America for him!). Because his fully functioning right hand could maintain full control of the steering wheel (required), and his 'useless' (what the person called it, which was not only rude, but also incorrect) arm easily changed up or down gears by his using shoulder movements.

For twelve months as this natural-born driver learned to drive, we all knew, he needed to be issued with an unrestricted manual driver's licence, nothing else. So the hasty assumption by the employee was incorrect.

Unfortunately, the employee arrogantly thought he knew what was best for my cousin and his disability, and refused to allow him to apply for the full unrestricted licence; wouldn't even give him the paperwork to fill out. My cousin and uncle had to speak with supervisors, all to no avail and then go through a lengthy appeals process before the department finally relented and allowed him to sit the practical driving test. Because they had applied an 'automatic fail' without letting him even sit the driving test the moment he stated he couldn't operate an automatic.

On the day he eventually got to sit his driving test, a very cranky and sceptical examiner made it quite clear that he was not in the mood so late within the day to put up with having one more inept learner nearly run down pedestrians, cut off other motorists or have dangerous near-misses and close-calls. So my cousin and his disability better not stuff things up or he will fail as fast as the examiner's pen could mark the paper. Again, a negative assumption that because my cousin has a disability would mean he would somehow be a less-able driver.

And thankfully my cousin proved the examiner wrong.

By the time my cousin had driven a kilometre in heavy traffic, the examiner turned less hostile and more pleasant. By the time they arrived back at the depot half an hour later, the examiner was positively smiling. My cousin proudly boasted for weeks that the examiner told him he had never felt so safe in the car with any other learner driver as what he felt with my cousin behind the wheel.

Part 2
Personal DETAILS

My cousin didn't quite get full marks in the driving test. He lost two points because he was a bit slow to put on his indicator or something, but still had plenty of other points he could have lost before it would have caused him to fail the test. The examiner was forced to concede that my cousin not only could be issued with a full unrestricted licence, but that their department and staff initial assumptions about his disability and correlating capability were wrong.

My point here is that my cousin knew his disability inside and out, and as such understood exactly what he could and couldn't do. He knew he could drive – he had spent the past year being allowed to learn and had never run into trouble he could not handle.

And, by the way, this cousin then spent the next fifteen years working as a courier, and a further ten years as a truck driver (which he still is).

Wouldn't it be terrible if he had believed he couldn't drive just because that's what other people were telling him?

Tax file number and bank accounts

Although an employer will require your tax file number (here in Australia) or other such taxation or social security number in other countries along with your bank account details to deposit your pay into, these are again **super-sensitive details** that jobseekers need to keep to themselves until they secure the job and have established that everything is completely above board with the employer and the vacancy listing.

A tax file number and bank account details will definitely need to be provided to the employer at some point **after being offered the job**, so that you can be paid and taxed correctly. But you need to do a background check on the business too, to make sure that the person or business is legitimate and therefore sufficiently trustworthy enough in your view that you can comfortably provide such sensitive details to them.

It is just keeping the detail out of your application tools (your resume and cover letter) that is the important part you need to follow during the early hiring stages.

Right Your RESUME

Summarised information sections

Part 3.

Right Your RESUME

Quote

"When you truly believe in what you are doing, it shows. And it pays. Winners in life are those who are excited about where they're going."
@Inspire_Us

Part 3
Summarised INFORMATION

21 Summarised information

In this section, I am going to revert back to my original intention of breaking the section into one of three distinct groups: a *'yes, you should include'*, a *'no, you shouldn't include'* and an *'optional, because it depends on…'* separation. I feel that this will be the best way to help you decide if you should include or exclude the section as a whole.

But, please remember, that like with the Personal Details section, even when you should include a section, there might be circumstances where you should leave out finer specifics. I will discuss precisely which details to include or exclude from your resume, which are optional, and why, as we get to each of the different chapters, to clarify the information given.

Common summarised information sections

Although there aren't all that many hard rules when it comes to writing resume content – because everyone has different skills, interests, experiences, attributes, values and capabilities, as well as differing personal preferences and styles, so rules aren't always going to apply to everyone – there are a few common 'sections' that most jobseekers include in their resume.

In the following chapters, we are going to look at some of those more common sections, and discuss ways and means of deciding if including the section is right for our own resume, and ways to handle and treat including such sections and its details when you decide they are fully relevant and completely appropriate for you.

As you should be convinced by now, you need to have a specific job in mind when you create the content of your resume; and with that job firmly in mind, now, as we start working in the prime resume real estate area, it is time to start convincing potential employers that you are potentially suitable for their role. (So if you have multiple job types that you are applying for, you'll need to pick one and create the content for that one job, and then repeat the entire process for each subsequent job type afterwards).

Assuming that the hiring manager has already formed a good impression as they pick up or open your resume for the first time (from their brain processing the visual structure faster than their eyes zero in on any specific text), you have now reached **crunch time** where you need to back that strong start up with providing the right details that will get the hiring manager to start checking mental tick boxes that builds their interest in you as a viable candidate.

The best way to achieve this building up of interest is to include details in a short summary, or snapshot, form.

What is a snapshot?

Imagine for a moment that you go on a two week holiday. Let's say you travel to a beautiful tropical island retreat, where you can have fun adventures water skiing, scuba diving, going on a bush walk and a helicopter ride. Where you can while away a few hours just sun baking upon a towel laid on pristine white sand and occasionally cool off by going for a leisurely dip in the clear blue-green water in which you can open your eyes and see into the distance even while underwater.

As you enjoy every moment of your relaxing heaven, you take plenty of photographs to capture certain moments of the time, fun and the activities undertaken, so that later, when you are back at home, you can show family and friends. And perhaps even create a scrapbook album so that from time to time you can bring it out and reminisce about your blissful break and never forget how great, how perfect, that two weeks was.

Now, if you were to gather up just a single picture from each of the different things you did while on that two week holiday, say perhaps just your favourite snapshots, and you put those favourites into a sequence, other people would be able to see the **range** of activities you did. They'd be getting the best pictures of the best moments, rather than having to sift through every shot taken. They wouldn't have had to be there to form an accurate mental picture of what you had done; those single images covering every aspect would tell that story progression for you – without any unnecessary 'filler' – that might inspire the reader to enviously express 'I want to go there, and do that!'

Well, this is what snapshots attempt to achieve in in a resume; except, instead of being precious best-of-the-best photographic moments from that treasured holiday, it is a capture of your essential work-related skills, experiences, licences, or position titles etc., that is being shown. A snapshot summary condenses a much larger period of time to provide a short story that paints an accurate picture of the person's employment abilities and history so that a hiring manager will be able to see that range to accurately compare what

Part 3
Summarised INFORMATION

is on offer to what they need, which hopefully enables them to reach the conclusion, 'This person might be suitable for our role!'

Because the focus will be clear about what that person will be like for the future.

So, within Part 3, we'll cover the best details easily shaped into a summary or snapshot form, namely:

- Career Objectives
- Career Snapshots
- Skill Summaries
- Personal Attributes Summaries
- Area of Expertise
- Licences, Tickets and Checks
- Training, Education and Qualifications
- Tools of the Trade
- Computers, Technology and Social Media Savviness
- Hobbies, Interests and Sporting Participation
- Achievements and Awards
- Referees and References

Note

We will deal with your work history in Part 4, because your work history requires listing in much greater detail.

For now, kick back and let's start going through each of those above-mentioned sections, to explore the decisions you can make and the particulars you can include; that have the power to convert a hiring manager from neutral skim reader, to either interested (and even excited), or have them start yawning, thinking about other things and quickly toss your resume straight over to their rejection pile unimpressed and eager to move on to other things or the next in the pile.

Hopefully, by the end of the following chapters, you'll learn some great tips, techniques and secrets that resume writers use, that can cause hiring managers think, *"We might have a winner here!"*. And so you can confidently right an existing resume that hasn't been getting you results, or write a good one from scratch.

22. Career objective

Include or exclude?

I'm listing this section as **optional**, because inclusion depends on the country you live in, and the industry and employer expectations – so you may need to do a bit of additional research / further investigating to work out whether you should include or exclude this section.

> * Include
> * Exclude
> ✓ **Optional, or It Depends...**

I don't include Career Objectives in the resumes I create for clients for entry-level or general worker type roles, and prefer to write a *Career Goal* or *Dynamic Person Statements* for my higher level clients, if they want this type of section. This is because as both a former hiring manager and as a writer I find the typical Career Objective on resumes I assess (and in most online samples and templates) *boring* and *unmeaningful*; and therefore a waste of valuable prime resume real estate space.

I have previously worked with both employers and fellow recruiters too who considered the Career Objective (or sometimes entitled a *Career Statement*) as yawn-worthy '*go nowhere*' or '*me, me, me...*' statements. That is, those important people making the culling decisions considered such a long sentences of text nothing more than rambling, self-focused wastes of their time, because for the majority of applicants their statements rarely **add value** or **lead anywhere** specific *for the employer*.

Yet, I've seen countless articles online and heard career advisors tell jobseekers to include a Career Objective.

So what should you do?

To help you choose if you should include this section or not, my advice is: if the position type you are going for is in any way competitive, sales or target driven, or higher than entry level (such as middle to upper management), then you are probably able to set yourself apart from your competition by

Part 3
Summarised INFORMATION

including a goal or dynamic person statement in your resume rather than a career objective. Because hiring managers will be looking for what sets you apart, for what makes you better than everyone else that applies. And a goal or dynamic person statement achieves this to a much higher degree.

But, if the type of work you are doing is early entry level, training, general worker or uncompetitive in basis, then it is probably better to *leave this section* out of your resume altogether, because many hiring managers just skip over this section anyway. If old habits die hard and you decide you have to include some sort of paragraph to kick things off in your resume even though I'm suggesting you shouldn't, then I encourage you to choose a goal statement or dynamic person statement rather than a career objective.

What does a career objective look like?

Here are two examples, with my hiring manager perspective commentary breaking it down, afterwards:

> To obtain a role as Receptionist / Administration enabling me to utilise my experience and qualifications in Administration whilst making a valuable contribution to my team, my employer and to society.

Can you see that this career objective is all about what the jobseeker wants: '*I want to obtain a role as receptionist*'; '*I want to use my experience and qualification in Administration*'? Yes, they are expressing desire to 'contribute' but what value to the employer are they expressing? None.

See it from the hiring manager's perspective: how does this statement set the person apart from the other candidates that apply. What do we learn about this person? How are they are good match for our role?

We have questions that aren't being answered. We have text, but it isn't demonstrating relevance or suitability. So we start to get bored, and form a neutral or negative opinion.

I see another mistake within this particular Career Objective also, which I know my former manager would have grumbled (*loudly*) over: "*Administration is not a position title; Administration is the type of work a person does!*"

What this candidate is ultimately seeking is a combined Receptionist and Administrative Assistant or a Receptionist and Administrator role; the jobseeker isn't applying to become 'Administration', so listing the position as Receptionist / Administration in this flawed way sets the tone of their entire resume as being one of poor quality.

Right Your RESUME

It might be a small, nitpicky detail in your eyes, but if the hiring manager notices and views the flaw negatively then they are likely to start noticing other little flaws too. Until a number of little flaws are viewed as big ones. And the assumption the hiring manager then makes is that this person is too careless and unsuitable for the reception / administration vacancy they have going. Because, in their view, the candidate doesn't have a high enough skill level or hasn't paid enough careful attention to details needed in such an administration role.

Let's try the next one.

> To find a suitable job that fits my past experiences, skills and previous jobs.

Again, the candidate is expressing what they want, not what value they would bring to the workplace if they were the successful candidate: '*I want a job*' and '*I want any job*'.

They haven't indicated what type of work they have done in the past, or what they want to do in the future. Many jobseekers apply for jobs which they would *like to do* but which they don't already have experience – and that is okay. But, 'A job that fits my past experiences, skills and previous jobs' could be *anything*; it is non-specific.

The hiring manager doesn't read a candidate's resume (like a lot of jobseekers want them to) with the view of '*how can we fit this person into our business?*'; they have **one vacancy to fill.** The candidate must use the small window of opportunity given to them to demonstrate how they fit in with that business and into that vacant role.

From a hiring manager's perspective, reading such career objectives is: *Yaaawwwwnnnnn!*

Yawning means you are failing to generate interest. Yawning means you are milliseconds away from having your resume moved over to and placed on top of the rejection pile (or have your electronic file closed down). This is BAD news.

> "... We still have the rest of the resume to go... and if this poor standard is all I'm going to get..."

What the hiring manager **wants** is to read something that ***brings them alive.*** Something that grabs hold of their interest, something that forces them to sit up straighter with increased interest as they move away from the tediousness

Part 3
Summarised INFORMATION

of sifting through resume after resume after resume after resume after goddamn boring resume.

As humans we naturally consider our own needs and wants, often before we consider the needs and wants of others, taking a self-focused approach to life and circumstances. I'm not saying this is necessarily a bad thing, just that when it comes to getting a job, such an approach works against us.

The hiring manager though, is going to take the same self-focused approach in deciding who they view as being potentially suitable. So, the way to stand out from the competition is to be different from the majority, to be YOUnique, and not come from a place of considering our own needs.

Therefore, if you are going to include such a statement, your words must add value and be meaningful to the employer, so that if the hiring manager reads your objective they are pleasantly surprised because it is not the same meccentric they expect to find.

But remember, not all hiring managers will read such paragraphs at all; and as such, you could decide to leave the section out of your resume without any detrimental effects.

As mentioned earlier, many hiring managers just skip straight past them because their purpose in viewing the resume is to quickly assess the quality of the resume and the person. When they do this, they aren't interested in the candidate, yet, to want to know anything about them. Not until they have made a preliminary determination about the candidates potential suitability. At this initial skim read, the hiring manager has one thing on their mind: *'Does this person have the skills, experiences and attributes we are after?'* and career objectives don't (often) contribute to answering that pressing question.

When I did the culling, I know I didn't bother reading them. And neither did my manager, or our Sales team. Actually, more often than not, if I handed the Sales team member the resume of a potentially suitable match to the vacancy and the resume contained a typical career objective, before the Sales Rep contacted or met with the employer, they quickly 'fixed up' the clients resume (or got me to do it); often, cutting the career objective statement straight from the resume as the very first change made.

Alternatives to boring career objectives and career statements

If you quality, or insist on wanting, to provide a paragraph of text for the hiring manager to read before they are permitted to jump in and start

Right Your RESUME

seeing the key details they hope to find, then there are two better options that you could use to fill in that space.

The first is to write a **Goal Statement**.

What is a goal statement?

A goal statement is a clear and concisely worded statement about what your goal is for yourself in the position, or the benefits you believe you will bring to the role.

For example

> My goal is to use my case management and persuasion techniques to motivate and inspire resistant longer term unemployed clients, to drive them towards action, to overcome fears and personal barriers that enable them to go on to find and maintain employment so I consistently exceed monthly placement targets and reach 13 and 26 week outcomes.

In this example, the goal statement is specific to the particular job role (Employment Consultant / Case Manager). It demonstrates to the hiring manager the candidates understanding of what can hold longer term unemployed persons back (fears and barriers) and what skills the position holder will need to use in order to succeed within the role (case management and persuasion). It also demonstrates knowledge of what is required in the role (job retention outcomes at 13 and 26 weeks).

From a hiring manager's perspective: This person has experience, and knows what the job truly involves; they sound like they might be a suitable candidate.

Because the resume is now off to a good start – their interest captured – the hiring manager is likely to *read* the resume rather than just *skim read*, too. And, if the candidate backs up their strong start with further quality details throughout the rest of the resume, the hiring manager is likely to conclude when they reach the end of the resume: '*I must interview this candidate.*'

(I know this particular goal statement worked, because the Human Resources Manager provided feedback that it was because of this goal statement – which they happened to read first and was so vastly different to what they usually had to read – that the application was placed in their 'contact immediately' pile. The HR Manager read the rest of the resume because the goal statement had already convinced them they had just found the type of candidate they were looking for.)

Part 3
Summarised INFORMATION

Let's try a simple one for a landscaper:

> My goal is to assist homeowners beautify their yards and gain gardens that are easy to maintain, so the homeowners and neighbourhood can enjoy their outdoor environment.

In this example, the goal statement is once again specific to the particular type of work (Landscaper). Their goal statement demonstrates the candidates understanding of why homeowners will spend thousands of dollars to have works done to their front and back yards. The words also hint at the candidate having an ability to work towards customer satisfaction, which is important to most businesses.

From a hiring manager's perspective: This person aligns well to our business goals, they could be a suitable match for our vacancy.

The second option is to write a **Dynamic Person Statement.**

What is a dynamic person statement?

A Dynamic Person Statement is a clear and concisely worded statement written from a third-person viewpoint that sells how great (dynamic) the person is.

For example

> A talented Case Manager with proven history in moving long term unemployed into employment, and driving strong results in gaining 13 and 26 week outcomes.

This Dynamic Person Statement demonstrates the candidate's strength and confidence in their abilities to do this specific type of job well, while maintaining the focus on their attributes rather than their goal if they get the job.

From a hiring manager's perspective: Oooh, we might have a top performer here. They sound like they achieve strong, consistent results. I want to know more about this person!

Again, because the resume is off to a good start, the hiring manager is likely to read the resume in full (rather than skim read) and, backed up by the rest of the resume to cause them keeping this high opinion because they start ticking off all the mental boxes for the skills and experiences they are expecting (and find), the hiring manager will have made the decision before they even get to the end: I want to interview this person.

Let's try another one, for a Salesperson:

> A high-performing Sales Rep who successfully builds strong networks and exceeds monthly sales targets, recently awarded Top Salesperson of the Year.

This dynamic person statement demonstrates the candidate's skills and achievements to perform in this type of work and uses top level skills to achieve good results. It uses 'highlights' of the person's career that would be of the most interest for future employers to paint a mental picture of strong performance and results.

From a hiring manager's perspective: Oooh, looks like we have a top performer. Their network and history suggests they could start getting high results for us very quickly. I want to know more about this superstar!

How to write

It is only possible to write compelling goal statements or dynamic person statements when you **know your own self** and **the job well**; either through having worked in the industry or in similar positions in the past, or from having researched the industry and job role thoroughly so you know exactly what is required. And knowing how your skills and attributes align well to the employers needs and wants.

All statements must be concisely written. That is, the statement should convey one key message, and the remainder of the sentence must support that message using the shortest amount of words, and framed in the most positive and impactful way.

How to list

If you decide to include a goal or dynamic person statement in your resume, then you need to spend time on constructing a good, powerful statement; because as discussed earlier, it has the power to set the tone and expectation of the entire resume, if the hiring manager reads the statement.

To list, use proper spelling, punctuation and grammar as you would for any similar paragraph writing, such as when writing letters or essays.

Part 3
Summarised INFORMATION

Positioning

This section, by whatever name or type you give it, belongs *immediately after* your Personal Details section.

You should list it in normal font size. And because the paragraph is by nature a 'blurb' you could emphasise this by making the text italic. (But be aware, that Italics both on a screen and in printed form are hard on the eyes when used for more than just the occasional word or short phrase).

My suggestion is to make sure that your goal or dynamic person statement is no longer than one or two sentences in length, and uses two or three lines from margin to margin. As one line doesn't provide enough detail (which means your message could probably be added elsewhere within the resume) and more than three lines will cause most hiring managers to ignore it (as it is likely to be too verbose in its wording or carrying too many messages).

I also recommend that you align the text to either the left or right margin, but avoid justifying or centring the text (because that just shows amateur-level layout and styling techniques). You could use indentation at both the left and right margins, if necessary.

23 Career snapshot

What is a career snapshot?

This section is a snapshot or quick summary of your relevant and useful employment history – a brief listing (a snapshot, as described earlier) of the position titles you have previously done, the full details of which appear from the second page of your resume onwards.

It may be helpful to think of a Career Snapshot as an 'appetiser', a sampler of what is to come, that can pique the reader's interest and build their desire to learn more about you, where the Work History section is the 'main meal' providing all the finer details.

During their skim read, the more details the hiring manager can see (and the faster those details come) that is important, relevant, related and appropriate for the position they are filling, the more it should grab their attention, build up their interest and lead them to logically concluding that you might be the person they are looking for. And, because it is too soon to convert them from skim reading to actual reading listing these 'short bites' of essential information is the best way to cause them to see your potential suitability.

Hiring managers don't want to waste time reading stuff they don't care about; they want to see important details upfront. They are a hungry lot and want to see details of interest after yet more details of interest as they scan your text.

Include or exclude?

I'm listing this section as '**It depends…**', because inclusion depends on the resume format you choose to use.

> * Include
> * Exclude
> ✓ **Optional, or It Depends…**

I mostly always include a Career Snapshot section because most of my clients have worked in a number of different roles, and the resume format

Part 3
Summarised INFORMATION

that I prefer is the multi-page Combination-style (discussed previously in this book).

Positioning

Assuming the resume format you decide upon gives physical room for you to include this section, such as your resume will be two or more pages in length, the ideal placement of the Career Snapshot section is in the PRRE area.

Mistake to avoid

I have seen jobseekers bury summary information and key details like this on the last page...

Why leave the best details for last; when the second page onwards may (or may not) be looked at?

Viewing a resume on a computer screen, readers don't bother scrolling the page to skim read the rest of the resume if nothing has grabbed their attention, captured their interest and the person isn't keen to learn more from the information they have viewed.

When viewing a printout of a multi-page resume, the reader isn't going to bother flipping to those subsequent pages if nothing on the first page, above where they are holding, has stood out to them as being of high interest either.

You need to make an *impact* with your wording.

Deliberately. Positively.

When learning to write, coaches and mentors frequently advise writers' to avoid writing in passive voice, citing that active voice causes the most reader interest and is far more compelling. So too is having placed key details up front more compelling.

Therefore, the best place to locate a Career Snapshot section is within the PRRE, i.e. immediately after your Personal Details section – to get the interest happening as soon as possible. (If you haven't included a Career Objective section; otherwise next best place to locate the Career Snapshot is immediately after the career objective or statement).

Right Your RESUME

How to list

If the resume format that you choose supports you including summary information to 'whet' a hiring manager's appetite, then you need to make the most out of including this section.

The purpose of including summary information is so that the short sentences guide the reader's eyes to travel *down the page* quickly rather than moving their eyes *across* the page. So, to create the best interest, the details should be:

- Listed in bullet form
- Written using short sentences
- Only include relevant job titles that (where possible),
- Match the type of work sought.

Some points to keep in mind when deciding what position titles to list include:

- Not having any more than 6 job titles per summary – to avoid inadvertently making yourself look like you job hop too frequently (as hiring managers might assume you won't last with them).
- Keep the details to the last ten year period (unless you have good reason for breaking this rule)
- If you didn't have a specific job title, then you should create a meaningful one that best describes what you did.

Notice how, in the first of those preceding two sets of bullet points, the shorter sentences guided your eyes down the page far quicker than the second set of bullet points, which you had to read across the page before you could move downwards or onto the next one?

I have on occasion advised clients they could include a career snapshot section, only to find when they resend their resume for a second look over that their sentences are long and verbose; which defeats the whole purpose of adding a *snapshot*.

Remember: Short lines (lengthwise across the page). Is. Best.

The same is not true *depth wise* (length travelling down the page). If you have only done the one type of work previously, say, forklift driving, then you wouldn't want to create a Career Snapshot section.

Part 3
Summarised INFORMATION

This would look silly:

Career Snapshot

- Forklift Driver

But you don't want to create really long lists either, just to get the hiring manager to the end of the first page. Because long lists lessen the significance of the individual points made, they can make you look like you can't last in a job, and are being needlessly repetitive or that you are trying too hard to make your history seem impressive when in factual basis it is not:

This also doesn't work:

Career Snapshot

- Forklift Driver
- Bobcat Driver
- General Labourer
- Warehouse Supervisor
- Data Entry Operator
- Machine Operator
- Power Tool User
- Customer Service Officer
- Salesperson
- Technician
- Pipe layer
- Job Estimator
- Shift Rosterer
- Cleaner

This is meant to be a snapshot of your *different positions held*, not all the different tasks you did as part of that role.

Pro tip

Each of the job titles that you include in the Career Snapshot ideally should have an entry in your work and development history section (discussed

Right Your RESUME

later in this book), thus providing the hiring manager with the 'main course' course information after having earlier been satisfied by the 'appetiser'.

Just as appetizers in the food world aim to work up your hunger so that you'll be more satisfied when you've finished the main meal, so too is the aim in providing this type of snapshot.

Pro tip

If a former position title isn't relevant to the type of work sought, the detail is unlikely to be impressive to the hiring manager.

For each item you want to have listed (or intend listing) you must decide, "*Is this a detail that I need to include in my snapshot?*"

Or is the detail something you can include within your work and development history; or, something you could leave out entirely?

Part 3
Summarised INFORMATION

24 Skills summary

What is a skills summary?

This section is a snapshot summary of your **relevant skills** for the type of work you will be applying for. These are the details employer's are most interested in; the last two sections have been 'tasters' aimed at capturing the hiring manager's interest.

Now that you have indeed captured their attention (under the AIDA Principle), it is time for you to back your worth as a viable candidate up by starting to cultivate that attention and convert it into the hiring manager growing interest in you as a potentially suitable candidate.

Providing a summary of the skills you have relevant for the type of work you are seeking is the way you can build a hiring manager's interest in you as being potentially suitable within your resume (after providing a career snapshot).

Therefore, this section can be 'make or break' time.

Include or exclude?

I'm listing this section as a must **include**.

> ✓ **Include**
> ∗ Exclude
> ∗ Optional, or It Depends...

Although a Skills Summary section can end up as the third or fourth 'section' in your resume, it is important to note that this section should **always** appear in the PRRE (never at the back of a resume like too many jobseekers place it). Preferably this section starting before the halfway mark of an A4 page document.

Great care must go into deciding which skills you list, and how you word them.

Right Your RESUME

Mistake to avoid

Not understanding the difference between a Skill and a Personal attribute.

A **skill** is tangible, something that can be put into practice or demonstrated through action. For example, driving a car, hammering a nail, or typing.

A **personal attribute** is an intangible personality trait, value or belief that you possess or hold about yourself. For example, being punctual, a hard worker, a team player.

The trouble with personal attributes is they are difficult to prove on paper; we can only claim that we have these attributes.

What I find in most of the resumes I assess is jobseekers often combine their skills and attributes into the same summary listing, and I've seen many online templates and sample resumes that steer jobseekers to doing this too. But I'm going to encourage you to focus on providing just details of your skills. And either separate your attributes into its own summary list or forget about including your personal attributes completely (see next chapter on personal attributes for reasons).

Now that I have made it clear this summary is for your *skills only*, let me discuss why I encourage you to include this section regardless of which resume format you use.

After gaining a quick idea as to what jobs you have done in the past, the next thing a hiring manager is going to want to know about you – to help them determine your suitability – are the skills you have developed while doing those roles.

When most hiring managers first see a printed page (well, I know I did), a heading with the word 'Skills' is generally one of the first things noticed because it is what the reader has picked the document up (or opened the document) to see.

So our alert brain zeroes in on the word we are subconsciously looking for the moment they spy it.

The very act of including the word 'skills' is, effectively, you 'grabbing the reader's attention' part of using the AIDA principle. (Apart from checking whether the candidates name is present, this is the information that most hiring managers are likely to read first. *Read*, no longer just skim-read. So the sooner you can cause the hiring manager to switch to actual reading,

Part 3
Summarised INFORMATION

and keep them doing that, the greater your chance of reaching the interview stage.)

The precise skills listed carry the power to help or hinder your application. As it can either build the hiring manager's interest in you as a potentially suitable candidate or cause them to conclude, quickly (and rather accurately), that the applicant is not suitable for their role.

As with the advice given in the Career Snapshot section, the Skills section has the power to permit the reader to see important, relevant, related and appropriate information in short bites that guide their eyes down the page instead of across it.

To cause the hiring manager to scroll down the electronic page, or to turn to subsequent pages in a multi-page application can depend on how far their reviewing reaches the end of what is in front of them. When they reach the bottom and are not bored by the contents, they should automatically turn to the next page or scroll down to keep assessing. But if nothing has stood out or generated their interest thus far, they could use this 'coming to the end' as a natural stopping point.

Positioning

As explained earlier in the book, it is important to use your PRRE well, and therefore the Skills Summary section needs to be located in this area either directly after your Personal Details (or after your Career Snapshot if you use a format that means you should include that section).

This is another section that some less savvy jobseekers tend to bury towards the tail end of their resume content instead of getting it upfront.

What skills to list

Like the Career Snapshot summary section, a skills summary is a snapshot or quick summary of the person's relevant skills gained from past (paid and unpaid) work history, and should be:

- Listed in bullet form
- Written using short sentences
- List skills that are relevant to the position being considered for
- Listed in order of highest importance to the least importance
- Can be from your personal background, not just your employment

Right Your RESUME

one

Some points to keep in mind when deciding what skills to list include:

- Carefully choose which skills you include / omit from this section
- Don't list any more than 6 skills (you need to leave the hiring manager with desire to know more about you, not tell them everything so they don't want or need to know anything further)
- Keep the skills, if possible, to those developed within the last ten years
- List in order of priority to the job and your capability in that skill
- Make sure that it is a skill, not a personal attribute, and you back this skill up by including further detail in your work and development history section.
- Don't use cliché phrases like 'Proven competence in… ' or 'Demonstrated ability to…', if you want to say you have customer service experience, write 'Customer Service' (Telling) and leave the explanation to demonstrating (Showing) how you use this skill to when you write your skill statements.

Later, in the Work and Development History section, I will discuss the importance of showing rather than telling. But for the Skills Summary section, the importance is on **telling** rather than showing. That is, you tell them in this section (concisely) what you are going to show them (in greater detail) within the Work and Development History section.

A forklift driver, for instance, might list:

Skills

- Forklift Driving
- General Labouring
- Workplace Safety

In the licensing section, I would want to see that the candidate has the required forklift licence ("Is the person licensed? Check!"), and in the employment history I would want to read a skill statement or two (that answers the questions "Do they have experience? Check!" and "Are they likely to do the job well?" Check!)

Wait staff, for instance, might list:

Part 3
Summarised INFORMATION

Skills

- Food & Beverage Service
- Customer Service
- Cash Handling
- Cleaning

In the employment history section, I would want to read skill statements that discussed 'serving customers' (correlates to Customer Service), 'processing payments' [Cash Handling], 'clearing tables' [Cleaning] (that answers the question "Do they have experience? Check!" and "Do they have the skills needed to do the job?" Check!", as well as specific details to help me draw the conclusion, "Are they likely to do the job well?" Yes!)

I used the 'Food & Beverage Service' detail as a means of tying the skills to the particular type of work where they were developed. I did this because people can gain customer service, cash handling and cleaning skills without having worked in a Food & Beverage service role; as one can develop customer service skills from any client-facing role, and cash handling skills from, say, having worked in a bank or in the back office preparing the banking, not just from operating a cash register. (Though, note that just specifying having a specific skill doesn't automatically equate to being proficient or accomplished in that skill.)

Pro tip

For every Skill listed in your summary section, ensure you have a *correlating skill statement* in at least one of your previous work history listings. This is so that your elements are tied together to better create a cohesive whole.

Most jobseeker simply toss in an impressive list of skills but don't back those skills up anywhere else in their resume – and that is where the problem lies. As a hiring manager, when you have just interested me about a particular skill, I might want to learn a little bit more about that, so I skip ahead to check out your employment history where I expect to gain a better idea about your level of ability and competency.

When the clarifying information isn't there, I'm left wondering, 'Where did all those skills come from?', and often have to conclude that the person has just thrown in random skills to try to make themselves look good. Which makes those skills meaningless, if if they are what we had hoped to find.

Right Your RESUME

Pro tip

Although you should definitely list this summary section in your resume document within the PRRE, I find most people write this section first because they write the content in the order they present it on paper. I believe it may be wiser to wait; and instead write this section after you have written your work history content. That way it can be easier to identify what your main skills are (the skills that you used in multiple positions) and can then simply choose to list the most relevant for the type of work you are seeking so that the section is more effective in generating hiring manager interest.

Pro tip

Remember to use strong, industry-relevant keywords matched to the position being applied to.

Part 3
Summarised INFORMATION

25 Personal attributes

Personal attributes are your *YOUnique* behaviours, ethics and values. Listing them in the resume is a favourite for jobseekers desiring to demonstrate their potential suitability to the job. Especially for those who don't have experience in that type of work and are looking to break in to a position, industry or with a specific employer.

Include or exclude?

If you are using my Resume Content Building template to help rewrite your resume content, then you will notice there is a section entitled Personal Attributes following the Skills Summary section, and it has room for you to write down all the personal attributes that you can think of which is relevant to and might make you suitable for the role. In the absence of instructions or explanations for using the template, one could easily *assume* that this personal attribute section needs to be included, and therefore would be located immediately after the skills summary section.

However, although I *do* want you to indeed knock yourself out to spend quality time filling out this section, with as many details as you can possibly come up with about how wonderful you are as a person and as an employee, I *don't* want you – yes, you read that right – I *don't* want you to include a personal attribute section in your resume (I'll explain why this section is on the template in a moment).

Therefore, I'm listing this section as **Exclude**.

> * Include
> ✓ **Exclude**
> * Optional, or It Depends...

But, back to your shock over my saying I don't want you to include this section...

What, you ask? Yes, you definitely read that right; your eyes aren't playing tricks on you. I *don't* want you including any of those attributes on your resume. (Well, not just yet, anyway).

Right Your RESUME

Why?

Telling versus showing

Whereas **telling** is a fantastic method for highlighting the important skills a person has so that it interests the reader to make them keen to read the expanded upon skill statements in the work history section, the same is not true for personal attributes, which are best **shown** rather than told. Because telling just makes these latter isolated details challengeable 'claims'. And those can backfire on a jobseeker very quickly.

Mistake to avoid

Unfortunately, the personal attributes listed in most people's resumes are just commonplace, cliché-style details that are so overused by so many jobseekers for over a very long period that they have now become meaningless and boring for hiring managers. And because the details only tell (without any later showing any particulars that substantiates the truth and accuracy of them), the listing simply doesn't provide any value for the employer. Making such a section a waste of the resume real estate used.

Also (and far too frequently), the personal attributes listed are often either fabricated (in an effort to make oneself look more employable) or self-delusions the person has about themselves (and employers are left scratching their heads wondering how on earth the person could ever have considered that they have the attributes claimed, when their behaviour and attitudes clearly demonstrate the opposite).

Over time, these negatives have resulted in hiring manager's not trusting what *any* person says about themselves, which has significantly devalued the believability of reading the details that can set one person apart from the next – negatively affecting all jobseekers who list their personal attributes in summary form.

So how can you show what sets you apart, what makes you *YOUnique* and potentially suitable for the role.

Create your list

Knowing what you believe to be your greatest attributes' *is* helpful if you instead **show** hiring managers the attributes you have. Hence why I encourage you to write them down, and list as many you can, so you know what they are and have a ready list for when you need them.

Part 3
Summarised INFORMATION

The more good things you can think of about yourself and what you would bring to the role, great! The more good things you can think of about yourself will give you a healthy dose of positivity and self-esteem to enthuse you during jobsearch. And, it will be great fodder for your cover letter and the interview too... just not so great for your resume. Yet.

Once completed, it might be tempting to go against my advice to include this list as a summary listing on your resume, I don't deny that the temptation won't be there to begin with. But hang in there; let me tell you how to use that list so it works.

So go on, please take some time out now to write your long list of personal attributes, and then come back to see how we can rework them so they go in your favour.

Got your list

Great, you're back and have your lengthy list of cliché personal attributes that are most relevant to the type of work you seek (even if you are fully delusional about your attributes).

You should now have a list that looks something similar to this:

Attributes

- Punctual
- Team Player
- Able to follow instructions
- Hard working

Does yours look similar to that? Excellent.

Now all we need to do is take your list a step further, to convert it into an evidence-based *skill statement*.

If we use an attribute that we want the hiring manager to know about ourself, and then think about each of our past roles and the work we did, we can then turn that ordinary, cliché attribute into something *YOUnique, employer-centric* and therefore details that are interesting to read.

And we end up with a listing that can look something similar to this:

Customer Service Officer

ABC Company

2011 – 2014

- Arrived to work on time to deactivate security system, perform security checks and allow staff entry so they can carry out pre-operational tasks like starting up computers and setting up ready for doors opening at 9 a.m.

- Pitched in to help colleagues out by serving clients or answering incoming calls during peak periods, and sharing ideas during meetings or keeping them informed of changes and updates upon return from absences.

- Read operation procedure manuals and follow required steps to complete unfamiliar tasks and safely operate machinery for the first time.

Let's re-examine that listing, this time with highlights and followed by my commentary, so you can convert your list into something similar:

Customer Service Officer

ABC Company

2011 – 2014

- **Arrived** to work **on time** to deactivate security system, perform security checks and allow staff entry so they can carry out pre-operational tasks like starting up computers and setting up ready for doors opening at 9 a.m.

In this first bullet point I *suggest* **punctuality** without directly claiming it through the use of specific, deliberate wording (the words 'arrived' and 'on time') and backed this up by providing a workplace example of how and why it was *necessary* for the person to be punctual. Thus taking an evidence approach making the attribute more believable (and less challengeable).

I could have just written the duty as a skill statement like this:

- Deactivate security system, perform security checks and allow staff entry so they can carry out pre-operational tasks like starting up computers and setting up ready for doors opening at 9 a.m.

But just those few extra words demonstrating personal attributes provide extra value for the hiring manager and allows them to visualise the person

Part 3
Summarised INFORMATION

arrive at and enter the premises, carry out security checks and deactivate the building's alarm before letting other staff in so that they can prepare for business opening.

The hiring manager would conclude that to have this responsibility, the person would indeed have to arrive on time because lateness would significantly affect others. So the person would have to arrive on time, or arrange for someone else to do this tasks for them on occasions if they are late or will be absent.

And therefore, the skill statement has just caused the hiring manager to *agree with the applicant* – a mental tick, that will go a long way into enabling the hiring manager to see the candidate as potentially suitable. Especially when more mental ticks and agreements occur, one after the other.

Let's assess the next bullet point:

- **Pitched in** to help colleagues **out** by serving clients or answering incoming calls during peak periods, and **sharing ideas** during meetings or keeping them **informed of changes** and updates upon return from absences.

In this second bullet point I *demonstrated* the person as a **team player**, again through the choice of compelling and deliberate word choice, and in the providing of an interesting example (of the tasks completed above and beyond the job description) to guide the hiring manager to assume this attribute as fact rather than the jobseeker outright claiming it.

Pitching in to answer calls and serving customers so that they aren't kept waiting also suggests a strong **customer-focus** which employers *like*, so you're demonstrating another trait without directly pointing it out. And rest assured, the hiring manager *will* note this strong secondary alignment as much as the first and think the better of you because of it, even when they don't consciously realise the statement is serving double duty.

What about the next statement:

- **Read** operation procedure manuals and **follow required steps** to complete unfamiliar tasks and safely operate machinery for the first time.

In this last bullet point, rather than state that the person 'follows instructions' a clear example is provided and deliberate word choice is used so that the hiring manager can again see the personal attribute, assume the person having it is fact, and make the judgement that this person 'aligns well for our role'.

Right Your RESUME

Not everyone does have the patience to read an operation manual or carefully follow the steps outlined within. Our statement not only suggests the person can follow instructions, but it also hints at them having high concentration levels, able to pay close attention to finer details and other such positive traits that might align the person well to employers wants and needs.

The details are unique and interesting to read, unlike one and two word listings that are just words on a page. There is nothing cliché or challengeable about the sentences, because they are **factually based**. And, they've successfully avoided causing the hiring manager a sceptical moment where they think or state '*Yeah, prove it!*' – which can send everything belly-up for the jobseeker, like when they say they are punctual and then show up for a job interview ten minutes late, cementing the hiring manager's disbelief already formed and causing them to think or mutter 'liar' even when the person has a genuine reason and calls to advise the employer of this ahead of time.

(You do realise, don't you, that almost every long term unemployed person seem to list that they are punctual, a team player, are customer oriented, a hard worker and have strong attention to detail in their resume for the hiring to be sceptical the moment they see these attributes listed? How many jobseekers do you think are going to write that they are 'lazy' and 'tardy' on their resume? Umm, zero, right?

The trouble is too many jobseekers just list the personal attributes like I got you to create earlier, writing what they think the employer will want to see rather than showing them the attributes the actually have.

So, over time, 'hard workers' have been fired because they go on to prove in the workplace that they aren't all that hard working in the slightest; employees rush through their work and make silly mistakes or cut corners, proving they don't 'pay attention to finer details' at all.)

You can't help it if the hiring manager **assumes** you possess positive traits from their interpreting your skills statements to mean you have them – and you're not going to complain if they make this positive judgement about you either. But, *you* gain peace of mind that you didn't make claims for the hiring manager to develop the want to test or challenge them.

So, think about what the *employer* wants. If an attribute is important for the work (you are applying for), write a (truthful) skill statement combining your attribute in a task, duty or responsibility within one or more of your past roles (paid or unpaid).

A 'hard worker' will naturally have a stable work history; and along with that, plenty of examples where they can demonstrate that they are hard working

Part 3
Summarised INFORMATION

and reliable as an employee. Meanwhile, our naturally lazy workers won't be able to back up their claim with evidentiary examples, because they have problems they need to hide, so will be left creating meaningless lists that don't carry any sway.

Actually, if you have strong work history, you will probably find that you have more tasks, responsibilities and accountabilities in a role that will be of more interest and benefit to potential employers. And therefore you may not even need to list any of your personal attributes because your skill statements will convey everything you want and need to say about yourself for you without you needing to specify the attributes too. And that is great!

But, if you are applying for a position for which you don't already have the skills and experience required, then adding a *few* personal attributes into evidence-based skill statements can be a good way to boost the employer seeing your potential suitability. Just keep in mind that although it is good to get some of your key and relevant personal attributes into your skill statements, hiring managers will be looking more for what you have done, so use this method *sparingly*. Perhaps just include your Top 3 attributes only – and leave the rest for your cover letter and the job interview.

How to list

To include any personal attributes in your resume, you must avoid creating a dedicated summary section and instead use careful and deliberate word choice to incorporate chosen attributes in with the relevant tasks, duties and responsibilities for your previous roles.

Positioning

As you will not be creating a section, and will be blending attributes into your work history section, the details will appear immediately after all the summarised information sections that you include.

26 Area of expertise

When you have worked in a particular industry or within specific job roles for any great length of time, you naturally become highly knowledgeable and proficient in certain areas compared to those who don't have the same skills and experience you have.

You may have developed a range of special or advanced skills that would make you significantly better for the role than those who do not have your particular skill set. When this happens, an Area of Expertise section might benefit you.

Include or exclude?

Therefore, I'm listing this section as an "**It Depends...**" section.

> * Include
> * Exclude
> ✓ Optional, or **It Depends...**

This is because, for the average jobseeker they don't *have* any areas of expertise and so a specific section is unnecessary. And thus, it would actually look silly and just cause a negative impression in the hiring manager if the person was to include one.

For those jobseekers, like perhaps trainers or community service workers for example, where within the same job you could develop specialist skills from having worked around a particular role or topic from a number of angles and levels, such a section like this might aid in differentiating yourself from your competition.

To help you decide if this section is for you

An Area of Expertise section is generally a **sub-category** to the Skills Summary section. You may want (or need) to separately draw attention to up to **two particular skills** that you are highly proficient in – that is **up to**

Part 3
Summarised INFORMATION

two areas of expertise within a specific industry or job role that demonstrates your value over other candidates.

For example

> In the employment services industry, consultants often have to use case management, customer relationship and advanced administration skills to maintain their caseload of clients. But they also provide training and post placement support, market clients to employers and deal with aggressive behaviours or personal crises, as well as needing to have a broad range of knowledge about how to write a resume and successfully apply to and gain jobs. Certain individuals are going to excel in one aspect of the consultant role and might have weakness(es) in other areas, all within the one position.
>
> But each of the many agencies (employers) put greater importance on different aspects; one employer I worked for wanted good '*all rounder*' skills, another expected strong ability in calming aggressive behaviours and with helping clients overcome their personal crises and meltdowns; another was *marketing, marketing, marketing* all the way; and another focused on the position-holder building up jobseeker skills and confidence levels by providing them with training and mentoring.
>
> When employers publish their job advertisements, they often state the type of person who would be most suitable for the role – this is not just to discourage candidates who don't fully meet the criteria from applying (they do need to keep the number of applications down if they can); it also provides valuable insight on what 'angle' the applicants who do apply need to focus upon within their resume and job interview answers if they want to be successful in gaining the job. That last employer with the focus on *educating jobseekers* would be more interested in consultants like myself who hold Training and Assessment qualifications and experience over those that don't; whereas the *marketing, marketing, marketing* employer would be more interested in candidates that have strong Sales, Marketing and negotiation skills, and would value and be impressed by high performance in KPI's and KRA attainment.
>
> Another example of a jobseeker that might benefit from using an Area of Expertise section is a Trainer. Trainers (and teachers) develop the skills to teach a broad range of subjects, and they can specialise in certain areas, for example, teaching people with disabilities, children or adults. You could further separate what they teach into subject area. For example, Maths, English, Art, Life Skills, Work skills etc. The scope for what they

Right Your RESUME

teach is large; and therefore, most specialise in only a handful of subjects (if they specialise).

My advice for deciding whether to include or exclude an Area of Expertise section in your resume depends on 1. Whether you truly possess an Area of Expertise, and 2. Whether you need to highlight this, because the details you include and exclude can be a double-edged sword[1] in that it has the power to either impress the reader or cause them to decide that you won't be a good cultural fit within their organisation.

If you have any doubt about whether you should include this section in your resume or not, I would encourage you to 'err on the side of caution' and leave it out rather than risk causing a negative reaction from including one.

How to list

If you can see that creating an Area of Expertise section could give you a competitive edge and possibly cause a hiring manager to want to know more about you to call you in for an interview, then by all means, go ahead and create an Area of Expertise section.

Positioning

And list it immediately after your Skills Summary in the PRRE so that your details are easily found when the hiring manager does their initial skim read.

Mistake to avoid

But a word of caution. To avoid inadvertently causing this included section to work against your intentions: don't list any more than two (2) areas of expertise. Or you no longer have an 'expertise' area(s) and are simply counter-intuitively demonstrating that you have a wider range of experience, making you a Jack – or Jill – of-all-trades within the role.

And if that is the case, it would be a better decision to just list those Jack or Jill details in your Skills Summary section as the topmost important details.

---

[1] Where a sword can be used to either save or take a life

Part 3
Summarised INFORMATION

27 Licences, tickets and checks

Some jobs may require a licence, certificate, ticket and other type of permit or check, either before the person is permitted to start in that type of position or by a certain date following commencement in the role (for example, within three months).

Include or exclude?

I'm listing this section as '**Include**' because providing a snapshot of the licences, tickets and checks that you have which are related to the work being applied for, helps a hiring manager to see your potential suitability.

> ✓ **Include**
> ∗ Exclude
> ∗ Optional, or It Depends...

There are many different licences, certificates, tickets and checks as well as different government departments that issue them (depending on the industry entered into).

For example, in Australia, people in NSW wishing to work in the real estate industry are required to obtain a Certificate of Registration (from Department of Fair Trading). Club and bar staff are required to hold a Responsible Service of Alcohol (RSA) and /or Responsible Control of Gambling (RCG) certificates (from Office of Liquor, Gaming & Racing). Anyone driving a motor vehicle is required to have a Driver's Licence or Learner Permit (where learners must be accompanied by a fully qualified licence holder at all times), but those that drive heavy vehicles are required to hold higher level truck driving licences, such as MR or HR Driver's Licences (from Roads and Traffic Authority).

High Risk Work requires the person to obtain a licence for the type of work e.g. scaffolding, dogging and rigging, crane and hoist operation, forklift operation or using pressure equipment. Other positions, like those with higher authority, may require a Police or Working with Children Check

Right Your RESUME

(WwCc) to be carried out and kept on file along with a First Aid Certificate to demonstrate the person is a Fit and Proper Person.

Most licences, tickets, permits and checks come as a result of having undertaken training and testing to have passed at or above a minimal level of competency, or from meeting specific requirements.

Employers of the particular type of work generally will know the types of licences, certificates, tickets, permits and checks that are needed for the industry and position type. With an emphasise on keeping costs down, and saving time and money when and where they can, an employer is going to be keener to consider applicants who are already in possession of the required (or desired) permits over applicants who don't have them.

This is another thing that I've seen jobseekers complaining about. But think about it: if you didn't have to pay for something and were on a tight budget, would you go out and buy that item? No, you'd spare yourself the expense so that you can spend that money on other, necessary things. Businesses are the same; the decision maker (and the business) is probably on a limited hiring budget, and so they aren't going to want to pay to get an employee suitably licensed when they can hire someone that has that licensing already. Not unless the person has a good and compelling reason to cause the hiring manager to want to hire them without their having the appropriate licence, ticket or check already – such as the person has the required skills and experiences already and just needs to obtain whichever ones are needed (none of these things are cheap, are they?)

So, if you have relevant licences, tickets, checks and other such permits that are either essential or desirable for the job you want, then you can make a great leap ahead of other applicants by listing them in your resume, preferably in the PRRE, as they can greatly increase a hiring manager's interest in you as a candidate and it is amazing how many people don't include these high-important details anywhere, expecting employers to guess that they have them.

Positioning

There are two ways you could handle including them in your resume: creating a specific section and listing the multiple licences, tickets, permits and checks; or, combining this section with Training, Education and Qualification History section (details follow in the next chapter).

Part 3
Summarised INFORMATION

For example

(Multiple Sections)

Licences, Tickets and Checks

- NSW Driver's Licence
- RTA print out
- Forklift Driver's Licence
- White Card
- Blue Card

Training, Education and Qualifications

- Certificate III in Warehousing
- Certificate III in Construction
- Higher School Certificate

OR

(Combined Sections)

Qualifications and Licensing

- NSW Driver's Licence
- Forklift Driver's Licence
- White Card
- Blue Card
- Certificate III in Warehousing
- Certificate III in Construction
- Higher School Certificate

I'll discuss deciding whether to separate or combine soon.

Right Your RESUME

For now, a few things to consider when listing the details of your licences, tickets, permits and checks include:

- **Use the proper title**

For example

Don't just write 'Driver's Licence'; instead provide the proper title 'NSW Driver's Licence', 'Victorian Driver's Licence', 'International Driver's Licence' or 'NSW HR Driver's Licence' so that the reader doesn't have to ask, guess or make assumptions about the licensing type, level or appropriateness.

- **You can leave out *unnecessary* details**

For example

If you are applying for a job as a Forklift Driver, the forklift licence and Warehousing certificate is fully relevant for that type of work sought, and will help hiring managers see that you have the skills and capabilities for that type of role.

Whereas, if the same person also completed a certificate in Horticulture and the position being applied for is as forklift driver in a clothing warehouse, then the certificate in horticulture is irrelevant (to the type of work being sought) and therefore the detail can be left off the person's resume (even though they completed that course of study, as including the detail reduces the focus being on gaining a forklift driving position in a clothing warehouse.)

But, if the person was applying for a forklift driving position in a Nursery or warehouse dealing in plants, then this same qualification *would* be a detail that could boost the person's potential suitability. Because the hiring manager will be able to see that this candidate has a personal interest in plants, and may have skills that will help them to move pallets of plants from one location to another that keeps the plants (precious stock!) alive and healthy compared to a candidate who knows nothing about plant life (thus the person could gain an edge over other forklift driver's applying).

As most industries have licensing or qualification requirements, you should learn what these are and endeavour to obtain them to help you gain that type of work. Otherwise you may find your jobsearch that little bit harder (takes longer) than those who have the necessary certification.

Part 3
Summarised INFORMATION

- **Be consistent with how you provide similar details**

For example

Don't write 'Certificate III in Warehousing' and then 'Construction Certificate' when the details should be listed as 'Certificate III in Construction' in a different entry.

If you aren't sure what the proper qualification title is, then check your licence, certificate, permit, ticket or the department or institute you gained it from.

A hiring manager might not notice the inconsistency in how you list the details, but it is these smaller *visually interpreted* details that can increase or decrease the professionalism of your resume (and you are trying to get more right than wrong, aren't you?)

The following list shows some of the common licences, tickets and checks that are available. But keep in mind that the list is not comprehensive:

Checks

- State Police Checks
- Federal Police Checks
- Working with Children Checks

Licences

- Driver's Licences
- Machine Operation Licences
- Licensees-in-Charge
- Certificates of Registration
- Tickets (Cards)
- Health and Safety e.g. White Card (WHS)
- High risk work (in construction and mining industries in particular) e.g. Confined Spaces, Elevated Platform, Tower Crane
- Handling of Dangerous Goods

Certificates

- First Aid
- Formal Educational courses

Right Your RESUME

How to title the section

How you title the section will depend on whether you separate details into specific groups or combine the details under a single heading. I suggest you read the Training, Education and Qualifications section (next chapter's discussion) before you make your decision.

If it is appropriate, you could create separate headings for each type you have e.g. Checks, Licences, Tickets, Training, Education and Qualifications. That is, you could create (if you have multiple details for each section) up to six separate sections, with which to emphasis these important details.

Or, you could combine into groupings, such as Licences, Tickets and Checks and then Training, Education and Qualifications (like I have done for this book). That is, you could create two separate sections, and divide each of your details into those two specific headings.

Or, if necessary, you could combine them all under a single heading. That is, you create a single section and list each of the different licences, tickets, checks, training, education and qualifications in the one place.

You don't have to title the sections like I have. You have the freedom to choose a Heading (or Headings), that is relevant and meaningful for employers while still using your own personal style and preferences. And how many sections you create will depend on the number of relevant qualifications you have.

Date acquired

Some jobseekers like to list the year that they *acquired* the licence, ticket or checks. And this is fine *if* the date is within the last five years.

Anything beyond that time period though, the course or requirements are likely to have changed (and can become less relevant to what is required or expected in the present day).

Expiry dates

Most licences, tickets and checks have an *expiry date*. And I know some jobseekers alternatively like to put this expiry date in their resumes, especially when they have only recently obtained it. Because it shows they have a long usage period before the licence, ticket or permit will expire.

Part 3
Summarised INFORMATION

But, like with everything else for your resume, including such additional can act like a double-edged sword; and gives rise to potential abuse of the detail for your having supplied it.

To avoid making a licence, ticket or check seem outdated, I recommend using the **renewal date** (expiry date) rather than the attainment date, because it is a date that lies in the future rather than the past (which helps keep your resume future-oriented). But also because the extra detail is not an absolutely essential one. My recommendation is if the employer wants or needs to know when your licence, ticket or permit expires, let them ask you this in a phone call or at the job interview.

28 Training, education and qualifications

Some jobs may require you to provide details of your educational and training background to demonstrate suitability for the role.

For example, trainer and assessors are not only required to hold a Certificate IV in Training and Education, but also hold a secondary qualification at one level above the certificate level they teach at, in addition to having five years (or more) experience in that industry. That is, to teach the Certificate III in Business Administration, the trainer assessor is required to have employment history and a Certificate IV (or higher) in Business Administration.

In Australia, until a few years ago, students used to have a choice about when they could leave school. They could leave when they reached a certain age (I think it was 16 years 9 months), which equated to most student being somewhere within Year 9 (or 3rd form) when they reached that age. Most students chose to remain at school to complete their School Certificate (at the end of Year 10) and then made the decision to either go on to complete Higher School Certificate (HSC) education (Year 12 or beyond) or find a job (with many parents insisting that if they didn't find a job they had to go back to school and get the higher education).

Changes introduced by the government a couple of years ago means students now have one of three choices:

1. they can leave without completing their HSC, if they obtain employment that includes a certain amount of training or study within it, such as apprenticeships and traineeships (this is so that the young adult doesn't stop developing employable skills).

2. they can leave without completing their HSC, if they take up a full time placement at an educational institute (such as TAFE) in order to complete a formal (workplace) qualification (the courses of which are developed in consultation with industry councils) for the field they are interested in (again so that they develop relevant skills), or

3. otherwise, they now have to remain in school and complete HSC studies.

Because of the former different educational 'exit points', it was commonplace for jobseekers to include the details of their education and training in their resumes, as the schooling levels were distinguishable from their certificate

Part 3
Summarised INFORMATION

titles alone. Students that struggled often dropped out of school the moment they became eligible, so didn't end up with a School Certificate or Higher School Certificate; and therefore employers could work this out just by seeing the lack of schooling certificates in a resume. Some employers, like trades, were happy to take lower educated jobseekers because the manual labour they needed didn't require the person to have any higher education to do the job well, and might view someone with higher education over-qualified. Other employers were happy to hire school leavers who had the minimum School Certificate. Yet others wouldn't consider any school leaver that did not have their HSC. (I know, I once missed out on a job with a company I thought I would be perfectly suitable to because of their having that policy).

But because of the above-mentioned changes to the system for when they can exit schooling, listing educational details now has become somewhat redundant for school leavers, because whereas HSC used to be just for a smaller number of 'academically minded' students, it is now 'the norm' for the majority of them.

Employers know about the less exit points, and that the certificate courses are a suitable *equivalents* to the HSC, making the section to demonstrate the person's schooling level completely unnecessary.

Include or exclude?

I'm listing this section as '**Optional**' because providing a snapshot of your educational and training background is not longer necessary (in Australia, and not necessarily needed for other countries), and is therefore used at your own discretion.

> * Include
> * Exclude
> ✓ **Optional**, or It Depends...

To help you decide whether you should include or exclude:

Information to support include

On the one hand, training, education and the qualifications attained can help hiring managers determine your suitability for a role. Remember, from your perspective the job you are applying to might look like you are a good match, but from the employers perspective you might not come

Right Your RESUME

anywhere even close to being the right person for the role. For this reason, you could have strong basis to include such a section in your resume, to demonstrate the educational background that has provided you with knowledge for that job or industry or shows your personal interest (because most students explore relevant subjects during their schooling).

Information to support exclude

But, on the other hand, for many positions, a person's schooling and academic achievements are not anywhere near as desirable to know about compared to what skills, experiences, attributes and permits the applicant has. Not all training results in formal qualifications, but most training results in increased awareness, knowledge or a skill developed. For this reason, you could have strong basis to exclude such a section in favour of increasing your employment skill statements instead.

My suggestion is: if the detail is relevant for the type of work you are applying for, then it is something that you can add to your resume; if it doesn't help you gain the particular type of work you seek, then it is an unnecessary detail that you should leave out.

If you choose to include

1. Assess each small detail related to licences, tickets, permits, checks, training, education and qualifications on its own and decide whether each of the individual details belongs in your resume or should be left out.
2. If you have details that need to be included, then move on to deciding how you will list those details in your resume.

How to list

- **Use the proper qualification title**

If you complete a formal qualification, then it is best if you use the proper qualification title in your resume because (in Australia at least) qualifications are developed in collaboration with Industry Councils, so most industries are familiar with the courses and units of competencies.

For example, if you completed the course 'Certificate II in Business Administration' then use that proper qualification title rather than 'Business Administration' or some other name – which employers could mistake as no

Part 3
Summarised INFORMATION

longer being current.

Note for non-Australian readers: the qualification titles provided apply to Australian jobseekers. The formal qualifications that you undertake in your country may look different to how the qualifications appear in the examples provided within this section. If this is the case, you may need to research how your courses are titled by visiting an educational institution or a government department that such educational institutions must register with. Please take possible differences for your country into account and make necessary adjustments before adding education and training details to your resume.

Format

I've seen many online resume templates that get you to fill in your educational details like this:

- Year – Year, Certificate Title, Institute, Campus and campus location

For example

- 2012 – 2012, Certificate IV in Business Administration, TAFENSW, Western Sydney Institution, Penrith Campus

I don't put the extra **date** and **institution** details in any of the resumes I create for clients, and I encourage you to not do this either. For the reason that the dates can reveal (directly or indirectly) the person's age, the additional details are the finer details that can aid a scammer to ultimately steal your identity, or cause a hiring manager to make a 'no' decision without needing to meet you first.

I list just enough of the details to help the hiring manager to see the client (or my own self) has the qualification, and closely guard all the remaining details which can be misused, for if offered the job.

Specifically, I list the:

- Formal certificate title only

For example

- Certificate IV in Business Administration

Right Your RESUME

And leave out the:

- Attainment dates
- Institute, and the
- Institute location

For example

- 2012 – 2014
- TAFENSW, Western Sydney Institute
- Penrith Campus

I apply this safeguarding method consistently for **all** licences, tickets, permits, checks, training, education and qualifications. Because the shorter specifics of the qualification enables the reader to keep skim reading (and making their mental 'ticks' without having to pause to read text that spans across the page) too. So if the client had multiple qualifications (like, I myself do), each of them are quick and easy to read.

For example

- Certificate III in Career Education
- Certificate IV in Training and Assessment
- Certificate IV in Training and Education
- Certificate IV in Small Business Management
- Diploma in Business

As you can see, the core details that answer the hiring managers question are there; and it will make a scammers job all the more harder to be able to steal a person's identity if they don't gain access to those additional details (that could lead to them obtaining a copy of your certificate, and or using the detail at banks and government departments that would expect that only you know the finer particulars of).

What if I haven't completed my course yet?

Although the section is usually for demonstrating the qualifications and relevant training that you have **fully completed**, sometimes you may

Part 3
Summarised INFORMATION

want to include details of a course you are **currently undertaking** but have not completed yet; usually because the course is studied over a longer than six month or one year period, like Diploma's and University degrees.

If this is the case, you could clarify the information quite easily, by writing the words '*currently enrolled*' after the qualification to prevent potential employers from mistaking that you already have attained the qualification. *For example*, like this:

- Bachelor of Education (Early Childhood), currently enrolled

You could also list it like this:

- Currently enrolled in Bachelor of Education (Early Childhood)

I prefer the first method because it is shorter, and is in keeping with how I list other qualifications.

For example

- Bachelor of Education (Early Childhood), currently enrolled
- Higher School Certificate
- NSW Driver's Licence

Because the following method would look slightly out of place / not in keeping with the rest of how you list things, even though you are providing the same information.

For example

- Currently enrolled in Bachelor of Education (Early Childhood)
- Higher School Certificate
- NSW Driver's Licence

The difference is small, but noticeable to those who review resumes all the time.

Self learning

If it is relevant to the type of work being applied for, you can include details of any self-learning activities that you have undertaken.

Right Your RESUME

For example, I once carried out online research over a few months to gain tips and learn techniques for how to turn 'boring' looking word documents into better laid out, visually more appealing ones. This self-study greatly improved the look of the documents I created compared to the same type of documents being created by fellow students (in a typing and word processing class I later took).

When I applied for a position as an admin assistant, knowing I produced nicer to look at documents, I added details about my self-learning activities that best demonstrated that I didn't just type text-based documents only; I also developed and used some basic graphic design knowledge to help me create attractive newsletters, business cards, business stationery and the like.

I did this because although the job advertisement stated that typing at 45 wpm was a requirement, the advertisement did not state the types of documents that would be created as part of the job role. So I included this self study and listed the various types of documents that I could create to help the hiring manager see that I was potentially suitable for their vacancy; to give myself a competitive edge. (It worked too; I interviewed and got the job. And, I have to say I probably wouldn't have received that successful result if I had not demonstrated the range of my typing and word processing skills in my resume, because that was exactly what the employer had been looking for).

At the time, I had not completed any formal qualification that could demonstrate my intermediate to advance word processing skills, so I had deliberately included my self-learning so that demonstrated my informal self development and advancing skill levels. And I listed it like this:

For example

- Certificate IV in Business Administration
- Informal study in Advanced Word processing techniques
- Informal study in Book Publishing, Editing and Proofreading
- Informal study in Graphic Design principles

Positioning

If you have chosen (or your country of origin requires) that you include a specific Education section in your resume, then I encourage you to list all such summarisable information within the PRRE (room permitting) or for the sections to appear **before** your employment and development history (if room wasn't permitting).

Part 3
Summarised INFORMATION

Expiry date

Unlike licences, tickets and checks, most formal education lasts or is held on file by the institution for thirty years. (Other countries this may be different, so non-Australian readers should check with their own institutions about this requirement – or whether it is even a requirement).

My suggestion is that if the qualification or training certificate is ten years or older in age, then it has probably already had an (significant) update and is no longer professionally current, so the qualification or training could (and most probably should) be left off your resume – especially when you have worked in a role consistently since obtaining it. For example, tradespersons who completed their trade certificate under an old qualification name, but have maintained licensing and professional currency for that type of work.

Special note

If that is the case, then I would just list the person's licence, ticket or check, and leave off the detail about their completing a course to obtain it altogether.

Do you need to include a list of the individual subjects completed or units of competency achieved?

If you have work history in a role requiring a course or units of competency then I would say it is unnecessary to list the individual **modules** completed of that relevant course or qualification, because your work experience is an extension from your learning and carries greater value to employers.

If you don't have relevant work history, then listing the units of competency completed is a common way of demonstrating you have the basic skills – because you have already undertaken training, passed its associated academic testing and were deemed competent at a basic standard level set by the industry – as well as interest in that particular type of role (otherwise, why else would you have completed all that training).

But, I would advise another caution here: including the subjects taken, whether they are by a school leaver who recently completed their Higher School Certificate (or equivalent title in other countries) or an adult that is undertaking a technical college course to help them get a foot in an industry, can cause the hiring manager to assume the person is a recent school leaver.

Right Your RESUME

Recent school leaver equates to young, which can translate into 'unreliable' for some people – hiring manager's amongst them.

Candidates under the age of 21 cannot afford to provide details that might cause an employer to discriminate based on their young age. Many younger persons find it difficult to obtain a job in anything other than the fast food industry or traineeships and apprenticeships (which pay lower) because of the long held belief that younger persons are not as reliable as older, mature workers. That a young person will be more focused on having a good time; that they will arrogantly think they can do something when they don't have the necessary skills. I'm not saying those viewpoints are true; but it is a long held belief by employers, recruiters and within the wider general public that is not going to go away. So younger people need to use good 'workarounds' to overcome those stereotypical images of what it is to be a young jobseeker.

Older candidates need to ensure that the impression they are creating in the employer is not one of them being unable to hold down a job, or that they experience other significant problems affecting their employment history and ability. Including a list of the units of competency in older candidate applications can inadvertently imply such negative connotations within a hiring manager, who will wonder why the applicant didn't provide better (and more) skill and workplace details for them to consider.

Either way, you need to weigh up the pros and cons of listing each of the subjects taken; maybe try including them for, say, a three month period, and if you don't get the phone ringing during that time, try taking them out and see if that changes the results you get. In the business and marketing world, this practice is called 'A/B Testing' and is where you try something one way for a short period and then try it in a different way for a similar amount of time. Then, after you have analysed the results of both methods used, you implement the method that brought in the highest positive results. A/B Testing is a great practice you should follow to your best advantage in jobsearching too!

Do you need to include details of academic result?

I would say that if you passed at Distinction level, and the qualification or units of competency is essential for the type of work, then listing your academic result could give you a competitive edge.

But, if you complete at only Pass or Credit level, then you don't *gain* anything by listing the detail, because you are only demonstrating yourself at a mediocre level. Which could go against you, because who wants ordinary if they can get

Part 3
Summarised INFORMATION

extraordinary? In this case, it would be better to simply list the course or unit of competency but leave out the result.

Mistake to avoid

The main thing to avoid is providing unnecessary information, in the Licences, Tickets and Checks and/or a Training, Education and Qualification sections. Particularly details which are:

- Anything that reveals the applicants age
- Anything that increase the risk of identity theft
- Anything that increases the risk of the hiring manager making a 'no' decision
- Anything that is irrelevant to the type of work sought
- Anything that makes it look like your focus is on education rather than gaining employment

Although I have already briefly covered these concerns earlier, I'll readdress them again now, while you are deciding how you will list your educational information.

Revealing age

Remember earlier, in the Personal Details section, I discussed how age can be inadvertently revealed either directly or indirectly?

Listing the year of your qualification, especially if that date is ten years or more previously, allows a hiring manager to calculate your age (or make a fairly accurate guesstimate).

For example

- 1989 Carpentry Apprenticeship

At the time of writing this book, it is late-2014. (Go on, grab a calculate, or do the Math along with me if you need to.) To calculate, the hiring manager would minus 1989 from 2014 to would work out that this person completed their qualification 25 years ago. Now, if the average age of a person doing an apprenticeship was around 16 to 20 years of age (and in all good likelihood they *were* in this age group), the hiring manager only has to add 25 (years ago) plus 'roughly' 18 years of age to reach the conclusion that it makes the applicant in their forties (43 years old, plus or minus two years).

Right Your RESUME

That might be okay if their ideal candidate is aged 'above 30, below 45'.

But, it is very likely to be the cause of a 55 year old (someone who completed a similar trade qualification in 1977) being discriminated based on their age. So although the candidate did not state how old they are, they have indirectly revealed it anyway.

Identity theft

Not only is a hiring manager (who you want to review your resume) able to calculate what your age is (which you don't want them to know), but so too can a scammer and identity thieves.

I imagine that over a 25 year period, the person no longer has the same residential address. But, the scammer or identity thief could attempt (if they have enough information about a person) to try to obtain a copy of that certificate (it wouldn't be easy, but they could pull it off if they are convincing enough). That copy, although completely out of date, could contain, say, your middle name which may just happen to be the only detail they have left to work out before they can go and open up a bank account in your name, and thereafter go on a very large spending spree at your expense – that will cause you years of hassles and financial mess. Or it might provide an old address that convinces an authority (like a bank or government department) they are 'the real deal' when clearly they are not.

Is this scaring you?

Good.

My aim here is to make you think twice about just tossing all these unnecessary details into your resume without great thought and careful deliberation like so many jobseekers do!

No decision

Apart from discriminating against you based on age, the hiring manager could just see unnecessary details on your resume and decide – without any discrimination whatsoever – that you aren't suitable to their needs: through both the details you have included as well as what has not been included.

If you have too many licences, tickets, checks, training, education and qualifications, you could inadvertently demonstrate that you are ***too* qualified**

Part 3
Summarised INFORMATION

for the job. Conversely, not having enough could cause them to see your skills and training gaps, so they conclude that you are *too* **under-qualified** for the role.

To overcome this, you need to fully understand the position and what is required, and then demonstrate your competence and suitability in the right proportions, so the hiring manager views your application as fully aligned.

Any detail that is irrelevant

When it comes to education, training and qualifications, you need to ensure that the detail is necessary for the role (sought).

For example, what is the point of providing details of a course you did, in say, floristry, if the job type you are applying for is Administration in an Accounting Firm? The floristry has no bearing and therefore no value for the role. Just because the person took the course, doesn't mean the detail must be included. Listing unnecessary educational and qualifying details not only wastes precious resume space, it can lead a hiring manager to wonder 'why is this person applying for this role when clearly they are better suited to [...a completely different] job role.' When hiring managers think that, the next logical action they take is to place this resume in their rejection pile, because their thinking the person would be better suited to something else automatically also means *'and therefore is not suitable for us'*.

The focus is on education (instead of employment)

This is not a common problem, but it is one that recently happened in two resumes I assessed, so I thought it appropriate to include here.

The resumes under question came from university students (and were almost identical in problem, so I only need to discuss one of the clients).

The resume was five pages long. The student had held three part time jobs (one after the other) starting back when they attended high school. And now, in their final year of university, they had relocated from another state (and transferred to a new university) and was looking to gain a new part time job in a supermarket or fast food outlet (great choices to suit their needs and matched their previous experience) within their new local area.

The trouble was: the student was a high *'academic achiever'*. Instead of showcasing those three former part time jobs, to demonstrate to potential

Right Your RESUME

employers that they had the very skills and experience for this type of work, this student's resume was so focused on their academic achievements, that their Educational History and Involvement ran to three and a half of those five pages. And their work history was almost non-existent.

In (both) these student's efforts to demonstrate how good they are, they failed to consider their audience.

If the student had been applying for an ***academic*** position, the resumes might have been perfect; but they weren't applying for an academic role, they were seeking work in retail or fast food, so the resumes were really missing the mark.

The students were each applying for a part time job, again. The focus of their resumes needed to be on ***workplace*** skills and experiences, not every bit of training and the subjects undertaken throughout their high school and university education. What was worse (and troubled me most) was that one of the students had gained help from one of her university teachers to create that incorrectly focused resume.

When we look at things from the hiring manager's focus, it is a case of 'what does an employer care that the student went on three school excursions when they were in Year 7 (nearing 8 years ago!) that earned them an Academic Achievement Award for Outstanding Participation in Extra-Curricular Activities?'

My point here is simple: you don't have to (and shouldn't) include every little bit of information about yourself in your resume. And you need to get the focus right.

The details must be appropriate, and relevant, and balanced. You must be careful not to focus on any one element too strongly; must avoid making your resume '*all about me*' when it needs to be powered by an 'all about the employers needs' focus.

When you are applying for ***work***, your academic achievement just isn't anywhere near as importance as your competency to do the role, and do it well. So if you are going make a mistake by focusing too heavily on something in your resume, let it be where it needs to be: on *demonstrating your competency* and *doing the job well*.

Part 3
Summarised INFORMATION

Listing the details

Whether you decide to include as six separate sections, two main ones, or even one section, there are a few things for you to consider:

- Only list 4 – 5 bullet points per heading
- Keep your sentences as short as possible
- List details in order of relevance and importance
- Avoid providing extraneous details

Positioning

As the licences, tickets, permits and checks, and qualifications carry more weight in developing hiring manager interest, if you create more than a single section to house your details then ensure that those more important details appear before the lesser weighted similar details (training, education). As a general guideline, include the section(s) after your Skills Summary but before your Work History.

Right Your RESUME

29 Tools of the trade

Some jobs may require you to use specialised equipment, and when that is the case, if you are already proficient in how to use those tools and machinery, letting employers know this can be beneficial.

> * Include
> * Exclude
> ✓ Optional, or **It Depends...**

Include or exclude?

This section is another of our '**It Depends...**' sections; as the section's inclusion really ought to depend on the relevance and necessity for the type of work sought.

A tools of the trade section *is* geared more towards jobseekers who are looking at gaining work in the building and construction industry where there are similar job titles that carry out completely different types of work, like when one 'labourer' might work with cement mixing and a different 'labourer' might use power tools.

The good news is that a tools of the trade section may also be suitable for school leavers, career changers and parents returning to the paid workforce, as it enables them to demonstrate their non-workplace acquired capabilities, which is most beneficial when the person has minimal experience within their particular choice of job role.

To help you decide to include or exclude

If there is a specialised piece of machinery or a particular type of tool that you use frequently in the workplace (or in your personal situation), it may have a place for inclusion in your resume for those with strong experience too, as differentiating the range of work and competence with specific tools and machinery can aid jobseekers in demonstrating their value to recruitment agencies and hiring managers.

Part 3
Summarised INFORMATION

Although we could reasonably argue that *all* industries have tools of the trade unique to that industry or job type – from doctors using medical equipment to diagnose and treat medical conditions to admin workers using computers and fax machines, from baristas using kitchen machinery to make coffees through to carpenters using power tools to build houses – I recommend only including this section if there is a **need** for you to demonstrate your greater value when you are unable to achieve this in just your employment related skill statements.

For example, take a recent school leaver who is perhaps seeking a cabinet-making apprenticeship. To support having an interest in 'Woodwork', the jobseeker might like to include details of their already possessing basic skills in using power tools (such as electric saws), planes and chisels etc. I see the inclusion of a tools and equipment section as completely relevant and appropriate to help this school leaver to gain an apprenticeship in carpentry or cabinet making.

Take also a jobseeker seeking work as a Forklift Driver. This jobseeker might do handy man type jobs around the home to have developed skills with power tools, planes, chisels etc too. The difference here though lies exclusively with the role being sought; listing the tools they are proficient in brings significantly less value towards demonstrating capabilities needed for a Forklift Driver, and is therefore irrelevant and not appropriate to help the person gain this type of work. Yet, if this person wanted to change careers to seek General Handyman work, then those same skills become immediately relevant and appropriate to demonstrate to employers of that type of work that although they don't have experience they still have good capabilities.

The key point of difference here, like every other aspect in creating your resume, is to strictly keep it focused on the type of work sought; so you need to think about the job role and match your skills and capabilities from the past to that work sought, to weigh up the detail carefully before deciding include or exclude. When the detail will enhance your application, include it without hesitation or doubt; if the detail doesn't demonstrate extra value, is unlikely to give you a competitive edge, or doesn't enhance your candidacy in any way then always choose to leave such details out of your resume.

What details to include

For those of you that identify that you could benefit from including this type of section in your resume, the main thing to remember is to list the details in 'snapshot' style. That is, using concisely worded bullet points.

Right Your RESUME

The best tools of the trade you should include, if relevant and appropriate, are those tools, machinery and equipment that you have become 'unconsciously competent' with using (*see section on Competency for further information) rather than tools you are not fully skilled in and still need to develop proficiency with.

And, tools of the trade don't have to be restricted to just carpentry related.

Admin Assistants use office equipment – like comb binders and laminators that they could list if the work involved publishing documents. Many office tools and equipment have 'home' or 'office' equivalents available at local department or office and stationery supplies store, which jobseekers without direct office work experience may be proficient in using, from having been a student or completing a personal (or community) project.

Parents returning to the workforce, perhaps seeking work as a Kitchen hand, Cook, or Chef may have developed skills with carving meats or peeling fruits and vegetables. Food industry related Tools of the Trade could include knives, peelers, food processors and ovens.

Think about the type of work you want to gain. What tools and equipment will be necessary on the job? Do you know how to use them already?

Positioning

And as you have probably already guessed, the best place to locate the details is within the PRRE, not buried towards the back.

Titling the section

You could call the section 'Tools of the Trade' or something similar, like 'Tools I've Used', 'Tools Used Snapshot' or 'Tools Summary'. The main thing to remember is to keep the title consistent in style and presentation of other sections you have included in your resume, and relevant to the details listed, so that the section doesn't feel out of place or 'hastily tacked on'.

Part 3
Summarised INFORMATION

30 Computers, technology and social media savviness

Just as earlier the Licences, Tickets and Checks section closely related to the Training, Education and Qualification section, so too is a Computers, Technology and Social Media Savviness closely related to a Tools of the Trade section.

Once again, it is possible that you treat the sections separately, or, depending on the type of work you are seeking, they are combinable into one.

Include or exclude?

I'm listing this section as '**It Depends…**'

As with a 'Tools of the Trade' section, inclusion really ought to depend fully upon the relevance and necessity to the type of work sought.

> * Include
> * Exclude
> ✓ Optional, or **It Depends…**

If you are seeking a job where you will be using or need advanced computers, technological gadgetry or social media skills and knowledge as part of your core tasks, then it makes sense to create a specific section with which to highlight those key computer-related competencies rather than bury the details within your work and education history where they might not be viewed.

To help you decide whether to include or exclude

Technology is so prevalent in our society that there is an expectation that people can operate computers and technology at the most **basic level** (such as turning a computer on), but there are many positions that require specific or advance level computer skills. And if you have those higher skills and competence levels it will greatly enhance your application and potential suitability, and give you a competitive edge, by ensuring you educate your reader of this fact. Hiring managers are not mind-readers, after all.

If you are seeking work as a typist, audio transcriber or word processor, then it would be completely relevant and appropriate for you to highlight your skills in and ability level of working with Microsoft Word on PC or Mac.

You could list the individual **advance features** that you are accomplished in (to generate a 'narrow' or 'close up' view of these skills) or, you could list your **broader range of skills** and the **different software** that you are proficient in like this:

For example

(Broad focus)

Programs

- Word
- Excel
- PowerPoint
- Outlook
- MYOB

(Narrow focus)

Advanced Word features

- Styles
- Tables
- Illustrations
- Headers, Footers & Page numbering
- Hyperlinks, Bookmarks & Cross referencing
- Mail Merge
- Track Changes
- Macros & Development tools
- Formatting text, paragraphs and pages

Part 3
Summarised INFORMATION

Indicating your *ability level* could also give you a competitive edge, if you have higher levels:

- MS Word, advanced
- MS Excel, intermediate
- MS PowerPoint, advanced

You could even provide a *subtle* graphical representation of your ability level (because as discussed earlier in this book, graphical elements are processed and understood faster by our brains than then words).

(Note: so long as the graphical representation is understated and maintains the professional appearance of your resume, like the following examples, a simple graphical representation shouldn't harm your application).

For example

- Microsoft Word   *****
- Microsoft Excel   ***
- Microsoft PowerPoint   *****
- Adobe Photoshop   ****

Or,

- Microsoft Word   *********
- Microsoft Excel   ******
- Microsoft PowerPoint   *******
- Adobe Photoshop   ***

Remember to always consider the relevance of include details. If you were seeking a forklift driving position, for example, even if you had these same higher level computer skill levels, you simply would not include this section in your resume. Because the details are irrelevant to the type of working being sought; and therefore unnecessary detail that is wasting the hiring manager's time and taking up valuable space (bloating you resume out to make it look more substantive than it is).

Social media savviness

Social media savviness is more than just using Facebook, Twitter or whatever social media accounts you have. Social media savviness encompasses the

Right Your RESUME

ability to create content (write posts, create graphics, visuals and/or audio), understand SEO, analytics, and content marketing strategies.

With more businesses having an online presence, possessing these current **high demand** skills and knowledge in using social media and creating content can give you a significant edge over other job applicants who don't have these modern skills.

If you just use Facebook to talk to family and friends and share the Meme's and viral posts doing the rounds, then your Facebook savviness is unlikely to be necessary for inclusion in your resume. However, if it is relevant to and appropriate for the type of work you are seeking, and you decide to include details about your social media savviness, then it might be best to create a list and use similar graphical representations (mentioned for computers) to demonstrate your skill level.

Some aspects about social media savviness that you might like to consider are:

- Number of site visits (to your blog or website)
- Number of Followers or Subscribers (to your Profiles, Pages and Accounts)
- Frequency of posting / tweeting
- The range and frequency of products you've sold online (e.g. running an Ebay, Etsy or similar store)
- Type of Content you have created (e.g. blog posts, podcasts, videos, screencasts, eBooks, infographics, sales landing pages etc.)
- Platforms used
- Budgets levels you have worked to
- Promotions and campaigns you have initiated/seen to completion
- Tools (or programs) you have used to track and monitor your results (i.e. analytics, keyword research, spreadsheets, databases etc.)

What details to include

As you can see, social media savviness proves a large scope of considerations that may help you secure a job in various roles and industries.

Part 3
Summarised INFORMATION

If you decide that a social media savviness section is applicable and might give you an edge, then there are a couple of ways you could handle including this:

You could create a 'Tools of the Trade' type listing with each proficiency listed in a bullet list, or you could use a 'Computers and Technology' style approach to list the skill along with a graphical representation of your ability level.

('Tools of the Trade' style)

- Write and publish keyword rich blog posts
- Create and distribute infographics
- Implement SEO strategies
- Marketing on Facebook, Twitter and other social media sites

('Computers and Technology' style)

- Blog posting ✯✯✯✯✯✯✯✯✯
- Creating infographics ✯✯✯✯✯✯✯✯
- Keyword Research ✯✯✯✯✯✯✯✯✯
- Social Engagement ✯✯✯✯✯✯✯✯✯
- SEO & Traffic Generation ✯✯✯✯✯✯
- ROI Tracking ✯✯✯✯✯

31 Hobbies and personal interests

We all have things that we do in our spare time. Watch television, read a good book, go for a walk, play a computer game, shop or browse online, do sports, go on picnics... you get the picture. Our hobbies might be anywhere from learning to play a musical instrument, to knitting and sewing, scrapbooking or card making, to cooking or gardening and doing home handyman projects or repairs, like restoring old cars or furniture – the range can be endless!

For most of us, those things are simply personal pursuits we do to entertain ourselves, to break out of the boredom of working or studying, to relax and unwind, to get things working properly again or to express our creativity and individuality. For a lesser number, those things we do in our leisure time can translate well into skills and interests for the type of work we seek, on top of being of personal interest.

But do these things belong in our resume?

I don't think they do.

Correction. Let me clarify that: I don't think **most** hobbies or personal interests do.

There are exceptions though.

Include or exclude?

Until now, I have been quite clear as to whether a section should be included, excluded or is optional because 'it depends on...'

For this section however, I'm going to break away from that pre-established convention to list it as '**Exclude, except if...**' (I'll explain the exception soon).

> * Include
> ✓ **Exclude, except if...**
> * Optional, or It Depends...

Part 3
Summarised INFORMATION

I've said it a few times already, but it is worth repeating again, right now: a (good) resume is not a document that details your *full* life story; that is the role of a Career Portfolio. Bad resumes are ones where the person thoughtlessly throws in any and every detail in a misguided attempt to help make themself look good or better on paper. A person's hobbies and personal interests is where too many jobseekers go woefully wrong: they read or hear the (generalised) advice or find a free online template that suggests that they can include details of their hobbies and personal interests; and so, willy-nilly, the jobseeker throws in every hobby and personal interest they have, 'to show employers who I am and what I do in my spare time.'

Remember earlier I said I hate resume templates, and prefer to follow a good structure instead? It is this Hobbies and Personal Interests section being included in most cheap and nasty templates is probably the biggest reason why I hate them as much as I do; because it is so easy to mindlessly throw in a section like this and all the details that go in it and resultantly slant the application in an instant to a non-effective *'it is all about me'* focus, instead of the *'what I can do, and what value I would bring'* focus that a resume needs to have.

I see this incorrect focus in 95% or more of the resumes I assess. Unfortunately.

Many of my clients have been unemployed and jobsearching for a very long time, and they have become increasingly frustrated by the jobsearch process and the lack of positive results proportionate to the effort they are putting in. And contrary to popular belief, they do review their resume frequently – like they are supposed to do – trying to *'tailor it to each job'* – again, like they are supposed to –and even get family and friends to look over it too. And nobody (except the hiring manager who rejects the application,) sees that the **focus** is all wrong.

Eventually, the person despairs, *'What's wrong with me? Why aren't I getting results?'* and I want to scream: *'Because you used a **cheap** and **nasty** resume template that is leading you down the destined-to-stay-unemployed path! You haven't had somebody **knowledgeable**[1] in how to get hired to get good feedback or an opinion from.'*

---

1   Meaning someone Labour Market or Recruitment knowledgeable from their having worked in the industry; not the opinionated individuals who think they have the answer to everything even though they have never been in the industry, never hired anyone, have never been in any way involved in the hiring of staff, especially those currently unemployed and not getting invites to interviews but who somehow think they can advise you on your jobsearching.

Right Your RESUME

A hiring manager doesn't have time to provide specific feedback (many businesses don't even have time to let you know you were unsuccessful); and you can't afford to pay for a resume assessment service that could provide you with the knowledgeable answers because of your backlog of bills to pay is now reaching crisis point. If only these people had of sought the help of a professional resume writer or good jobsearch coach at the *beginning* of their jobsearch and they might not have ended up in the dire financial position they are in today! But I've digressed.

Most hobbies and personal interests that those jobseekers have included are unnecessary details that achieves the opposite of what that jobseeker had hoped to achieve when they decided to include them – there, now it has been said.

To help you decide if you an exception applies

For most jobseekers I have no hesitation in saying a Hobbies and Personal Interests section is completely irrelevant and therefore inappropriate to be included in their resume. But of course, there are exceptions. I hope you understand me enough by now to see what that exception is. Come on, let's all say it together, now:

- *Only if the details are relevant for the specific type of work sought*

(Well done if you correctly guessed that! It means you are starting to understand the importance of carefully and fully assessing every tiny little detail before you include or exclude it from your resume, and that my intentionally repetitive message is getting through! I'll try to stop now.)

But, I'd take that exception slightly further, too.

- **And only if the jobseeker has low skills for that type of work sought.**

What I'm suggesting is that a Hobbies and Personal Interests section is useful more for jobseekers with little to no work history or a lower skill set level (for the type of work) rather than those with higher skills and or plenty of workplace examples in that type of work, such as **recent school leavers** attempting to gain their first job and **career changers** attempting to demonstrate interest and basic competence to gain a foot in the door for the new industry.

With a 'Hobbies and Personal Interests' section included far too frequently and in too much detail over the years, and the information listed in the

Part 3
Summarised INFORMATION

section being mostly irrelevant to the job, hiring managers have come to associate such a section as the hallmarks of a poor resume and poorly-suited candidate. Quality applicants don't *need* to include these 'lesser' supportive information sections because they have sufficient workplace examples and history, licensing and qualifications to demonstrate their potential suitability without it. And often these jobseekers need to cut back on less important details in order to keep their resume length to an appropriate page count, so this type of additional information (rightly) ends up first to go.

There are better ways of demonstrating your potential suitability for a role, namely providing a targeted skills summary in the PRRE and writing evidence – or achievement – based skill statements in your work history listings.

Quality applicants do this, so I would caution any jobseeker, who has worked for five years or more, in particular, against including this section. Actually, for these jobseekers, including such a section could be the cause of the hiring manager deciding against their application, because the hiring manager could mistakenly assume the person does not have strong work history. (Remember, during a skim read, **key words** jump out at them, so the words Hobbies and Personal Interests might stand out more than the quality skill statements listed on subsequent pages).

I'm a school leaver, parent returning to the workforce or career changer and could include this section. How should I handle it, Char?

Even school leavers, parents returning and career changers should give considerable and careful thought about which hobbies and personal interests they include, because if the details do not align well with the type of work being sought the hiring manager can use that information to reach a 'no' decision.

When included, it is important to remember the section is not supposed to be a listing of **all** the person's personal interests and pursuits; it is a place where an unskilled or inexperienced person can list the hobbies or interests that *best demonstrates* their interest in or ambition to follow that particular line of work. No more.

For example, a school leaver who is interested in gaining a **carpentry apprenticeship** could list their hobby in creating **woodwork projects** on weekends or having done that subject at school; and may benefit from providing details about a few of the projects they have built as the personal pursuit brings high value of their capabilities and interests in the role.

In essence, this jobseeker is demonstrating that they haven't wildly decided *'I want to try carpentry'* without ever having dabbled in carpentry at all; the person has already developed an interest (and some ability) in working with wood from their personal pursuits, and carefully sets out how this interest aligns them well to that type of work – to persuade potential employers willing to provide them with opportunity to give them a go which will allow them to further develop those skills, interests and abilities so they can take them to a higher, professional level. (Many employers *are* happy to employ inexperienced people who demonstrate a strong interest and commitment for that particular type of work, if the person's application is strong enough! I know, when I worked in Employment Services, I met them with *great frequency*.)

But, that same school leaver would best leave out the details about their personal interest in, say, water skiing, as this type of personal pursuit *adds little or no value* to the potential employer (unless the employer is into water sports, because of the 'common ground' – but you won't know this at the application stage (unless you know the person or learn this while doing employment research!)).

Remember that although a resume is about the person it must be relevant to the type of work sought; and the resume is not the document to list you full personal history.

Double-edged sword details

The crucial part is to think about HOW the information can be perceived by the hiring manager, and question, *'Does this detail project the right message I want to convey? Will it accomplish what I hope to accomplish when including it, or can it be viewed in a different way and be used to make a no decision?'*

For example, let's say you want to list '**reading**' as a hobby or personal interest of yours. Great! Reading can show that you are broad minded and that you have higher reading and writing skills than other applicants.

But it is a solo pursuit. So listing this detail on your resume could go against your intentions if you were, say, applying for a position that relies upon strong team work. As it can be viewed that you are more an individual player than a team one. And the detail (reading) can send out the unintended message that

Part 3
Summarised INFORMATION

the person is idle and inactive, which goes against a position that involves physical activity or frequent movement.

Listing the hobby 'reading' isn't quite as innocuous as it first seemed now, is it?

When you ask those questions I listed a moment ago, and you tie how even a detail like reading can be interpreted wrongly, then you can assess all other hobbies and personal interests that you may have in (or be considering putting in) your resume and start to see that most of what is typically included is better left off a person's resume.

What details to include

You need to take this same approach for each of the many different hobbies and personal interests you might like to list in your resume to support why you would make a good candidate, and think about how a hiring manager could view each intended detail in a negative way before you include it in your resume.

If creating a hobbies and personal interest section in your resume, then there are a few things to keep in mind:

- List in bullet form
- Include only hobbies, interests and participation that is essential or desirable for the type of work being sought; and only after you have considered whether the detail is necessary and won't inadvertently cause a no decision.

Positioning

When you have reason to include this section in your resume, you need to position it well. The logical place to position the section would be on the first page of your resume. It probably won't fit into the PRRE area – not if you have already included the other more important sections we have discussed so far – so I would say aim get it on the first page of a multi-page resume, as close to the PRRE area as you can. If you intend creating a one-page resume, you might not end up with enough room to include this section anyway. And for those creating multi page resumes, the first page only is your summarised information page; from page two onwards is your work history listings.

32. Achievements and awards

Instead of being an average worker like most of your current or former colleagues, you have worked extra hard or shown exceptional ability and proficiency in the role(s). So much so, a past employer (or few) recognised that good performance of yours. Perhaps rewarding you with bonus payments or issuing you with some type of Achievement or Merit award. Well done, you!

This **high performance is what employers want to hire**. They want the best of the best. They want to hire the person who will give them the greatest bang for their buck.

Therefore, they want to see these higher performance details in an applicant's resume. And, if you omit them (when you have achievements and awards), then you are foolishly wasting the single-most best opportunity you'll ever get to impress the heck out of the hiring manager and make yourself their preferred candidate.

Include or exclude?

Without doubt, listing your exceptional and notable higher performances and achievements should be a 'no-brainer' – an absolute **must** in your resume.

But, does it need to be its own section?

I say 'yes!', **Include** this section. Even though I don't see this section very often – or perhaps *because* I don't see enough of it.

> ✓ **Include**
> * Exclude, except if...
> * Optional, or It Depends...

Most of the resume advice I have ever read (or heard) over the last ten years or more talks about the importance of writing strong evidence- and achievement- based skill statements (you'll learn more about this in the

Part 3
Summarised INFORMATION

section on writing your employment history). But those skills statements are usually buried on subsequent pages, because they are attached to each previous job position.

And when they are compelling enough, the hiring manager will read them (if they happen to flip to subsequent pages and a detail catches their; remember not all do flip to the next page, so the great detail isn't seen).

Earlier we discussed the AIDA principle, and the necessity to convert a reader from skim reading to actual reading. It is these 'superstar' details that is almost guaranteed to convert the reader from just catching their fleeting attention, onto their moving to becoming 'highly interested' and then further onto 'getting excited' about the application and this particular candidate. And eventually onto growing in 'desire to want to know more' about the person so much so that they are spurred into taking action to contact them.

All candidates, with stand out performances and achievements, need to capitalise upon the power those 'super details' as early as they can in their resume. Causing a hiring manager to feel compelled to jump straight on the phone and call the person in for an interview – before some other business snaps them up (and very much scared that this could very well happen if they don't act quickly) or else face the prospect of having to choose from only 'second pickings' as consolation prize – is the ultimate compliment a jobseeker could ever receive. Because once shown that The Best is interested and potentially available for the vacancy, no hiring manager in sane mind wants to fill it with a runner up!

Put yourself in the hiring manager's shoes again: If you were an apple connoisseur keen to snack on a Red Delicious apple, you wouldn't be quite so satisfied – despite eating an apple – if you could only eat a Granny Smith apple when you really wanted the Red Delicious, would you? Some people might try to tell you 'but you at least ate an apple', and you would reluctantly agree; but a small part of you would always regret that you didn't get the Red Delicious that you really hankered for.

Well, for the hiring manager, they wanted the Best Person for the Job, and if that person has already gained a different job – and they will be very scared that this is a realistic possibility because of how exceptional their application is – they will end up having to choose from and offer the role to the Second Best Person for the Job.

What. A. Huge. Letdown!

If you aren't already, aim to become Best of the Best.

Right Your RESUME

(And, being the preferred candidate can help a person get passed any interview 'stuff ups' the candidate might feel they made with how they went with answering questions – because it takes a sizeable stuff up to bring a good first impression down when compared to what it takes to 'come from behind' to knock the favourite out from contention, which is why preferred candidates often go on to receive a job offer. Hiring managers overlook 'interview nerves' that cause stumbles with answers.)

It takes hard work, dedication and great effort, as well as sometimes having talent and strong capabilities, to become the Best of the Best. So, although this next advice once again steps away from writing the content of your resume for a moment, I want to ask: what can you do to become the Best of the Best now, or in the future?

Do you need to love what you do? Do you need to go that extra bit that others don't do? Does it mean being helpful and friendly and doing the tasks that others don't want to do or grumble loudly over?

Aim high and you reach high! Don't just aim to get **a job**, aim to obtain a job in which you can thrive and excel in the role. Take a lesser job for now if you have to, but keep working to become the best of the best, and you will surely get there. The rewards go so much further than just finding work quickly; there is a real sense of pride in knowing that others can see and appreciate what you have done.

Positioning

I say, what a waste of a valuable opportunity if you don't get those 'better than the rest' type details listed up front where the hiring manager can easily see them – in the PRRE area – so that hiring managers work out that they have received an application from The Best.

What details to include

Although you should certainly demonstrate your achievements **in your position history** by writing strong skill statements, if you have special Awards or significant other Achievements, you might like to **create a section** titled Awards & Achievements (which is listed in the PRRE) to bring these details into greater prominence (rather than leaving such valuable successes 'buried' on subsequent resume pages which we know may not be read or even looked at).

But, I want to encourage you to be cautious and **selective** about what awards

Part 3
Summarised INFORMATION

and achievements you will list in the section and to think of the impression including the section will have upon your reader. It is essential that you only bring attention those awards and achievements that are **significant** in some way; perhaps hard fought for, rarely received, important industry type awards, not daily or weekly 'merit' certificates or academic achievements. No offense to the many great universities, colleges and schools, but the education sector readily dishes out awards and merit certificates with great 'dime-a-dozen' frequency, to motivate students and keep them engaged. But in a jobsearch context, some of those awards and achievements just aren't really all that special. (Even though they are important to the person and the school). Which ultimately lessens the value of including an awards and achievements section, if the details provided within the section misuses or abuses the purpose for including it.

Case Study

Earlier I told you about the educational-focus mistakes made by two university student jobseeker clients, who I assessed resumes for.

One of those students had listed so many of the extracurricular studies and school life involvements, that for every one of those activities completed they also gained an Academic Achievement Award for Excellence in that topic, class or participation (or so it seemed, anyway). The student's employment history and skills had been included, but only in such a small way that they appeared almost as an afterthought. In short, the overall (unintended) impression gained when I read the resume was one of *'look how much study I have done'* along with *'and how I beat all the other students too'* instead of the needed *'look at how much experience I have for this type of work'* along with *'and how well I did in the roles'*. If that was the impression I gained, it would surely be a similar one for employers. And the student had been applying for work, unsuccessfully, for many months without being contacted by employers to prove that employers weren't forming the 'wow, isn't she great' impression she thought she would create.

Only three topics of study that this student had listed were in any way related to the retail work this person sought; and it took a lot of persuasion for me to convince this student to release all except those three achievement awards from her resume.

Perhaps if the student was applying to become a teacher, or work in the education section, I might have believed she could keep more of that long list of awards and achievements in; but she was embarking on obtaining part time work only, and that work was not related to their university course, or entering the education sector in any way. I feel that my job in agreeing to assess a clients resume is to provide them with **honest** feedback on what I see as the reasons why their resume is either effective or not effective towards gaining the type of work specified – to work out possible reasons why the client isn't getting invitations to attend interviews. Either to prevent months of applying for suitable jobs without any success before they even start, or to help turn the situation around for those who have struggled unnecessarily so the negative results don't keep happening. To do that, I need to draw on my experience as a resume writer, and as the hiring manager who had to think about the employers' needs and wants, and what was required – even for job roles that I had never worked in my own self. In other words, I'm paid to *think like* an employer, so I can *help* the jobseeker.

The real problem undermining that student's resume – though the student could not see it – was they were applying for customer service roles (which involved strong teamwork and needed demonstration of retail experience), yet the 'message' and focus of the resume conflicted with that because it was all about their academic achievement and the extra-curricular activities they participated in. We resolved the problem by removing all but five awards and achievements in the end, and then adding a lot more detailed content about her former work history. The client gained work within two weeks following that simple change in focus.

Mistake to avoid

If you don't have Best of the Best type details, **please don't make them up**. Lies have a habit of rising to exposure in the end. For now, just realise that you are competing with candidates that could be the best of the best each time you apply for a position, and because of this, a less than stellar performance could result in your jobsearch taking a while longer. So factor that in.

So, no false achievements. No fancying up ordinary information.

If you want the right to include this section you have to earn it.

Legitimately. Through strong performance.

Hiring managers will see through thinly disguised ordinary performance that has been puffed up to make the person look better than they are. And no great impressed lasts as a result of it.

Part 3
Summarised INFORMATION

What details to list

If you have Awards that you are going to include in your resume, they must be relevant to the type of work you are seeking, or otherwise be significant in its prestige.

Use the proper Award title, and list the year (and perhaps even the month) received.

For example

   2013 National Young Australian of the Year Award

Or

   January 2013 National Young Australian of the Year Award

If you were presented the award by a **notable authority** or **personality**, then it can enhance the prestige of your having received the award if you include the 'presented to you by' detail.

For example

   2013 National Young Australian of the Year Award, presented by Prime Minister, Julia Gillard at an Australia Day ceremony

(Of course, not all of us receive prestigious national awards like the above examples; most of ours will just be industry or employer based. But there could still be notable people with an industry that employers have heard of.)

Mistakes to avoid

Listing the year you received the award can cause problems, if you aren't careful. You don't want to inadvertently reveal your age (so that discrimination could occur without your knowing it), and you need to avoid inadvertently showing yourself as a *former* **achiever** that is no longer achieving.

The best way to avoid inadvertently revealing your age is to remember to limit the details you include to the last ten year period (unless you have good reason to break this rule); and the best way to avoid showing lack of recent achievement is to make sure that you have recent achievements.

Right Your RESUME

For example

A fast food worker might receive an 'Employee of the Month' Award in June 2014. If it is still 2014, then this is a great achievement to list in your resume, especially if the person also receives a bonus gift card payment in, say, November for receiving 100% mystery shopper score, as this demonstrates that even though the prestige isn't as high as the Employee of the Month award, achievements are still being consistently attained within the role.

And it could be listed like this:

Achievements

- June 2014 Employee of the Month
- November 2014 100% Mystery Shopper score

On the other hand, if the fast food worker received an 'Employee of the Month' Award in June 2010, and they haven't had any further achievements within the role, listing the past achievement can cause the reader to assume the achievement was a one-off event.

As mentioned often throughout this book, you have to think about things from the hiring manager's perspective and look at how an innocent element, even one as positive such as an Award, could be seen in both a positive and negative manner – that each element sits on a double-edged sword that can (metaphorically) save lives or take them away – so you want your details to work for you not against you.

Part 3
Summarised INFORMATION

33 Referees

For reasons you will learn later within this section, employers' rarely hire any person without first meeting the person face to face (at a formal or informal interview) and carrying out some research to learn more about them.

Desperate jobseekers often resort to lying, fabricating, exaggerating and embellishing the truth to try to gain an upper hand securing a job, perhaps because they don't trust that the hiring managers will see, or they just don't have, the required skills and experience required. So they decide the only way they'll get the job is if they lie or try tricking their way in.

This practice is so disgracefully prevalent it is commonplace; and because of this, hiring managers aren't going to blindly trust *any* applicant's sole word for it – ever. So, they have developed the policy and practice of seeking the opinion from an independent source (or few). And spend time building a portfolio that provides a bigger, truer picture of a candidate, to enable them to make a well rounded decision rather than narrow one (which happens if they just use a jobseeker's slanted viewpoint alone, as presented to them in the application).

There are two common ways for hiring managers to gain that broader picture about what a candidate is really like that directly affect our resume writing: their carrying out background checking research (in particular, a person's online presence which I briefly covered in the Social Media section earlier), and the contacting references to obtain an unbiased, arm's distant viewpoint from independent people.

> *Definition*
> Reference: a referee; a person prepared to testify verbally or who provides written testimonial, as to the character, abilities, qualities, etc. of another person, especially a job applicant

Include or exclude?

Other resume writers, career advisors and the like may not agree with me, but inclusion of your references on your resume is **optional**, and that decision needs to be made on an application by application basis:

Right Your RESUME

> * Include
> * Exclude, except if...
> ✓ **Optional**, or It Depends...

There are strong, compelling arguments for both including and excluding references on your resume, and because the arguments for both sides are equally strong and logical, this is the only section that I would prefer to leave it up to you to decide rather than my encouraging you to choose one over the other. But, as a general guideline, I would say, if you are applying for a government job, or to a big name business (like a bank, or chain supermarket) that is trusted and well known, then I would go with a 'yes, by all means include' the details of your referees (because these organisations are likely to treat your details properly and securely more than not). But, if you are applying to smaller businesses, and especially when you don't know anything about the business you are applying to, then I'd go more with maintaining a 'think twice' attitude.

I have worked with some hiring managers that stubbornly refused to interview any person if they haven't included their referees on their resume; and I have worked with more hiring managers who were laid back and easy-going so didn't care if referees weren't listed on the resume or not, because they knew they didn't need them at this point in the hiring process and would just simply ask for them during or after the job interview if they were still interested in the person and had reached the point of needing them.

You never know which type of hiring manager you are going to get. So have a read of the reasons for both including and excluding, and then weigh up what you think is right for you. Like with previous optional sections, I will let you make up your mind and will provide details of how to list if you decide to include, with no hard feelings if you decide not to.

Reasons to include...

Inadvertent red flag indicator

If you have work history, you could inadvertently send up 'red flags' if you don't provide references from your past employment, especially roles you held within the past five year period, as this can be viewed as an indicator that 'all was not well' within a past role.

Part 3
Summarised INFORMATION

Think about it: no jobseeker (except perhaps one deliberately sabotaging their chance of getting the job for whatever reason) is going to tell the hiring manager, 'I have an attitude and behaviour problem', 'I don't know how to get along with co-workers, especially the idiots in authority' or 'I do really shoddy work', are they?

After a five year period, it is generally accepted that people can lose touch with former employers and supervisors, as other staff move on too, not just you; and as such there might not be any person left at a former workplace that remembers or can vouch for the applicant.

Jobseekers who have negative attitudes, behaviours and performance often 'burn their bridges' with former employers and their managers or supervisors, and either end up with no referees to provide the details to potential employers at all, or are unable to provide them with referees from certain positions from within their work history – which becomes noticeable on paper, so the jobseeker leaves off the section entirely to try and mask this. And often hoping they won't be asked for them.

Experienced hiring managers know jobseekers use these types of tricks and are wary of them. For this reason, hiring managers may want to see details of referees on the resume, because on a subconscious level it can satisfy them that independent people are prepared to vouch for the applicant. Which immediately prevents any concerns arising and causes them to make a last mental tick, because they can see that the details are already on hand for when the time comes and they want to use those details to contact the referees.

Other applicants will include them

On top of omission acting as a red flag indicator, not all jobseekers are aware that including References is optional. Most jobseekers I've met think, because crappy templates have led them to believe, they must include these details. And, those that have good references, or plenty of them because they have no problematic background and therefore nothing to hide, might willingly list their referees on their resume without any qualms or second thoughts about doing so because they don't know they can do otherwise, and are proud to let potential employers see they have referees.

You've worked hard at writing a quality resume so that you get to this point of the hiring manager being interested in you as a potentially suitable candidate. And, although congratulations are in order for your putting in that extra time and effort to achieve that, you don't expect to be the only potentially suitable candidate that the employer may want to interview. As such, any person with plenty of referees listed could be your greatest competition.

Right Your RESUME

As mentioned a few moments ago, some hiring managers will want to see the details are present, others won't be fussed. If this application you have sent in happens to be to an employer that is fussed about seeing the details and you haven't then that could affect your application. Especially when other similarly impressive short listed candidates do provide their referee details. You would hate to miss out on a suitable opportunity simply because the wearied hiring manager assumed that your excluding of referee details (done wholly to safeguard against potential misuse) meant you possibly have a problematic background, so they reject your application based on this (negative, wrong) assumption formed.

Reasons to exclude...

Not an essential detail during the application stage

Let's face it; you are only applying for the job because you are interested in it, so therefore you are simply sending out an Expression of Interest to be considered for the job. Just because you are interested in this type of work, and are probably fully skilled and experienced, doesn't mean you are perfectly suited to this vacancy, and the job might not actually be perfectly suited to you in return. You've read the advertisement, and have assumedly done a bit of research about the industry, the job type and this employer to feel that the role may be right for you. Now that you've applied for the job, it is the employers turn to assess whether you are right for them.

But, the hiring manager shouldn't be making a final hiring decision yet, should they?

As discussed elsewhere throughout this book, the hallmark of a good, quality resume is one that balances providing sufficient detail to enable the hiring manager to see your potential suitability, enough to want to know more about you against not wasting resume space with unnecessary details which can be used against you or misused for purposes that don't match your intention in providing the detail.

You've read all that advice, understood its importance and now you are (correctly) asking the question: "Is this detail absolutely essential at this time, or can I leave it off?" And you've been able to answer that question with an unequivocal, "No, it is not essential right now; therefore it is an unnecessary detail that I can and should happily omit."

You are right. There is no need for the employer to have this detail right now.

Part 3
Summarised INFORMATION

And, you have not yet ascertained that the employer is who they say they are, that they are above-board and will use the information purely for the purpose for which you have provided it – that is, to contact these people who are prepared to vouch for you so they can see that you are as good as you say you are; and no other reason.

So you have justification for having reservations about providing details of your referees just because that is what other candidates do – so humph, more fool those candidates! You have nothing to hide and are happy to provide the details when you attend the interview, and even have a list already typed up and ready to take with you and will hand over as soon as you can see that everything is as legit with the business and the vacancy as it ought to be. Protecting oneself against risks does work both ways, after all.

Misuse of information

There is potential for scammers, identity thieves and shonky employers (or an untrustworthy employee) to misuse these referee details every bit as much as they can misuse your own personal details.

For example, some recruitment agencies (which many jobseekers automatically trust) enter the particulars provided into a database, so they can market their services to those referees and the businesses they work for. In those recruitment company views, you've provided them with the names and contact details of possible decision makers. They aren't out to hurt you – the jobseeker – it's just business, they are under pressure to obtain new business from their bosses and this can help them reach their targets and KPIs.

How?

Now that they have these details they can bypass cold calling by tricking an unsuspecting receptionist into believing that the person knows them (and vice versa), so the receptionist doesn't act as that dratted gatekeeper always blocking access to their 'target'. Having a person's name allows them to act as though they are making a warm call instead.

(A cold call is where the recipient person doesn't know the person and is not expecting the call, and might not want the call; a warm call is where one or more of the 'cold' factors have been removed. For example, the recipient might be expecting the call while not knowing the caller and not being happy to accept the call, or may know the caller but is not expecting but are happy to take the call because of the 'warm' factor.)

The problem mostly arises when the referee doesn't want such cold calls. See

	Know	Expect	Happy to Take
No problem	✓	✗	✓
	✗	✓	✓
	✓	✓	✓
Unhappy Referee	✓	✓	✗
	✗	✓	✗
	✓	✗	✗

figure below:

Think about it from your referee's side, because this is a relationship you want (and need) to preserve. You've asked that person (and they have agreed) to act as a referee for the exclusive purpose of *helping you* gain a job. (They didn't have to give their consent). But what they get instead are annoying and disruptive phone calls from recruitment agencies trying to get the referees company to use the recruitment agency's services to manage the hiring process for them – and the referee's company might not even be hiring and are pressured to then do so, or 'Head Office' might handle all that! So, a recruitment agency calling them is just a pestering phone call.

Some businesses also sell their database 'lists' to other businesses as a revenue stream (don't we hate it when our own details are sold and we start getting nightly telemarketing calls, right on dinner time!), so not only do your referees start getting recruitment agencies phoning them, they also might start having other business-to-business marketers trying to sell them a range of products they may or may not need – stationery and toner marketers phone with annoying frequency!

If your referee is, say, just the duty supervisor whose job it is to make sure the shift runs smoothly and they don't have product purchasing decision-making authority (or responsibility), how quickly are they going to become annoyed when they keep getting phone calls to their business extension, interrupting important tasks, or to their personal mobile phone number which your referee only gave you so it increased the chance of an employer reaching them? A number that they don't usually like sharing out.

Part 3
Summarised INFORMATION

You and your referees might not realise what has caused this sudden influx of unwanted calls; but you have the power to spare your referees all this potential 'harassment' that you wouldn't want yourself, simply by providing a list of your referees only to employers seriously contemplating hiring you and no one else. Thus decreasing the risk of the details being misused.

What are hiring manager's looking for?

Back in the Before We Start Righting Your Resume chapters, I discussed the different perspectives: you as a product, and the reasons why hiring managers don't just take jobseekers sole word for what they are like as a person and as a worker. That they want (and need) to speak with an independent person or few so they gain an impartial third-person opinion. Employers will trust the word of another **business person**, because that professional will know where the hiring manager is coming from (and is in the same situation when they hire).

And, as Arthur Weasley so eloquently quoted Shakespeare in the Harry Potter and Order of the Phoenix movie, the *'truth will out'* in the end; lies have a habit of being discovered, the truth a way of revealing itself to those not doing the lying (and possibly affected by the lie). Do you really want to be the foolish jobseeker candidate who misses out on a job offer, or is humiliatingly dismissed from a new job, because they lose all credibility when the shit hits the fan?

If you've decided that you will leave this section off, then without guilt you can now jump straight to the next chapter where you can read about writing or righting your work history.

But, for those of you that decided you'll include your referees, stick around, also without guilt. We'll now discuss the how's, what's and why's to listing your references in your resume.

Referees and references

As discussed at the beginning of this chapter, the reason hiring managers ask for references is because when they are seriously considering offering you the job they now want to gain opinions about you from independent and external sources who can confirm or deny that what you've said so far is a true and accurate representation of your skills and abilities.

But it is important to note that reference checking is only *one* prior-to-employment background check options available to them, though it is the

Right Your RESUME

most common and well known practice to most jobseekers.

We've already touched on that references can be:

- Written or
- Verbal

But, they can also be:

- Professional or
- Personal

Let's briefly discuss each of the types.

Professional references

Professional referees are people you know from within your previous employment and development – preferably past bosses, managers, supervisors or even community leaders who you used to work under, or fellow colleagues you used to work alongside.

These people have witnessed you within a workplace (or in a work-like environment) and can therefore provide a firsthand, independent perspective about your skills, attitudes, strengths, capabilities and weaknesses. The work environment can be from your paid and unpaid history. These referees generally are not a part of your close-friendship circle, though you may get to know them well due to the working relationship.

Because of their impartial and business-oriented viewpoints, their testimony carries much greater weighting compared to personal referees, because hiring managers view them as a more trustworthy source.

Personal references

Personal referees are people you know, who you have never worked with (or for), that might be family, friends, acquaintances or community members who are prepared to vouch for you as a person. That is, they are usually people who are part of your close-friendship circle and can only provide testimony as to your personality, characteristics, values and ethics on a close and personal level because they know you so well, or for a long time. But, they are in no position to discuss workplace skill levels and capabilities.

Part 3
Summarised INFORMATION

Because you have close relationship or connections with these people, their testimony doesn't carry much weight compared to professional referees.

But both your professional and your personal referees can provide their testimonies either verbally or in writing.

Written references

A written reference, otherwise known as a Letter of Recommendation, is where the referee takes the time to put their endorsement or testimony in written form. That is, they decide what they want to say about you, and then put that in writing. Which is then given to you in either print or electronic form (usually print, so that no changes can be made to an original document).

When a person provides written reference from within their professional capacity, they often use the company letterhead and sign off with their name and position title.

Authorised people are usually a manager or supervisor who you've worked under or been accountable to. The focus of their letter talks about your strengths and weaknesses as a worker, and uses keywords to impart the intended message.

A personal referee probably doesn't have a business letterhead, and of course the difference in what they say about you is based on never having worked with you so they discuss more your positive personality, characteristics and attributes rather than workplace skills and experiences.

Verbal references

A verbal reference is where you simply provide the referees name and contact details (either verbally or in writing to the hiring manager), and when contacted the referee answers the hiring manager's specific questions and gives their unscripted, unrehearsed opinion on the spur of the moment. Both the hiring manager and the referee influence the outcome of what is (and isn't) discussed during the call.

A reference check phone call might last for only a few minutes, or it can end up a lengthier discussion.

The hiring manager is likely to establish whether your referee is personal or

Right Your RESUME

professional *early* within the conversation.

Which type should you use?

Most hiring managers will require the details of at least two (2) referees (some companies prefer three (3)) and prefer those referees to be professional references over personal ones. And, preferably your professional referees will be past managers or supervisors, rather than colleagues.

You should always aim to provide these preferences to give yourself the best chance of success in gaining the job.

How to list

Now let's look at how to provide your verbal and written reference details in your resume.

Verbal references

The essential aspect that the hiring manager will want to know is firstly, what is the name of the person, quickly followed by questions like what is the connection, and in what altitude or authority level are they acting from, along with how do they contact them.

The best way to structure referee details is to follow a similar format to how you provide your employment and development details, like this:

- Name (bolded)
- Position Title
- Company
- Contact number or email address
- Best time to contact (optional)

For example

Joe Bloggs

Manager

ABC Company Pty Ltd

0411 119 922

Part 3
Summarised INFORMATION

The referee's name will be the most important element, followed closely by the contact number. The rest of the details are just supplementary to help the hiring manager see the connection or you are being helpful. The position title suggests the authority level.

In the interests of maintaining consistency in how you apply styling of elements throughout your resume, I recommend that you bold the referee name like you did for your position titles, and list the remaining details in the above order (only this time, without bullet points).

Depending on how much room you have left in your resume document, you can list the details of *multiple referees* one after the other, like this:

Joe Bloggs
Manager
ABC Company Pty Ltd
0411 119 922

Jane Doe
Managing Director
ZYX Business
0410 600 900

Or, you could position the details side-by-side in columns, like this:

Joe Bloggs	**Jane Doe**
Manager	Managing Director
ABC Company Pty Ltd	ZYX Business
0411 119 922	0410 600 900

(Note, in this example I used Tabs to divide the information, but you could use a hidden table instead. Actually, a hidden table will better enable you to rearrange details than using tabs.)

Obtain permission first

Right Your RESUME

It is important to ensure that *you* contact your referees *before* you list them in your resume to a) obtain the person's permission to act (or continue to act) as your referee, and to b) obtain all necessary particulars so that you can supply accurate information and supply all details (to enable you to apply the elements consistently), and c) so the referee is not surprised or blindsided by an unexpected call.

One referee from each position

In an ideal resume world, you would include at least one professional referee from each of your previous two or three positions – at least for the last five years worth of employment.

For example, because ABC Company Pty Ltd and ZYX Business are listings within your employment and development history, you would obtain permission and provide the professional referee details for both of those former employments, not just one or the other.

But, again, most jobseekers don't live in the confines of that ideal resume world. It is not just candidates that change jobs; referees can do this also. And, we don't always stay in contact with staff at former jobs.

So now, I want to cover a couple of common questions I'm asked about referees, from those who fall outside of the ideal resume world, even though, once again, this advice falls outside of resume writing.

What if my referee no longer works at that company?

Let's say Joe Bloggs was your manager while the two of you worked at ABC Company Pty Ltd. You are aware that Joe, who is happy to keep acting as your referee and only has wonderful things to rave about you, has now moved on also.

In the interests of providing accurate information and not confusing the hiring manager when the receptionist answers the phone with a different business name to what they were expecting to hear, it would be best to list the name of the company that Joe Bloggs currently works at – for example, let's say he moved on to become Area Manager at A2Z Products – when the number you provide is the new workplace number.

If you need to provide the referees new employment details, you could

Part 3
Summarised INFORMATION

provide clarifying 'formerly employed at' details to keep the association to your employment listing, like this:

Joe Bloggs

Area Manager

A2Z Products, former Manager at ABC Company Pty Ltd

02 9600 3010

But, it sort of makes the Company details line a little bit too long – the information looks out of place, and is inconsistent to how you have listed other specifics, so you could break the information up to make it look less noticeable, like this:

Joe Bloggs

Area Manager

A2Z Products,

former Manager at ABC Company Pty Ltd

02 9600 3010

However, if the contact number you provide belongs to the referee, then you could keep things simple by listing the detail matched to your work history and not provide the new employment detail, and list it like shown earlier using Joe's former position title and company name, like this:

Joe Bloggs

Manager

ABC Company Pty Ltd

0411 119 922

What if I no longer have any referees from a previous company?

If you no longer have referees from a previous company, then you may need to not include a Referees or References section in your resume.

If it is just one position and you have two or more referees, then perhaps the hiring manager won't notice if you list two referees from ABC Company and no-one from ZYX Business. But, it will always look best if you have at least one referee for each former job role though. That was something I checked when culling applications.

You might need to try and contact the people you are still in contact with who also know the person you are trying to contact, to see if they know where the referees might have gone to or someone who might know. The goal would be to try and track the person down as soon as possible in the early stages of your jobsearch, in preparation for when you need them.

What if I have never worked or been out of the workforce for a significant period and do not have any referees?

This is probably the biggest hurdle for school leavers and parents returning to the workforce. The best thing to do is develop good relationships and participate in external activities well ahead of needing to look for work, so that you gain them.

School leavers can approach their teachers, who will know them well, or any other community leaders for activities they have been a part of. Parents returning to the workforce may need to seek voluntary work or participate in a community organisation to help develop referees. If they can, parents returning to the workforce need to undertake preparatory measures well before they need to find a job, to rebuild skills and redevelop employment contacts. And it would be helpful to try and maintain contact with a few workplace contacts throughout your non-employment period too.

Written references

If you have decided to include a Referees section in your resume, then you are deciding to mostly include the particulars of your referees so that the hiring manager can obtain *verbal* references.

Although written references are useful, they are not ideal.

For those of you who have written references, **do not** attach them to your resume or send copies in as part of your application, simply because you need to remember that you are only at the *application stage*, and references are for later stages within the hiring process when you are seriously being considered for the role.

To send them as part of your application can be negatively viewed as a statement that you don't feel that the hiring manager will see your worth and benefit without those additional unrequested documents. And if that is the case, then you need to fix up your resume so that hiring managers will see your worth and benefit without the 'back up' of other people during this

Part 3
Summarised INFORMATION

beginning of the process.

There is **no** competitive edge gained by including scans or copies of written references as part of your resume or application; actually, it is a common practice of those with less than stellar work history, so (most) hiring manager's only see this as another form of trickery that the jobseeker is using to make them self look better on paper than what they are in person. That it is the jobseeker trying to sell themselves to the hiring manager before the hiring manager is ready to be sold to.

How to let hiring managers know you have written references

Obviously, you've weighed the pros and cons to decide that you want to include a References section in your resume (and that decision is perfectly fine) but you now know the actual written references do not belong in your resume.

To correctly handle letting hiring managers know your references are written (and that you will bring to the job interview if you are offered one) without ruining the good impression you have strived to ensure for your resume, you need only write a summary, like this:

Written References

Joe Bloggs
ABC Company Pty Ltd

Jane Doe
ZYX Business

Leaving out the contact details make it clear: you have references, but the hiring manager does not have permission to contact them by phone at this time, and that you have not provided a copy of those written references with your application.

If you do this though, then you **must** take a portfolio of the original documents with you to the job interview if you are offered one. That way, if the hiring manager is interested, needs to keep a copy on file to help them with making a final decision or needs to keep accurate personnel records they will be able to request and photocopy them. And they will be able to mark that they have sighted the original and taken a **true copy**.

Right Your RESUME

Written vs. verbal.

As hiring manager, I get answers to the questions at the heart of what I most want to know more from speaking to a referee over the phone than I would ever get from just reading a written reference. It's a 'the hiring manager's agenda trumping a 'what the referee has to say' thing.

It is great when referees take the time to write out a reference; on the one hand, the person must genuinely have some respect, admiration or affection to put in the time and effort to write about another person's character, abilities and qualities that they have been most impressed by. But the referee can be 'glowing' in one direction while the hiring manager wants to know about things from a completely different direction; the referee can touch on an aspect that the hiring manager wants to explore in-depth; and let's face it, with accessibility to computers and printers, anybody could have written that reference, including a dishonest candidate. So for this reason, hiring managers value verbal over written references.

Okay, we've covered verbal and written references and potential problems. Let's now continue with how to list your referees in your resume.

Positioning

The first consideration you need to be aware of is where to position your referee's details.

Although I am addressing this section in the Summarised Information chapters that **does not mean** that your Referees section belongs in the early parts of your resume.

On the contrary, the Referees section, if you decide to include one, is best left as the **very last section** on your resume. That is, you physically locate it *after* your work and development history listings.

Next is, what title do you give this section?

Do I use the word referees or references?

The words Referees and References are often used interchangeably.

But, from my viewpoint : Referees are the people, and references are the documents and what referees provide.

Part 3
Summarised INFORMATION

For this reason, when I am including details of Referees on a resume – that is, I am providing the names and numbers so the hiring manager can make verbal or email contact, then I use the word 'Referees'.

Whereas on the occasions when a client doesn't have Referees but has a couple of written references, then if the client wants details of their references included on their resume I entitle the section 'References'.

And, when the client has a combination of both Referees and References, I entitle the section References.

Optional details...

Best time to contact

Not everyone works 9 to 5, and even those that do might have certain times when they are just un-contactable. For instance, in one of my employment services roles, I trained jobseekers from 9 to 12. The site receptionist just took messages during that three hour period, and I could only return calls after lunch, because my role was to assist jobseekers with their jobsearch, not manage my caseload during that time block. My own family were aware that they would not be able to reach me during that time so knew to only call me during those times if it was an emergency.

A former colleague asked me to be referee for a job they had just gained an interview for, and, in the interest of not wasting the hiring manager's time trying to reach me while I was training, I let the person know that they should advise the hiring manager that I was only available after 1 p.m. A couple of days later, sure enough the hiring manager rang. And, they were able to reach me without too much trouble because they had best time to contact information.

If you are aware that one or more of your referees might be difficult to get in contact with, then you could ask them for a best time to contact and list that on your resume, like this:

Joe Bloggs

Manager

ABC Company Pty Ltd

0411 119 922

Best time to contact: after 1 p.m. weekdays

Right Your RESUME

Jane Doe

Managing Director

ZYX Business

0410 600 900

Best time to contact: before and after business hours

You could also use the abbreviation 'BTC' or 'BTTC' to signal best time to contact, rather than writing it in full, to conserve space.

For example

Joe Bloggs

Manager

ABC Company Pty Ltd

0411 119 922

BTC: after 1 p.m. weekdays

Or, you could use the word 'Available', like this:

Joe Bloggs

Manager

ABC Company Pty Ltd

0411 119 922

Available: after 1 p.m.

When hiring manager's see these types of *helpful* details, it automatically creates a good impression. Because they realise you are considering things from *their* perspective; that you are trying to make things as easy and convenient as possible for them.

As most jobseekers don't do these 'little things', you doing so could be that one small thing that sets you apart from your competition, to tip the odds in your favour.

Pronunciation of difficult names

Does one of your referees have a difficult, unusual or foreign name that is difficult to pronounce? Another 'little wow-factor thing' that you can

Part 3
Summarised INFORMATION

do is provide instructions on how to pronounce the referees name to take the awkwardness away for the hiring manager. For example, a former manager that I worked with first name was Weina, which was pronounced 'Way Na', not 'We In A' or 'We Ner' or any other way you might see her name and think it is pronounced.

If I was in a situation to want or need to ask her to act as a referee for me, then I could simply clarify the pronunciation of her name, like this:

Weina Surname (pronounced 'Way Na')

Former Title

Former Business name

Mobile contact number

It irks me sometimes when too many people call me Char using the hard ch sound (like when saying charcoal), because my name is pronounced Char using the soft 'shh' sound. (Yes, 'ch' can be pronounced 'shh' – one only has to look at names like Charlotte, Charmaine and Cheryl and words likes chalet, chamois, champagne, champignon and chandelier (to name a few), to hear the softer shh sound and see evidence that not all Ch words use a hard ch sound!)

Mistakes to avoid

Once again, we need to consider what can be done wrong when writing our resume, so we can avoid those mistakes. The main ones for the Referees and References section are:

- Half provided details
- Written references attached as a scan at the rear of the resume
- Irrelevant references
- Personal referees

Do not half-provide information

Do not **half-provide** information that is included: that is, don't create a Referee or References section in your resume and then not provide the full details, to instead replace the specifics with trite and condescending phrases like 'Available upon Request', or something similar. That is half-providing details.

Right Your RESUME

Be decisive when including and excluding your information in your resume. If you choose to include a section, then you must provide *all* the accompanying details; if you choose to exclude a section, then you must omit the entire section and all associated details. Follow through on the decision you made, don't change your mind halfway in.

Unlike movie and book promotions, 'teaser' style information **does not work** in a positive way when it comes to resume writing. Phrases like '*Available upon Request*' are cliché, and redundant – of course you will provide details to a hiring manager if they request them. That is a given. Because if you don't (or can't), they'll just reject your application. So to state 'Available upon Request' just makes you look foolish or unthinking, and is wishy-washy decision making, as you are effectively insulting the hiring manager's intelligence that they won't understand sub-text.

From the hiring manager's perspective, it is a strong sign of a poor quality resume or that the person has used a cheap resume template. Both negative perceptions, which don't help your application proceed further.

Actually, when I was culling resumes, even though I didn't often look at subsequent pages of a resume as a general rule, sometimes I often partially flipped the top page to view the References section underneath because it is mostly listed as the last item. I judged the resume not on whether the section was included or excluded but, when the section was provided in full, on whether the particulars were provided or a variant of the cliché phrase had been used.

Because 'Available upon Request' is mostly associated with jobseekers who don't have any referees at all, and the person probably used that phrase to distract the hiring manager from noting this, and I *was* aware of this trick I checked the Reference section during my initial skim read. If I didn't already have a reason to reject the application, I used this as my last 'test' to whether they were potentially suitable or not.

And, I never rejected applications where the candidate didn't include the section – because I knew we could ask for the details when we met the person. In other words, omitting the section wasn't a criterion for us to reject, only the cliché phrasing was. (Which makes it sad (and frustrating) when you hear career professionals advising jobseekers to write those phrases).

Part 3
Summarised INFORMATION

Written references attached to resume

As discussed in the how to list section, **do not** scan your written references and attach to the end pages of your resume. This not only increases the document file size which can make it difficult when it comes to emailing and uploading your resume when you apply to jobs, but the details are not necessary during the application stage, and as discussed can cause a negative impact towards your being considered potentially suitable for the job.

If you have written references, then only provide them to interested hiring managers at the interview. Take them as a portfolio of evidence to choose your brand and let the hiring manager decide if they want to see them or take a copy.

Actually, now that I think about it, the majority of applications I culled used the words 'Available Upon Request' rather than omitting the section – so maybe jobseekers ARE more aware that the section is optional than I originally gave credit. And if this is the case, then those jobseekers were just handling the situation in the wrong way! Either way, at their own expense.

Irrelevant to the type of work sought

When you take written references, be sure to only take along carefully selected ones that are relevant to the type of work being sought. What is the point of taking a written references that discusses, say, how great you are at solo sports endeavours, if you are trying to get a job as, say, an Accountant.

You are allowed to be good at solo sports, but your participation in physical activity, the lack of demonstration towards teamwork or any task performed by an Accountant, doesn't bring anything of value to the potential employer; whereas a reference from a community group leader where you have tutored disadvantaged children Maths for the past three years, which discusses your extraordinary ability with and love of numbers completely supports your application for an Accountant role.

Just because you have written references doesn't automatically mean they are relevant and should be used.

Personal referees

If you have professional referees, use them over personal referees.

If you do not have professional referees, do not attempt to trick hiring

Right Your RESUME

managers into believing you have them by providing the names and contact details of family members. Family members have a vested interest in you obtaining the job, and therefore are only going to say positive things about you to help you secure a role.

It is better to be honest and let a hiring manager know that you do not have professional referees during the interview, and ask them what alternatives the employer is willing to consider. For example, instead of needing the usual (and preferred) three referees you might negotiate that they might accept just the one professional referee and the other two as personal ones.

Of course, you will have to provide a reason to the hiring manager, so there must be a *reasonable explanation*. As hiring manager, I would rather you tell me the truth, with something like 'I've been a stay at home mum for the past seven years, and am trying to re-enter the workforce. I only have one professional referee, but I can supply you with a couple of personal referees to reach your number, if required,' rather than have you try to trick me by getting a family member or close friend to pretend to be a professional referee.

If you have never been employed (at all, in this country, or for a number of years), hiring managers understand that you don't have professional referees with which to make independent assessment about your skills and capabilities. This is when having good, personal referees does become important.

The best personal referees therefore, if you have no choice but to use them, are 'external' referees that have good standing within the community: community leaders, such as police officers, priests, teachers and community group organisers such as sports coaches. These people need to know you quite well enough to be prepared to vouch for you on matters like honesty and reliability; but there are many areas in relation to the workforce that they will not be able to vouch for.

It is important if you list both professional and person referees on your resume that you distinguish what type of reference they are (i.e., professional or personal). And you can do so easily, like this:

Professional

Joe Bloggs

Manager

ABC Company Pty Ltd

0411 119 922

Part 3
Summarised INFORMATION

Personal

Jane Doe
Managing Director
ZYX Business
0410 600 900

Or, similar to this:

Professional	*Personal*
Joe Bloggs	**Jane Doe**
Manager	Managing Director
ABC Company Pty Ltd	ZYX Business
0411 119 922	0410 600 900

What can referees discuss?

This will depend on the country you live in, but in general, a hiring manager and referee can discuss **factual details** about you. The referee may need or be required to withhold any information that could be perceived as breaching privacy laws, such as disclosing personal details like your age or date of birth, but the factual information they can discuss broadly includes:

- Whether the referee believes you would be suitable to the vacancy
- What your strengths and weaknesses are, and your effectiveness and performance level within that past role was
- How you got along with other people – colleagues, managers and customers
- How you deal with situations like working under pressure or meeting deadlines
- Your leadership and management abilities
- Your technical ability and skill level, and any areas you need to improve upon
- Your reasons for leaving – did you leave of your own accord, or were you terminated and why
- Your honesty, integrity and punctuality
- Whether the referee would rehire you

Right Your RESUME

What can't a referee discuss?

The referee and hiring manager are not permitted to discuss anything that could be discriminatory (such as asking what your marital status or sexual preferences might be) or could be slanderous (like 'they are ugly and mean').

And referees will be cautious against providing factual that are unknown (such as providing them with your middle name or residential address) as those types of details the hiring manager needs to obtain directly from you rather than third parties, and if the referee provides them then they may be breaching your privacy.

Testing a referee

Not sure what your referee will say about you? Have you been successfully gaining job interviews but not getting the job, and can't work out why you keep missing out?

Then you might want to check what your referees say about you, to make sure they are saying positive things and your story is matching the one they give to the hiring manager.

Let me tell you of two personal experiences:

> When I was employed with one job service provider and wanted to get a job closer to home, I let my manager know that I was looking but intended being picky about what I would accept. The manager was happy to give me time off work to attend interviews, and was happy to act as a referee, fully understanding my situation. She didn't want to see me go, but told me there would be no hard feelings if I went.
>
> I successfully got invites to the jobs I applied for, but became confused when I didn't get the job offers for a couple of them, especially a couple that I had felt were my best interviews ever. It took a couple of rejections before I worked out that my manager was saying negative things about me during reference checks. When I confronted her about this, she sheepishly admitted that she had deliberately sabotaged my changing jobs efforts because I was her 'star performer' and it would be difficult to replace me. I was angry and shocked at this.
>
> With her showing no remorse and my being unable to trust that she wouldn't keep doing this even though having been caught out, I initially decided to just remove her as my referee and go back to an old one – but

Part 3
Summarised INFORMATION

that didn't work. Employers wanted a professional referee from within my current employment. This manager was the only person I could ask.

So what I did instead was to leave her name and contact details on my resume, but I listed her last, and I provided my quality referees upfront. Next, to combat her being able to sabotage future applications, I mentioned during the job interview that the top two listed people would be the easiest to get in contact with, and put a best time to contact my current manager as being 'between 5 – 5.30 p.m.' (when no one answered the phones!) It worked. The next employer wasn't prepared to waste time chasing my current referee, so chose to contact my good referees instead, and I was offered the job.

In another situation, I left one employer because I didn't like how I was treated, and when I handed in my resignation, my manager stated that he was upset to see me moving on and offered to act as a referee – they knew I didn't have another job to go to, because I stated this as part of my resignation. Because of my really horrible experience at the company, I was highly concerned that I might end up with a repeat of my former manager (above) deliberately sabotaging me, so I waited a couple of weeks during my notice period and then got a friend to phone up to do a dummy reference check.

Once again, I was surprised. But this time, pleasantly. For I learned that this manager not only had nice things to say about me but also that he went out of his way to try and make sure I was the chosen candidate by stating to my friend that they 'wouldn't find anyone more suited and capable to the job' than me. I rang this referee a few days later, and thanked him for the positive reference; but that I had worked out that the position wasn't right for me so turned the role down. The referee expressed disappointed for me and stated he was happy to keep acting as my referee. I kept him as my referee now that I felt confident that his testimony would be favourable.

Other background checks

Prior-employment reference checks aren't the only checks that hiring managers carry out to get an independent perspective about who you are, what you are like, and what you can do. Hiring managers will often perform other 'background checks' before they ever consider offering a job to their preferred candidate. These could be:

Right Your RESUME

- Criminal history checks
- Qualification and Licensing checks
- Social media and online presence research
- Credit checks – (mainly for positions in the accounting and finance industry)

Some employers, before they can progress an applicant to the 'next stage', will also require candidates to undergo:

- Drug and alcohol screening
- Physical exams, and or
- Skills and knowledge testing

I mentioned it earlier in the book, and now is a good a time to reiterate the point: check your online presence and set your social media profiles to private before you start applying to jobs.

Last words of advice

If you have decided to exclude this section from your resume, or you are going to include or exclude on an application-by-application basis, you will still need to be prepared for when hiring managers want your referee's details.

My suggestion is **don't wait to be asked** during a job interview. If all is going well you should raise the topic of referees and hand them a separate document which contains them yourself, before the hiring manager asks.

That separate document with your referee details should **use the same fonts and formatting** as used in your resume. I encourage you to build two versions of your resume: one with your referees listed on its own page (use a section break, if necessary) and the one you will use to apply for jobs that is without referees. That way, if you change your mind for a particular application you don't have to spend time adding them to your resume (or need to remember to delete afterwards, too). And the reason for using a section break is that this will allow you to keep the page numbering consistent, and continue using the same running header and footer (if used).

Before you attend an interview, you would simply open up the version that has your referees and just print that last page only to take with you.

Employment and development history

Part 4.

Right Your RESUME
Quote

"Don't cheat the world of your contribution. Give it what you've got."
Steven Pressfield

Part 4
Employment HISTORY

34 Employment and development history

The following pages in this book will now deal exclusively with righting or writing the content for your work history; therefore the instructions are best suited to jobseekers that will use a Chronological or Combination resume.

Those that intend creating a Functional Resume can skip over the writing of Skill Statements for each position previously held, but as stated before, if you are serious about getting a job, then I believe a Chronological or Combination resume is the better option.

Include or exclude?

In previous parts of this book, I have broken down the details into three distinct groups: a 'yes, you should include', a 'no, you shouldn't include' and an 'optional, because it depends on...' separation.

I don't think you need me to tell you that providing details about your previous employment is essential for a good resume. So, as a section, you should **include** this.

> ✓ **Include**
> * Exclude
> * Optional, or It Depends...

What is the hiring manager looking for?

The reason for including this section is that it forms the backbone to helping hiring manager's understand who you are as a person and as a potential candidate; and, it can help them decide whether the skills and experiences you have equates to your being capable and potentially suitable for the vacancy they have, in their view.

The specific information that the Hiring Manager expects to find answers the question: what has this candidate done in the past? That is, what positions did they hold, how long did they do that job for? What tasks were involved, and (the main one), did they do a good job?

If you haven't already generated the hiring manager's interest from your earlier sections, they might not even skim read your work history. But if they are interested and they do read it, you have this last opportunity to convince them that you are worth interviewing.

But like every other section in a resume, there is a lot that can go wrong in relation to what finer details you choose to include and exclude, and how you go on to present that information.

And, from having seen hundreds of resumes, I think this is the section where most of what can go wrong goes wrong, and this then is the main cause of rejection because the mistakes negatively impacts upon the effectiveness and can cause the candidate to look less skilled and capable than they might otherwise be.

Naming this section

You don't have to entitle this section 'Employment and Development History'; you could just call it the traditional 'Employment History' or 'Work History' section. What you name it is up to you.

I have called this section 'Employment and Development History' or 'Work and Development History' purely on the basis that I feel it more adequately describes the type of information I am encouraging you to include in this section.

Because, what I find with many resumes, especially those from longer term unemployed, school leavers and returning to work parents, is that because of their little or no paid work history, they tend to end up with just one page worth of content spread out over two pages. Rather than digging deeper to find more 'meat', instead some bloat out their resume to make themselves seem like they have more skills and experience (in misguided attempt to achieve two pages or more, common in chronological and combination style resumes) by ineptly increasing font size, narrowing margins and inserting larger than normal spaces between lines and paragraphs. This ruins the look of the resume as well as causing the resume to stand out in a noticeable, negative way. As it highlights the candidate's ineptitude in computer and word processing skills and the lack of value they would bring to the role being shown! (The lack of computer skills might be okay if the job didn't involve using them; but is detrimental to and a nightmare for applicants applying for admin-based roles.)

Part 4
Employment HISTORY

Hiring managers can see through those sorts of poor tricks, too; so the person just enables the quick rejection of their application.

You will soon learn that I value listing much more than just skills developed during paid employment. You will learn legitimate ways to increase the content instead of bloating it out with meaningless fluff or trickery. You will learn to right or write the content that hiring managers are interested in; learn what sets the applicant apart from the other candidates in a positive way, so you might make the shortlist.

Things to keep in mind

There are a couple of things to keep in the back of mind before we move on to the actual righting or writing your resume content.

These things include:

- Keeping the type of work you are seeking firmly in mind to decide if the detail is relevant and appropriate, or not
- Listing each position in reverse chronological order
- Keeping the details to just the last ten year period and having professional currency
- Showing, not Telling the details
- Working in stages

Type of work sought

Although I discussed this earlier in the book, I want to remind you again now that it is important to keep the position you are attempting to gain firmly in mind as you work through your employment history, to ensure that you stay on track with including only the details that will be of interest and benefit to the hiring manager for them to consider you a potentially suitable candidate.

Reverse chronological order

In the 'big picture view' of this section, employers want to see your Work History listed in reverse chronological order. That means you start with your most recent (or current) position and work your way backwards towards the first ever job you ever held.

Hiring managers want to know what job titles you have held, who you worked for, what duties and responsibilities you held and when you did this work for them. Most jobseekers understand this part.

As we will be including formal and informal work and development history, you should end up with a number of positions to write down details about. Just because you are listing it in reverse chronological order on paper when you get up to that stage doesn't mean you have to work backwards like that now. If you would prefer to start with the first job you ever had and then work your way forward, then do so. If you want to work out of chronological order, then that is fine too.

I suggest that you record each position on a separate piece of paper, and that way you can put them into reverse chronological order afterwards.

Show, don't tell

Whereas in the Summarised Information section you used a Tell, Don't Show style, now you must do the opposite of that and use the more common Show, Don't Tell writing rule.

Because what hiring managers really want, more than to just learn about what you did, who you did it for and when you did all that is for you to also demonstrate your competence, rather than telling them you are capable.

There is an art to showing not telling. I'll cover this in more detail a little further on when we reach writing Skill Statements because this is the bit that the average jobseeker doesn't do, or they get very wrong, while it is the part that employers get most interested in candidates over and are hoping to find when they first pick up the resume.

Professional currency

Employers like candidates that have professional currency. That is, the candidate's skills, knowledge, experiences, competence and history are recent and fresh, because it costs them less to employ the person, and because the experienced – those with strong background in that type of work – candidate might have tips and techniques that are more efficient and cost effective that the employer didn't know about.

Part 4
Employment HISTORY

Keep to the last ten years

But remember the rule discussed earlier in the book to not make your resume more than ten years in history? Skills that are over ten years old may not be relevant or should not be used any more.

For example, let's choose the analogy of riding a bike. 'They' say that once you learn how to ride a bike, you never forget. I agree. But, if you haven't ridden a bike in, say, twenty five years, you aren't going to be as confident or competent if you now hop back on a bike compared to had you remained a bike rider throughout the past twenty five years, are you? Those that use an old skill will be shaky, and might have a few falls as they relearn the skill; whereas those who've remained riding throughout the twenty five years are likely to be able to ride with their eyes closed, and perhaps even be able to demonstrate their higher competence by doing things like take their hands off the handlebars or standing on the seat, all without falling or crashing because they know how to keep their balance. They're fully unconsciously competent in doing that.

The same is true for much of your core employment skills. Yes, you have done something in the past – but if it is an old skill you may go through a shaky period while you redevelop that skill. If you have strong experience, you may well know little tricks that you can use and bring to the role for the benefit of the employer.

The point I am making here is although it will help your jobsearch if you can successfully demonstrate that your skills are current, and can disguise your age by keeping your resume content to a ten year history, you may have developed skills relevant to the type of job you are seeking from earlier than this.

You must be clear about the job you are applying for and what is required, so you can present the information that will most likely cause the employer to become interested in you. And, only use skills and experiences that fall outside of the previous ten period if it is absolutely necessary.

Work in stages

So you are now ready to start working on your work history section. Just as earlier I advised that when writing your resume you should break the writing a resume process into two parts – creating the content, and then afterwards creating the electronic document – you should also aim to break the writing of your work history section process down into manageable stages, rather than try to achieve 'everything at once'.

Right Your RESUME

Work on one past position from start to finish before moving on to the next relevant previous position held. And, for each position, break the process into stages.

You will need plenty of spare paper to scribble down ideas and thoughts as you go.

Stage One

Start off by creating a mind map, or spending quality time just generating a long list of every possible duty, responsibility and accountability you can think of about the particular job role you are working on. My DIY Resume Builder template should be a great help with this. Don't worry about spelling, or whether you are sounding repetitive. Don't worry about anything else except to get as much down about the role on paper as you can.

It might help to get into the task by asking yourself questions, like 'what did I do?', 'what was I responsible for?' and 'what was I held accountable for?' because our brains don't like having unanswered puzzles so it throws forth the answers. (Admittedly, not always immediately!)

Write those answers down as you go; or, if you aren't a pen and paper type of person, you could try typing the list directly into your word processor, or perhaps voice record your answers so you can transcribe them later. Whatever process you are most comfortable with (and have the tools for).

You will probably come up with the main tasks, responsibilities and accountabilities first. And then, the more time you spend on this activity, the more secondary things you will come up with.

I suggest you start with using the Telling method, e.g. serve customers, complete paperwork etc., and then move on to working towards showing those details in stages.

Stage Two

Once you have your grand list, it is time to look over the details. To see if you have missed anything, but mostly to see where you have repeated yourself so that you can then scale back whatever you can and combine points if necessary. For example, you might find that you have written 'serve customers' twice, or in two different ways where it means the same thing, e.g. 'serve customers; and 'customer service'.

Part 4
Employment HISTORY

Stage Three

Once you have your revised listing, it is now time to give each item a ranking, to mark them with a number (starting at number one) which prioritises the details from highest in importance and desirability for the type of work sought through to least importance, or of little interest to your potential new employer. The best way to do this is to have reviewed job advertisements to work out what details the employers are prizing most, and to just think about what is really required for your type of work (even if you are only trying to break into a job role for the first time).

Stage Five

Your next task is to turn your list of basic duties, responsibilities and accountabilities into good skill statements, which showcases your achievements, accomplishments and the positive benefits and the value you bring to your future employer.

Use the Skill Statement Formula (provided later in this book) to transform your basic list into powerful, interesting evidence and achievement based skills statements that show rather than tell and will therefore be more meaningful to hiring managers.

Stage Six

The last stage, which I need to mention now, will be to edit, revise, and or rewrite as much as you can until you are happy with how each of the skill statements written. And then, once you've reassessed and compared your draft skill statements, to check one last time that you are matching the work you seek rather than focusing too much on what you have done in the past.

Once you have created your electronic document, you will also need to proofread as part of this stage to ensure you have spelled and punctuated your statements correctly. And, before you reach final draft, get your document looked over by at least one other person, preferably someone who has strong spelling, punctuation and grammar skills, before you start to send your resume out into the world.

Right Your Resume

Deciding upon details to include and exclude...

Skills and experience

Jobseekers have complained to me, "I don't have any skills" because they haven't developed any, or recent, work experience for a particular role. These jobseekers are mostly school leavers, long term unemployed, returning to work parents, persons with English as a second language, and career-changers.

Please believe me: you have skills. You might not have professional currency, you might not have experience in that type of work, but you do have skills. You just need to recognise and value them, and find good examples in which you gained and used them, even if that is from your personal history rather than your work one.

Employers are generally going to favour, and possibly place higher value on, skills and experiences gained within similar previous positions, because it generally means the person is better equipped to deal with problems when things go wrong; because such problems are likely to have presented themselves to that person when they acted in those similar roles. The person will know how to handle it if such problems occur again in the future, and hopefully the problem won't be a bad as it could become for a person who hasn't faced it before.

You can successfully demonstrate your ability using situations that occurred outside of the paid work environment too. And, when you examine your informal work history, you may discover that you have more experience than you first believed. And, if you truly don't have any skills or experiences for the type of work you seek to gain, then you may need to address this first; or your jobsearch could be unnecessarily prolonged.

Types of employment

The type of work that can be included in this work and development section can come from either paid or unpaid (otherwise called formal and informal) work.

Part 4
Employment HISTORY

Paid work

Paid work can be skills and experiences gained from:

- Employment
- Self Employment
- Agency Work

Paid work, also known as formal work history, is any previous job that you have held for which you were paid money. That is, you received salary or wages.

It is 'formal' because the employment is recognisable as a conventional and accepted part of your work and development history to most people – jobseekers and hiring manager's alike.

Unpaid work

Unpaid work can be skills and experiences gained from:

- Voluntary work
- Work Experience
- Community participation
- Personal situations

Unpaid work, also known as informal work history, is any job that you have done in which you weren't paid money. That is, you didn't receive money or any type of financial compensation for having done this work.

It is 'informal' because this type of employment is not always recognisable, valued or accepted as forming a conventional part of work and development history to most people. Hiring manager's don't usually have a problem with it; but jobseekers under-utilise this invaluable part of their history – generally to their own detriment.

The details of each type of work and skill and experience development can belong in your resume, if they are relevant to and appropriate for the type of work you are now seeking.

The capacity with which you did the paid or unpaid work can vary in nature. You might have worked just one hour a day, a few hours or full-time hours; the role might have gone on for just one day, one month or for years. You could have been hired directly by the company or via a recruiting agency.

The important thing to recognise is that you develop and use skills all the time in the many different things that you do!

Let's examine each of the 7 types of work in a bit closer detail.

1. **Employment**

This is when you are formally employed. That is you are on a businesses' payroll, which is paid to you in cash or by electronic funds transfer, and work for the business (whether that business is private enterprise, commercial organisation or a government department).

You may have worked in just the one position since the day you started or may have worked in different roles within that same business. You could have worked for just this one business alone, or could have worked at a few different ones. You might even have held just one job at a time, or you held two (or more) jobs simultaneously.

The capacity within which you were employed can be:

- Permanent, or temporary
- Full time, part time or casual
- For a fixed term, or an ongoing basis
- Under a state or federal award, or under an Enterprise Agreement

In righting or writing your resume, the capacity of how and why you were hired is not necessary. Therefore, its inclusion is an unnecessary detail which enables a hiring manager to possibly make a decision without speaking with you.

2. **Self Employment**

This is when you have worked for your own self, such as being a Freelancer or Contractor. You aren't on any external business or company's payroll. You can be a sole trader, in a Partnership, or operate under your own Company in its legal structure. Your business usually has to invoice the other business or consumer under the pre-negotiated terms and conditions of your

Part 4
Employment HISTORY

agreement or contract, and that business or consumer pays the bill (your invoice) for your time and services rendered.

The capacity of your freelance, contract or project work can also be:

- Permanent, or temporary
- Full time, part time or casual
- For a fixed term, or an ongoing basis

Again, in your resume you do not list the capacity for which you were self-employed. To do so can hinder your application.

3. **Agency Work**

Some people are hired directly by Recruitment Agencies and are then assigned out to employers. The difference here is that the person is employed and paid by the recruitment agency not the business or company where they work at.

The capacity of agency work can be:

- Permanent, or temporary
- Full time, part time or casual
- For a fixed term, or an ongoing basis

You can be assigned to:

- Short or long term projects, and or
- Out at the premises of host employers (normally), or on-site at the agency (rarely)

In your resume, if you are employed by the Recruitment Agency, it is better for you (and is technically correct also) to list the Recruitment Agency as your employer; and the businesses and companies you worked for can be listed as your projects undertaken or your host employers. This can eliminate unnecessary employment gaps from creeping into your resume.

But, if you just find your job via a recruitment agency (as part of their recruitment service), and are employed directly by the business or company, then you would list the business or company as your employer, not the recruitment agency, and again don't need to provide any explanatory detail about how you gained the position or the capacity you worked in within your work history details section.

4. **Voluntary Work**

A lot of community-minded people 'give back' or 'pay it forward' by volunteering their time to do work for a charitable or community run organisation. Quite a number of those organisations follow a similar hiring process to employers and require volunteers to apply for vacancies before they take volunteer workers on. The only difference being that they take on workers without paying them.

For example, you might volunteer as a 'Meals on Wheels' driver. In this circumstance, you could gain skills and experience in driving, food preparation and aiding elderly or disabled persons. And if the work you are seeking involves driving, food preparation or caring, then this 'position' voluntarily undertaken would certainly support your application rather than hinder it.

The basis of voluntary work can be:

- Permanent, or temporary
- Full time, part time or casual
- For a fixed term, or an ongoing basis

But just because the work is unpaid does not mean that the experiences and or skills gained are any less significant than those gained from within paid employment.

Skills are skills, experiences are experiences.

If the voluntary work you have done in the past will demonstrate your potential suitability for the type of paid work you now seek, then please list the voluntary work in your work history section.

And, list it in the same style, manner and structure as you would all such relevant paid work history.

5. **Community Participation**

Closely related to voluntary work, community participation is anything else that you have participated in that is not part of your personal situation that best helps you demonstrate your potential suitability for a role,

Part 4
Employment HISTORY

often to support that you have knowledge or the personal attributes to be a good fit rather than having developed skills and experiences.

For example, you might donate blood every couple of months. In this circumstance, you might not have developed any skills or experiences but your voluntary participation speaks highly of your personality and good character. If the work you seek involves demonstrating your community spirit or participating in good causes, then list this type of participation. And when doing so, list it in the same style and manner as you do for all other details you include within this section.

But, the decision to include or exclude depends on how much work history you have, and if your community participation is needed. When you have lots of work history, just a small mention within your resume, positioned in the Summary section can be more than enough to show that you are generous with your personal time. However, if you don't have a strong work history, then you could create its own listing here in the employment and development section, so you can provide greater detail about your participation.

A community involvement listing is especially useful and suitable for school leavers and other jobseekers with long breaks in their employment history, as it can demonstrate that although you did not have paid employment, you didn't just sit around idly at home watching television or doing 'nothing' as a lot of people imagine unemployed people doing. Including details of your participation in community groups reveals that you made effort to either keep up skill level or develop new ones while you studied or looked for work.

But remember, it is best only included if it is relevant to the type of work sought, or when you have little other work and development history. If your resume will end up longer than four (4) pages as a result of including Community participation (or Work Experience (discussed next) then you don't need to use much – or any – of your unpaid work history.

6. **Work Experience**

Sometimes, when you do a course or while you are at school, you are able to do so many hours in a workplace as a work experience opportunity to help you decide if that type of work is what you would like to do in an ongoing capacity.

The basis of work experience is often:

- Temporary
- Part time or casual

- For a fixed short term

If you have completed a stint of work experience, then you may have developed some skills and or gained some limited experience, and as such could also list that opportunity within your work history section. And, as with voluntary work, community participation and personal situations, you would list it in the same style and manner as you treat any paid work history. The main thing to remember is that the work experience must be relevant to the type of work sought, not just be a listing to show you did this activity.

If you do a stint of work experience, it is often helpful if you request a written reference at the end. Because staff are unlikely to remember you once some time has passed, it can be difficult for hiring manager's to confirm you have done this and or to gauge how well you did completing tasks.

7. (a) **Personal Situations**

Just because you learned how to do something from within your personal situation in an unpaid capacity doesn't mean that the skills and experiences gained aren't valuable either. Actually, if you develop certain skills and experiences from within your personal situation, it is probably a strong indication that you enjoy doing those types of tasks, events and projects. When you enjoy doing things, you tend to do better at them. When they are meaningful, you tend to put more effort into doing a good job (rather than just an average one). Therefore, it makes sense to list these things if they are relevant to and might help you get the job you are after.

Perhaps you have organised an event, such as a wedding or other special occasion. Maybe you carried out home renovations as an owner builder, or other such building projects. These types of events and project plans, done for personal reasons, can provide you with much needed skills and experiences, or help keep your professional currency.

If you are a parent returning to the paid workforce or have been a Carer, don't dismiss your time being at home as not having much value. On a day to day basis, you've developed way more than just cooking, cleaning, caring, financial management, organisation and time management skills.

What things have you done as a stay at home parent, or Carer, that are relevant to the type of work you wish to gain? Include them. List your time doing 'Home Duties' or "Caring' in your work and development history. You don't need to write a gimmicky title, or fluff up the tasks you did. Give yourself the simple position title of 'Home Duties' or 'Carer' and write up a list of appropriate skills and experiences, then work out which ones are relevant and appropriate for the work you are now seeking to gain.

Part 4
Employment HISTORY

Case Study

I recently fixed up a resume for a client who was attempting to change careers. The client was applying for work with an airline, as this was the client's dream job. She had no immediately apparent skills or experiences for this type of work as she had worked in legal reception and admin roles since she had left school about five years earlier. Yet, this client received a phone call inviting her to attend an interview in under an hour from the time she submitted her application.

Why?

While communicating with her, I discovered that she had 3 highly relevant pieces of educational and personal history that supported her career goal, and I decided to list the last detail as part of her work and development history.

The first detail she had was that she had obtained an RSA certificate (Responsible Service of Alcohol). I visited both Qantas and Virgin Airline web pages while researching what airline employers look for in candidates (never having written a resume for that industry before). I quickly discovered that this certificate was a requirement for both airlines – and could logically be a requirement for all other airlines, including the overseas airline that she intended applying to. Therefore, it was the first qualification that I needed to ensure was listed in her resume, and I did, placing it in the PRRE.

The second detail was that the client had also completed a non-accredited Hair, Beauty and Makeup course. I didn't care that she had completed this training for personal interest's sake; she now had a personal grooming qualification. As each of the airlines placed emphasis on staff personal appearance, we included this otherwise irrelevant training (for other industries) to support that the client was a well-groomed individual, and additionally possessed advanced skills to ensure she always looked her best – completely aligning her well to employer wants and expectations.

The last (and probably most significant) detail that we included in her resume though, was that of her former participation as a teenager in Army Cadets. During that youthful participation, the client had undertaken leadership, fitness and survival skills training. From my thinking from the hiring manager perspective, that particular Army Cadet training demonstrated her potential suitability quite well towards the airlines 'unvoiced' requirements.

Right Your RESUME

The main reason airlines have cabin crew is not so that passengers are served food and beverages; they are there in case of emergency to provide authority and instructions to help keep passengers calm and safe. The food and beverage service they provide gives cabin crew something to do during the 99.9% of times when the craft isn't experiencing a critical or emergency situation. Airlines provide Cabin crew with that type of survival training to ensure they can handle in-flight and crash scenario emergencies so that they can keep calm and provide leadership to passengers. Therefore, this clients prior knowledge and competency, although gained from a difference circumstance, was more than just 'useful' within that type of role, it possibly equated to meaning the airline wouldn't have to put her through as much training as someone who had never done this type of training at all before.

To me, it best showed that she was a candidate worth seriously considering, so I paid particular attention to ensuring I wrote good skill statements for this role.

And, it worked: the airline not only contacted her, they were keen and contacted her quickly! (Under 2 hours).

7.   **(b) Content Creation**

One such personal situation that can lead to developing good skills for the workplace in our modern world is social media, and in particular, content creation. That is, the creating of text or graphical information that is used in blogs, websites or for initiating social media engagement.

Most businesses have an online presence, and as such could need help with building their online engagement. If you have a personal blog, or have managed websites, created content and the like, then rather than simply listing your skills within your skill summary section, you should probably go into greater detail by creating an entry within your employment and personal development history section.

The social media and online business world is only getting stronger and larger. And that trend is only going to continue. Employers, even solo entrepreneurs can't do everything on their own. At some point, they are going to need fully capable people to entrust completing the tasks for them. You might land doing this as employment or self-employment the opportunities are becoming so prevalent.

Contrary to my earlier stance in advising you to limit other details to only what is relevant, I now encourage you to break this rule for content creation

Part 4
Employment HISTORY

and list it on your resume even when it is not fully relevant to the position sought, because it is a truly valuable and growing area. Including the details could give you a strong competitive edge over other applicants.

The common, essential details

We've explored the idea that you can create a list of your skills and experiences from both your paid work and unpaid work history, now we will discuss ways and means of writing that employment history content.

Structuring your history

The best structure to use for Work and Development history section is one that includes the following foundational elements:

- Position title
- Employers Name
- Date range
- Skill statements

How you present and layout those elements is up to you, as there are a number of different styles or looks you can use to make your resume attractive in its appearance on paper and on-screen. I'll use my favourite styles as we progress through this section.

But first, let's discuss the why's and why not's for each of those four foundations.

1. **Position Title**

Details of your previous position title(s) help employers to know what jobs you have done in the past, for a whole gamut of different reasons. For one thing, the position title can suggest whether you have done that type of work previously or not; for another, the position title can hint at the type of skills you possess. And, as the hiring manager reads through the various listings within the employment and development section, it will become clear if the candidate has continuously done this same type of work, or whether they have worked across different types of job roles.

Those little things all paint a picture and help the hiring manager to see you as a potential candidate or not.

Right Your RESUME

Now, notice how in the bullet list above I listed the Position Title first? I did that for a reason: the type of work you did is more important than who you worked for.

Yet, too many jobseekers emphasise who they worked for over what their job title was. I'll discuss this in greater detail in the Mistakes to Avoid section.

How to list

Because you can end up with multiple previous positions held listings on the same physical page, you need to find a layout style that best presents that information.

Either still not quite ready to read your details just yet or happy to start reading now if particular details stand out, your previous position titles are going to be the first detail hiring managers are hoping to see as they scan down the page. I recommend that you emphasise this specific so that it catches the reader's eye using a simple layout. Let's use an example where a person with forklift driving experience from two former positions lists them, like this:

Forklift Driver

ABC Company

2011 – Current

- Skill statement 1
- Skill statement 2
- Skill statement 3
- Skill statement 4

Forklift Driver

XYZ Business

2008 – 2011

- Skill statement 1
- Skill statement 2
- Skill statement 3
- Skill statement 4

Note: There are many, many different layout possibilities. For this book's purpose, I am only going to continue using that one particular style while

Part 4
Employment HISTORY

addressing the rest of the topics and considerations. But, just quickly, here are 2 often used alternatives.

Alternative 1 indents the skill statements, so that everything aligns flush to the left margin, like this:

Forklift Driver

ABC Company

2011 – Current

- Skill statement 1
- Skill statement 2
- Skill statement 3
- Skill statement 4

Alternative 2 uses a hidden Table type formatting style, where all except the date range is indented, like this:

2011 – Current **Forklift Driver**

                    ABC Company

- Skill statement 1
- Skill statement 2
- Skill statement 3
- Skill statement 4

Notice how no matter where the position title has been physically located on the page, the bolded words 'Forklift Driver' still stand out, and grabs your attention?

I do this deliberately in the resumes I create because it stands out from the other text on the page. The text before and after the emphasised words in that example is in normal text; that is, the font plain and standard across all non-emphasised details. Because of this, our visual brain interprets the bolded text as an 'ooh, an important detail' element long before we focus in on reading the words.

As I am encouraging you to list your position title as the most important or significant detail than any other within each previous job listing, hence the bolded text ensures the detail stands out, in a professional aesthetically pleasing way.

Right Your RESUME

Unknown position titles

Most jobseekers that I have crossed paths with know their position title when they have had paid work but many struggle with this when they have been self employed or gained the skill from informal activities.

If you don't know what your position title is, or even didn't have one, then don't worry yourself about it. Just give yourself one; but not just any old title. Use a meaningful one that is fitting to the type of work you did, are applying for and so that it perhaps reveals some of your skills, abilities and personality.

For example, when I worked in Employment Services, I did stints in each of the following position titles: case manager, post placement support officer, employment consultant, jobsearch trainer, jobseeker solution coordinator. In each of the roles I performed a range of tasks; each position included administration, reception and switchboard relief, telephone marketing, and report writing as well as the specific tasks exclusive to that particular role. Those job titles are meaningful within the Employment Services industry. It instantly tells potential employers the different roles, and the skills used. For example, for case manager, I often had to work with difficult clients, where I needed to give 'tough love' and or undertake non-compliance action, when required; but, with post placement support officer, I needed to demonstrate patience and understanding, and be focused on dealing with problems and resolving conflicts so that it reached a successful outcome for all parties (jobseeker, employer and our agency). Tough love was the opposite of what I needed to do. But those jobs and their titles aren't necessarily meaningful for jobs I might have wanted to apply for that lie outside that industry.

Sometimes the job title you have doesn't fully represent the type of work you performed. For example, for those outside of the company, can you guess at what tasks I performed on a day to day basis when I was Jobseeker Solutions Coordinator? No, it was simple: I was receptionist. With greater than average responsibilities. I answered the agencies incoming calls, managed the office petty cash and stationery supply, and 'coordinated' jobseekers attending the office for appointments and training (solutions) by directing them to the right training room, or getting them to take a seat while I let their consultant know that they had arrived for their appointment. I wrote reports and marketed jobseekers to employers by phone, and I culled applications for each of the vacancies our agency listed. The position title appropriately described what I did within that organisation; but, the core role and meaningfulness outside that one employer was receptionist, switchboard operator and administration officer.

Part 4
Employment HISTORY

Now when I started applying for jobs so I could find work closer to home to cut down on my travel time and costs, depending on what type of position I was applying for, I changed that positions title to make it relevant and meaningful to the job I was applying to. For example, when I applied for a different position at a different branch within the same company (each branch was run as a separate business and staff were unable to apply for a transfer so employees had to apply for roles just like external applicants did; and there were a few branches closer to home), I listed my actual job title on my resume because the Jobseeker Solutions Manager's of those branches would each understand exactly what job I had been doing.

However, I also applied for jobs with other employment service companies that used different job titles and therefore didn't understand what my job entailed, as well as positions outside of the employment services industry entirely. And I knew my job title did not mean anything to those external employers, in or outside that one industry.

Handling unclear job titles

Having experience as a resume writer, I knew there were a few ways, any of which I could use, to handle making my job title more meaningful for the hiring manager.

These included:

1. Provide clarification (in brackets)
2. Rename my job title to something more meaningful
3. Provide a job summary statement clarifying that the title was a frontline management role
4. List my first two duties as Reception and Switchboard operator

If you want or need to change an unclear job title to one that is more meaningful and clear to the reader, then pick the method that you feel will work best for your circumstance.

1. **Provide clarification (in brackets)**

With this method, I could simply list my position title like so:

Jobseeker Solutions Coordinator (Receptionist/Switchboard Operator)

Right Your RESUME

Or,

> Jobseeker Solutions Coordinator (Receptionist/Switchboard Operator)

With both these methods, you are keeping your official job title (that your current or former employer has entitled it), along with the clarifying information in brackets, so that it enhances the readers understanding. (The only difference between the two samples is the level of emphasis I have placed on the job titles).

But as you can see, the job title was already quite long in and of itself; and adding the extra detail made it even longer. (I probably wouldn't choose this method because of how long the title is.)

Depending on the layout of employment details in the resumes I create (for myself and for clients), I intentionally do not allow a job title fall across two lines in the document – it just looks bad! If I needed to use the clarification method, I either would use a resume layout structure that is aligned to the left margin – which allows me to use longer job titles, or when I use a layout that is indented, I use the shortest job title that is clear and meaningful but which fits on the one line.

Some title varieties, based on level of indentation:

> Jobseeker Solutions Coordinator (Receptionist / Switchboard Operator)
>
> Jobseeker Solutions Coordinator (Receptionist / Switchboard)
>
> Jobseeker Solutions Coordinator (Receptionist)

2. **Rename my Job Title**

With this method, I could simply list my position title with a title that is understandable to most hiring managers, even though it is not the position title given by the employer:

> Receptionist / Switchboard Operator

As you can see, you change your official job title (it is only what that one particular employer called it, after all), to instead provide a job title that a wider readership understands; which subtly suggests the tasks involved without having to specify them.

Using this method helps an unclear job title to become clear; an unknown title to being understood. The decision to change a job title is up to you.

Part 4
Employment HISTORY

Is this lying, Char? Because you made it clear earlier to never lie in your resume.

I don't classify changing a small detail for the purpose of making it better understood to be lying or dishonesty for the simple reason that you still did that job no matter what title the employer gave it. You are just making it easier for the hiring manager(s) (of the future) to see, at a glance during their skim read, what you have done, for them to come away with the right impression about you and your capabilities.

3. **Provide a job summary statement**

With this method, you would list your official job title and then after the basic employment details but before the job duties and responsibilities etc details, you give a short blurb or written statement about the business or role. In this example, that the Jobseeker Solutions Coordinator role is frontline management in nature, and is listed like this:

Jobseeker Solutions Coordinator

ZYX Company

This was a Receptionist / Switchboard role in a busy employment service office servicing over 1,200 local jobseekers to develop skills and confidence to gain work and get off social security payments.

As you can see, with this method you state your official job title provided by the company and provide a brief explanation after the employer name but before the skill statement (not shown in this example) for readers to help them gain understanding about the company or your role.

The blurb adds more detail to your resume. And, if you do this for one position, then you must do the same for every other position you include in your document to maintain consistency of style and elements, which adds to your resume writing workload. I wouldn't use this method if I was applying to employment service providers, only if I was applying to other industries. Because I don't want to inadvertently imply that hiring managers in ESP don't know anything about the industry.

4. **List my first two duties as Reception and Switchboard operator**

With this method, you would list your official job title and then after in your employment details, the first job duties and responsibilities listed would be the clarifying information to demonstrate the work you do.

Right Your RESUME

Jobseeker Solutions Coordinator

ZYX Company

Duties:

- **Reception**: greeting up to 150 clients each day, marking off their attendance to appointments, jobsearch or classroom-based training and arranging for the client to be seen by their case manager, trainer, work experience supervisor or job interviewer, and accepting activity record sheets needed to be kept on file and particulars data entered.

- **Switchboard**: answering up to 200 telephone calls each day on an eight line, multi-office telephone system and connecting the caller with the person most appropriate to assist them with their enquiry or resolve their problem.

**Notice within this example that I don't tell readers that the job is very busy, I demonstrate (show) how busy the role is by using numbers and specific details) – But, more on this when we come to writing your skill statements.

Mistakes to avoid...

Now that we have discussed the position titles importance, we now need to address the problems that must be avoided in relation to position titles.

Positioning

As mentioned briefly earlier, I have seen and assessed a lot of resumes, and what I have found with surprising frequency is that jobseekers list the employer name and emphasise this detail instead of the position title. Why list and emphasis a specific which carries less weight, is less important, in comparison to another specific detail?

For Example

ABC COMPANY

Forklift Driver

Or

ABC COMPANY

Forklift Driver

Part 4
Employment HISTORY

The better way to list your details is:

Forklift Driver

ABC Company

I've said it before: from a hiring manager's perspective, when they skim read a resume for the first time they have a particular job position in mind. They are looking to see if the candidate has the skills, experiences and capabilities to do the job they are aiming to fill. Second to that, they are looking to see if you could do the job well. They are going to be much more interested in your past position title, your duties, responsibilities and achievements and in learning how much experience you have over who your former employer was – unless it was such a high ranking company or so special that it is this single most important detail that will impress most, which is rare (for 99.9% of businesses, the hiring manager will be more interested in your job title).

Over-emphasising

Bolding the text is the quickest and easiest way to signal to a reader 'this detail is important'. And because it visibly stands out more than normal text, most reader's eyes will jump straight to the bolded text – if there isn't too much of it on the page, that is.

But, a word of caution about emphasising text: **never use any more than two emphases on any piece of text**. That means, you can *bold and enlarge*, or *bold and italic* certain text like Headings, Sub-Headings and important words or phrases, but you should **never** *bold, enlarge and italic* (or more) at the same time. Because that is overkill; and is distracting.

Too much emphasis diminishes the importance for all other emphasised details.

Enforced reading

Have you ever gone somewhere with someone who constantly likes to point things out to you, while you just want to stand and take it all in slowly? They want you to notice all the little things that they are noticing within the larger scene, and thus say, 'Oh, look at that,' as they point to something they are looking at because it is a detail that is important to them; and then, as soon as you've looked, they point somewhere else and say the same words.

Right Your RESUME

Before long, you find that you've turned your head this way and that way, and you've seen everything that is high and low, to the left, to the right and what's behind. No angle is left uncovered. But you can be left feeling a little overwhelmed, because none of those smaller details were as important as the one thing that was grabbing and holding your interest, the bigger picture. And you realise, the other person took control over your experience and what you came to see because of their incessant 'you've got to look at this' attention-stealing.

This is a significant problem in resumes too: jobseekers can try to force employers to notice everything they think is important about them self – usually by using lots of bold or italic text emphasis, as a way of constantly signalling 'look at this' and 'look at this too', and 'what about this?'

That is the **wrong approach**. Instead, let the hiring manager see what they came to see, and let them decide on what reading action they'll take next; don't try to enforce any specific reading action upon them.

As writer's, you have to trust that the reader will understand your message and back off from trying to bring too much too their attention. In novel writing, the process of over-emphasising in effort to force the reader to understand the point you are making is called **sledge-hammering**. As the word suggests, doing this is akin to whacking the reader over the head with a sledge-hammer and saying, 'notice this point', because they treat the reader as being not smart enough to 'get it' or work it out for them self without the writer deliberately pointing it out. And as your resume contains the written word, you are a writer; and therefore must not behave like the person above pointing out too much.

For this reason, I encourage you to bold only your position title, and leave everything else within the listing as *normal text*. That way, the one element consistently applied catches their eyes, and the hiring manager can choose whether they wish to stop to read the details in the listing, or to continue on in their skim reading to see what other position titles you've had before coming back to read those finer details later, if they so desire.

If your resume or the template you've used means you have lots of bolding and italic text throughout your employment and development history, de-emphasis everything else and stick to the principle of only bolding main headings (such as your section titles), and this one key detail only.

In other words, don't try to force the reader to notice all your sub-points. Don't sledgehammer your details (like I am deliberately doing here because I wanted to show you how annoying and repetitive sounding it is on top of making sure you get my point).

Part 4
Employment HISTORY

Let the hiring manager decide what details they want to read. Trust, I know it is hard, that hiring managers will gain a lot of information – more than you think possible – out of skim reading just one position title.

I touched on it earlier: the position title of your current or last job title will indicate whether you are applying for the same type of job role or something different. That position title will indicate the level you have been working at (e.g. general worker, supervisor, manager etc.). And can hint at your interests and personality (for example, the title 'Nurse' hints at someone with a strong caring side to their personality, whereas 'Forklift Driver' hints at someone who likes operating machinery and can be emotionally tougher. Both job types hint at the person being up for working different shifts, whereas an Admin person suggests a preference for the 9 – 5 lifestyle).

Employer

Now, I just pointed out that hiring managers prefer to read your position title over who you worked for; but please don't misinterpret that to mean they don't want to know who you worked for at all. This detail is still important to them – just not as much as the position title in its weighting.

Where possible, use the proper name of the business, company or organisation. For instance, if the company's name is ABC Company Pty Ltd, then write it as ABC Company Pty Ltd, not ABC Company.

Some businesses use a trading name. For instance XYZ Business might trade as 'Words on a Page'. In this case you could just write that the employer is Words on a Page, or if you want to be particular about the details then you would list the employer as XYZ Business t/as Words on a Page (where the abbreviation 't/as' means 'trading as').

The main point here is to provide this detail after your position title.

Who you worked for – especially if you are applying for jobs in the same industry – can tell employers things about you that you might not have even mentioned.

For example, one employment service provider I worked for provided staff training every week. The company had strong focus on ensuring their staff developed a range of higher level skills to enable all levels of personnel to be productive and efficient in their roles, whereas another company only hired staff that were fully trained already and only gave new employees four hours induction into how they did things and what their record management system looked like before the staff member was supposed to dive in and start

Right Your RESUME

'doing their thing'.

People who work in the employment services industry do a lot of job-hopping.

With this in mind, it would be fair to assume that this second employer upon seeing the position title 'Employment Consultant' would immediately stop skim reading to deliberately look for the employer detail – attention grabbed and interest now building! – and because of how many different companies are around, locally and nationally, the hiring manager would know a fair bit about their competitors (maybe they have worked their themselves in the past, or hired other people from that company) and would be impressed if they know or had a fair idea of the inner workings of the company listed. It would help the hiring manager to know – fairly accurately – what this candidates skills, experiences and capabilities would be, without their even having to read a word of the applicants included position skill statements.

But even if the company is in a different industry, and the hiring manager doesn't know much about the company's operations, they may still have heard about the company's reputation (or lack thereof) through the news or via networking. And the companies name can suggest a number of things about the person's knowledge, even if their skills and experiences aren't immediately apparent.

So the point here is to include the details of who you worked for, but don't make the details the predominant element within the section compared to what you did.

Special considerations

List all relevant self employment, recruitment agency, voluntary work, work experience, community participation and skills developed from personal situations in the same style and manner as what you choose for your formal employment positions. That is, follow the same structure of using a position title, employer name, the date range and strong skill statements.

Self employment

Use an appropriate position title, followed by your business name.

I don't recommend listing your position title as 'Director', 'Proprietor' or any other title like 'Business Owner' if you are applying for positions with no or significantly less authority, as it can make you look over-qualified or otherwise unsuitable for the role sought.

Part 4
Employment HISTORY

For this reason, it is best to match your position title to the type of work sought. For example, if you owned and ran a Retail Store, and you are now applying for Retail Management positions, then I would choose Retail Manager because it demonstrates the industry and the level hiring managers for retail would be familiar with, rather than 'Director' which puts you at arm's length to the position and its (lesser) authority level, creating a mismatch

Recruitment agency

For agency work, use an appropriate position title followed by the recruitment agency name when the agency is your employer. Though, it might be a good idea to list the names of your host employers, which you can do like this:

Forklift Driver

ABC Recruitment Company

2011 – Current

Host Employers:
- XYZ Business
- AtoZ Warehouse
- B2B Distribution

Skills & Experience:
- Skill statement 1
- Skill statement 2
- Skill statement 3
- Skill statement 4

Notice, in this example I have italicized the sub-headings to separate out the host employer details from the skills and experiences. The position title becomes the Heading, and the Host Employer and Skills & Experience a Sub-Head, which also need slight emphasis to signify that the detail is not normal text. Whereas **bold** is used to draw the eye to it, *italic* is subtle so your eye can skim right past it.

Applied consistently to multiple sub-headings, it becomes clear that the detail is more important than normal text but less important than the bolded text.

Right Your RESUME

Voluntary work

Use an appropriate position title followed by listing the charity or community service organisation where you volunteer your time. They will generally have a registered business name, or be well-known by a specific, recognisable name.

Work experience

Work experience is not really a job that you held; it is more a short term activity that you participated in. Most work experience (here in Australia) have you doing a few simple tasks that don't require much training to perform, but the main reason you do the work experience is so that you can test out the type of work and observe workers to help you determine if this is the type of work you would like to do on an ongoing basis.

It depends on how long your relevant work experience went for and or how many different work experience opportunities you undertook as to whether I would include the details as a summary section positioned in the PRRE (or as closely afterwards if room isn't permitting), or would include as a listing in the employment and development section. So this is something you will need to think about too.

If, say, you did work experience with three or four with different employers and or different industries, then I would be more inclined to list this in summary form. But, if say, you did work experience for a few weeks with just one employer or just one job type, then I would probably be more inclined to include the details of this activity within my work and development history (see, told you I named this section for good reason!)

You will have to weigh up the best way to incorporate relevant work experience into your resume. For instance, I once did four week's work experience in a retail store when I was completing an adult education course. But, although it was an activity I completed and enjoyed, it was irrelevant to the administration work that I later applied for; and because it was a component of the module in the course that I had detailed, the work experience component didn't need specifying, so I did not include it in my resume.

Work experience is particularly useful for those with little to no paid work experience though.

Part 4
Employment HISTORY

Community participation

Like work experience, community participation is something that you do but doesn't necessarily mean that you develop skills or experiences as a result of that participation.

But, say you were seeking a position and the following personal participation would support your application for the type of work you want to get into:

- Regular Blood donor
- Volunteer Deliverer of Meals on Wheels to elderly persons

There are a couple of ways you could handle including this community involvement in your resume.

The first is that you could go back to the summary section and create a listing entitled 'Community Participation' and position the listing in (or close to) the PRRE and include anywhere between 3 to 5 bullet points of the titles you give yourself and possibly even the community organisation, like this:

Community Participation

- Blood donor
- Volunteer Meals on Wheels Deliverer

Or,

Community Participation

- Blood donor
- Volunteer Deliverer, Meals on Wheel

If you create its own section and list a handful of bullet points, then you will need to decide where about the section will appear on your resume. The sections placement will definitely need to occur after your personal details, career snapshot and skills summary, but you will need to decide if the section is more important – for the type of work you will be seeking – to appear before, say, tools of the trade or computers and technology. My suggestion would be to list it after Licences, Tickets and Checks and Training and Qualifications sections, but before the Employment and Development History one.

The second way of handling your community participation is to again list it within your work and development history, and using the structure and style

Right Your RESUME

of the other listings in the section.

Listing it in this section might enable you to close up noticeable employment gaps, and subtly demonstrate your active involvement as a choice, as well give you opportunity to demonstrate your value as a potential employee by providing accompanying strong skill statement details. Like this:

Blood Donor

2010 – 2014

- Give blood twice a year

Deliverer

Meals on Wheels

2010 – 2014

- Pack prepared hot meals into satchels
- Navigate local area using GPS and deliver run sheet.
- Deliver meals to elderly persons living at home
- Spend time with the elderly person to provide them with company and to report back on any potential health or safety issues they face which they need external help with
- Collect previous days meal containers for reuse

Personal situations

Because you won't have an employer name to list, you can follow the same basic structure for the rest of your history but simply leave out the employer detail, like this:

Wedding Planning

2010 – 2012

- Skill statement 1
- Skill statement 2
- Skill statement 3
- Skill statement 4

Part 4
Employment HISTORY

Or, you could list the position title with an event name, like this:

Event Manager

Rose and Thorn Wedding

2010 – 2012

- Skill statement 1
- Skill statement 2
- Skill statement 3
- Skill statement 4

The key to helping you choose is to consider what the most appropriate position title for the job you are seeking is, and then let that then guide you to how to handle the remainder of the information.

For example, if you were trying to gain work as a Wedding Planner, then you would probably be better of listing the position title as Wedding Planner, and then, if you have event managed more than one wedding list the bridal party events.

As with the recruitment agency work, you might have multiple times that you have completed similar projects. Let's say you organised three family weddings. In this case, you could make the one entry, and list the multiple projects, like this:

Event Manager

2010 – 2012

Wedding Parties:

- Rose and Thorn
- Black and White
- Chalk and Cheese

Skills and Experiences:

- Skill statement 1
- Skill statement 2
- Skill statement 3
- Skill statement 4

Or, if you handled them at different times, you might list it like this:

Event Manager

2010 – 2012, Rose and Thorn Wedding

2008 – 2009, Black and White Wedding

2006 – 2008, Chalk and Cheese Wedding

Skills and Experiences:

- Skill statement 1
- Skill statement 2
- Skill statement 3
- Skill statement 4

It is okay to **not** include an employer name, for example:

Home Duties

2007 – 2012

Skills and Experiences:

- Skill statement 1
- Skill statement 2
- Skill statement 3
- Skill statement 4

Carer

2008 – 2010

Skills and Experiences:

- Skill statement 1
- Skill statement 2
- Skill statement 3
- Skill statement 4

If you get stuck and have any problems with coming up with a position title or how you handle an employer name, you are welcome to contact me to seek

Part 4
Employment HISTORY

my advice. To do this, just head over to my blog and use the contact form, and I'll do my best to reply as soon as possible.

Employed by recruitment agency

A lot of jobseekers who gain lots of different work through a recruitment agency and can frequently have breaks between work, often make the mistake of listing the host employer as their employer, and the date range of when they worked at that host employer, which makes it seem as though the person has frequent employment gaps – which can be interpreted as though there is something negative with regards to the person's work performance.

If you gain work through a recruitment agency and are paid by the recruitment agency, then you should list the recruitment agency as your employer (because they are the one paying you). But, if it becomes important that you need to provide details of which companies you have been assigned work to, then by all means create a list. For example:

General Labourer

ABC Recruitment Company

2008 – Current

Short and long term assignments with:
- Fox Couriers
- Eze Wholesale
- Peterson's Distribution

Duties:
- Pick Pack
- RF Scanning
- Data entry

Notice how listing your employment in this manner shows your continuous employment status (you are still on the recruitment agencies books while you are between assignments). Be aware that if you list the recruitment company as the employer, you will most likely need to list one of the consultants as a **referee** either on your resume or as a list that you hand over during a job interview.

Right Your RESUME

Case Study

When I was in one of my Disability Employment Service case manager roles, I once gained a client who was between assignments and required to look for work because he was in receipt of social security payments. This man had a resume, but although he had been applying for many positions either directly to employers or to other recruitment agencies, he was not successful in gaining interviews and was becoming frustrated by his lack of success.

When I had a look at his resume, I noticed he had frequent employment gaps, and at first aimed to work with him to disguise how many gaps he had from changing jobs so frequently. Like hiring managers, I saw all his job-hopping and assumed there was a problem with either his quality of workmanship or within his attitude or behaviour, and wanted to minimise the negative impact the problem was now causing him in gaining work.

At some point though, close to my finishing reworking his resume, he mentioned in an off-handed, dismissive manner that he was still employed with the recruitment agency that he had been with continuously for the past five years and was only looking for short term, temporary work until he started the next long term assignment which he would commence in a month's time that the agency had already found for him.

It was at that point that I stopped what I was doing and admonished him for not telling me this sooner as I now realised what he had been really doing wrong in his resume. And that I had just wasted the last half hour in fixing up his resume.

He had erroneously listed each of his 'projects' (or 'host employers') and the periods he had worked at each of those different companies as his employment history. This was the cause of him appearing to have frequent employment gaps – which he did not have! – and was the underlying cause of employers rejecting his applications, because it made his work history seem unstable (when it wasn't!).

What he should have been doing all along was only listing the recruitment agency as his employer as it rightly showed his stable five years continuous employment in being assigned to eight different host employers (with month or two long gaps and no pay between assignments).

As soon as we reworked his resume again, to this time correctly show that he indeed had stable employment, he started getting invites to interviews immediately. (Note, I didn't make *any* other changes to his resume except reworking how he listed his employment).

Part 4
Employment HISTORY

The annoying part, for me, was then learning that his former employment consultant had been the one to write his original, non-effective resume – and that consultant had been fully aware of his continuous employment status! Oh well, my gain. He was one of my quickest placements. And, it probably explains why that consultant didn't get the amount of placements expected by that employer too.

Date range

In a big picture view, employers want to know how long you have worked in your previous position because it provides them with an indication of how experienced you are in that type of work.

Including the specifics of when you worked in a particular job enables hiring manager's to compare your level of experience against other applicants, and provides them with a range of insights to help them evaluate your potential suitability and or make an immediate decision, like:

- How long they have lasted in their previous roles: Does the person job hop or have they 'parked' them self into one position or with one employer for any significant period of time? Is this normal or unusual? Is this a concern?

- Whether the candidate has employment gaps: Does the candidate have gaps; if so how long are they, how frequently do they occur? Is this of concern? Is this a cause to decide no, or is it something we need to discuss during an interview?

- The level and amount of experience with performing particular key tasks that might be relevant to their vacancy: Will this amount of experience mean the person can do our role? Will we have to provide additional training or will they be able to hit the ground running? Does their experience match closely, or are skill or experience gaps evident?

The next detail you will need to include is the specifics of when you worked at the company. Again, it is an important detail, but it is not as important as your position title and actually may be a detail that you don't want to draw too much attention to – especially if you have gaps in your employment history.

Listing date ranges

How the date range is listed on the resume is up to the jobseeker and their style preferences. However, in an 'ideal' resume world, hiring managers prefer it when the jobseeker lists the month and year they started and finished rather than their using any other different date range format.

As you can see by the following examples, each of the examples is essentially stating the same thing:

Month Year to Month Year format

- 01 00 – 04 00
- Jan 00 – Apr 04
- Jan 2000 – Apr 2004
- January 2000 – April 2004
- January 2000 to April 2004

The choice is yours as to which style you prefer to use.

But of course, using the Month Year format exposes employment gaps, which is why hiring managers prefer it:

February 2012 – Current

September 2010 – January 2012

December 2008 – February 2009

Notice that in this example, the candidate has a 1 month (January 2012 to February 2012) and a 19 month (February 2009 to September 2010) employment gap.

As a hiring manager, I wouldn't be too worried over that one month between jobs – I could reasonably assume that the person most likely just took a few weeks holiday break between finishing with one employer and starting with the next, or possibly that it is actually less than a month if they finished up in, say, late January but started early February – but that 19 month employment gap would raise concerns. Why were they unemployed for that long, and what did they do during that time?

If you possessed all the skills and experience we need and we invited you in for an interview, it would certainly be a topic that we would raise during the job interview. It's just that, if there are a lot of other candidates that don't have large employment gaps, we might end up favouring one of those other applicants to interview over a person with such a large gap.

So we have three often cited basic rules for resume writing here that come into conflict for the jobseeker: don't show employment gaps in your resume,

Part 4
Employment HISTORY

explain your employment gaps, and don't provide unnecessary details. No wonder jobseekers get confused about what they are supposed to do and can make the wrong choice!

Don't worry; there are ways to handle them.

Employment gaps

An employment gap can occur for any number of reasons. For example, women leave the workforce to stay at home and raise their children, workers are made redundant and may spend a couple of months trying to gain a new job. People travel, get sick and injured or need to look after a close family member who is sick or injured, requiring them to take extended time off work. Workers leave without having an alternative job to go to because of upsets and disputes; people are fired over misbehaviour or poor performance; criminals are sent to jail over their having broken the law and getting caught.

All resulting in employment gaps.

Although hiring managers understand that employment isn't always continuous, they want to be able to see that as an employee you are stable: that the reasons for your leaving are either fully understandable, not your fault, or when they were your fault that you've learned and grown from the experience and the same issue won't be a problem if it were to reoccur if you were employed with them.

Glaring employment gaps, therefore, not only alert hiring managers that something happened, but also enable them to quickly form a negative opinion about you, especially if there are multiple employment gaps. But this doesn't mean you need to provide the reason in your resume. Actually, if you have employment gaps, then you may need to de-emphasis or disguise this fact.

Disguising employment gaps

It is possible to disguise employment gaps, but be aware that hiring managers know these tricks when they see them, and when they appear it can still raise concerns for them.

The first method is to drop the Month detail to use a Year to Year style.

For example

- 2008 – 2009
- 2010 – 2012

Or

- 08 – 09
- 10 – 12

But, the negative side is that hiring managers look at this date range and don't get a feel for how much experience the person has.

What looks like a two year period (2008 – 2009) doesn't necessarily equate to two years experience. The person could have started in December 2008 and finished up in January 2009. Therefore, although the candidate has technically not lied on their resume, it does inadvertently or intentionally misrepresent their level of experience as being one year instead of one month.

Recruiters know that a lot of jobseekers who don't have much employment history often do this intentionally to make their experiences seem greater than what they are. Apart from inventing skills, experience and history in outright lies, intentional misrepresentation of factual details is common. (And jobseekers wonder why employers don't trust their word and need to do reference checks and the like!)

The second method is to drop the dates of employment and provide details of length of experience instead, leaving the precise period of employment unknown.

For example

- 6 months' experience
- 18 months' experience
- 10+ years' experience

In this method, hiring managers don't learn when you were employed (or even when you developed the skill); only how long you were employed or developed the skill for, as a total accumulation.

Although it clarifies the breadth of a candidate's experience, some hiring managers (in particular, recruiters and HR professionals who review resumes for a living) will still be suspicious as to the reasons necessitating the candidate to hide their employment dates. But most of the employers I worked with

Part 4
Employment HISTORY

were happy with this style of formatting, and if they wanted or needed to know how recent that experience was, they asked during the job interview.

This method is great for, and mostly used by, parents returning to the paid workforce, migrants and those who are attempting to change careers, because it allows them to show skill and history while disguising gaps and the out of date currency level.

You could try testing it out for a month or two to see if this method is acceptable to employers of the type of work you hope to gain. If it works then keep using it. If it doesn't, try one of the other methods.

Mistakes to avoid...

Explaining employment gaps

If you are going to have to explain an employment gap to a hiring manager, my suggestion is don't do it upfront on your resume. Leave it for the job interview.

Why? Providing this information in your resume can lead to the employer making a no decision without ever having spoken to you or met you. If the hiring manager is otherwise interested in you as a potential candidate to fill the role (and that is your entire aim, is it not?) then they are more likely to ask you to explain when they phone you or meet you face to face if they are concerned enough about your employment gaps.

What jobseekers need to realise, and I discussed this earlier, is that they shouldn't be trying to control what information the employer should focus on, and should instead let the potential employer or hiring manager control what information they want to know more about.

By explaining gaps on your resume, the jobseeker is insisting on addressing an area of potential concern – but if the employer doesn't notice the gap or isn't too worried about it, by the jobseeker insisting on explaining, it could lead to the hiring manager making that unwanted no decision. By all means answer to the best of your ability when asked about something directly, but don't unnecessarily cause concerns by emphasising issues that might need addressing. Or you are deliberately sabotaging your jobsearch.

Why explain something you don't have to? Why plant concerns in the hiring manager's mind for them to have to overcome? Why bring to their attention something negative which they hadn't noticed?

Right Your RESUME

Skill statements

Not all job titles make it clear as to what tasks you performed in a current or former job role. For this reason, listing your duties, responsibilities, key accountabilities, accomplishments and results is the best (and only real) way to help hiring manager's better understand who you are, why you are applying for their vacancy and, most importantly, why you would make a good person for the role.

Some people call these things duties lists or accomplishment statements. I call them Skill Statements because they list the skills along with evidence and achievement based specifics to support and substantiate the skill level. No matter what people call them though, it is how you write them that can make all the difference between the hiring managers developing increased interest in you as potentially suitable for them, or dismissing your application while they skim read without any further or deeper assessment.

Okay, be honest. If you were an employer, and you received the following two resumes, which applicants work history would you rather read? Which candidate would leave you with a better impression about them as a potentially suitable person for the role? And which applicant would you want to learn more about once you've finished reading their resume?

Candidate 1

Duties:

- Industrial Cleaning
- Time Management
- Customer Service

Or,

Candidate 2

Duties:

- Cleaned 3 commercial premises each weeknight ensuring that facilities were sanitised, rubbish was removed and floors were vacuumed.
- Planned the order of jobs and site visits to ensure tasks were completed on time, rubbish would be collected in the quickest possible time-frame and that tasks were fully completed before

Part 4
Employment HISTORY

building security alarms automatically activated at 11 p.m.

- Liaised with customers to agree upon cleaning requirements and service deadlines, and to discuss any issues that arose.

Did you choose Candidate 2?

(If it wasn't, then boy have I got a lot of convincing to do!)

Not all job titles make it clear as to what tasks you performed in a former job role. In the above example, I didn't provide you with a position title, yet when you read through the second candidate's skill statements, it becomes clear exactly what the person did (it doesn't for the first candidate). And it also demonstrates the person's performance within that role.

The reason Candidate 2's resume is better is because it provides the reader with those greater details about the type of work previously performed. You immediately gain a fairly accurate picture of their ability level and the range of duties, as well as the benefits Candidate 2 would bring to a Commercial Cleaner role.

From a hiring manager perspective, firstly I've switched from skim reading to actual reading because my attention is grabbed by those numbers and action words. Next, I can see that this candidate has put in time and effort into creating their resume – with the aim of educating me on who they are, what they can do and how suitable they are for this type of work. They were successful and have done a good job in that; and, this sounds like the type of person we are after: Candidate 2 has the skills and experiences, and it would be good for me to now see if this person has the personality, attitude and characteristics to match what our organisation is seeking. So, my logical choice is to put this candidate's application off to one side for me to come back to, or, if the candidate's application stands out as the person being the Best of the Best compared to the quality of all the other applications, I might feel compelled to take immediate action to contact them, to make sure they are still available (this is true if I don't review resumes as I receive them).

Meanwhile Candidate 1 is telling (again); they have just listed a couple of cliché, typical, basic bullet points (skills that were already listed in their summary section, I might add), and therefore has clearly not put in much time and effort with creating their resume as they ought to (and are now just repeating details to fluff out their resume length rather than providing quality content). Although I can guess quite a lot about what their personality and attributes are (mostly negative), I'm still not any the wiser about what this person can do or why they would be suitable to our Commercial Cleaner vacancy.

Right Your RESUME

What a waste of an opportunity.

As the hiring manager, I've been able to continue with my bored skim reading of resumes, and with this one nothing has captured my interest or gotten me excited to cause me to want to read any of the bullet points. So I come to the end of the document and my decision is easy. This person is clearly not suitable for our vacancy; so their application is automatically tossed onto my rejection pile. I started out – and remained – bored by that applicant's resume; that's why I wouldn't want to learn more about them.

And even if these two applicants were applying for, say, a Customer Service role rather than a Cleaner one, it would simply be a matter of both candidates rearranging the order of how those skill statements are listed, and I would see the beginnings of benefits that Candidate 2 would have for a Customer Service role too.

Again, Candidate 1 does nothing to convince me of their potential suitability for this type of role either.

Candidate 1

Duties:

- Customer Service
- Time Management
- Industrial Cleaning

Or,

Candidate 2

Duties:

- Liaised with customers to agree upon cleaning requirements and service deadlines, and to discuss any issues that arose.
- Planned the order of jobs and site visits to ensure tasks were completed on time, rubbish would be collected in the quickest possible time-frame and that tasks were fully completed before building security alarms automatically activated at 11 p.m.
- Cleaned 3 commercial premises each weeknight ensuring that facilities were sanitised, rubbish was removed and floors were vacuumed.

Part 4
Employment HISTORY

As a hiring manager I have developed too many questions that are left unanswered over Candidate 1.

- *How and where did you develop customer service skills?*
- *What things did you do to build and maintain relationships.*
- *Anyone can serve customers but were you good at it?*
- *Did you go out of your way to provide good service.*
- *How do you manage your time?*
- *What range of industrial cleaning work did you do?*

Unanswered questions are bad. Not providing some clear details is bad.

As you can see, the difference between having a poor resume, a so-so resume or a fantastic one ultimately depends on whether the person adequately and effectively demonstrates their competence to do the work. And that is achieved by answering the hiring manager's mental questions *before* they start asking them.

Take an evidence and achievement based approach

Demonstrating competence on paper is the writing of evidence and achievement based skill statements. This is achieved through the inclusion and use of:

- Examples from a wide range of relevant tasks (duties), responsibilities, accountabilities, skills and experience from your previous position to demonstrate your capabilities for the type of work you seek to gain
- Strong, active words
- Quality descriptions of specific details
- Numbers and quantities
- Results and outcomes
- Past achievements and accomplishments
- Targeted, positive language

This is why I recommended using a **combination** or **chronological** resume structure rather than the **functional** resume style.

Right Your RESUME

Functional resumes by their very nature do not include these key duties, responsibilities and accountabilities skill statements at all, which is counter-productive when the majority of employers are looking for these very specifics! And it is that absence of details which can lead them to thinking the applicant has low skills, low performance and or problematic history the person is trying to hide.

Work in stages

Remember earlier I advised that you work in stages. The skill statements that you see in Candidate 1's skill statements are what you are aiming to write down when working in Stage One. Things like:

- I served customers
- I had to manage my time
- I needed to juggle competing priorities
- I had to clean to high standards
- I had to finish everything before security alarms kicked in at 11 p.m.
- Etc.

The difference between Candidate 1 and Candidate 2 is that Candidate 2 then spent additional time to rework a basic list, spent time converting those bland points into effective skill statements.

During stage one of creating your skill statements you need to write down as many statements as you can. To do this is easier than most people think. Ask yourself the question 'what were my....?' and then look at each of the following areas:

- Duties
- Accountabilities
- Responsibilities
- Achievements
- Accomplishments

Part 4
Employment HISTORY

So your questions become:

- 'What were my duties?'
- 'What were my accountabilities?'
- 'What were my responsibilities?'
- 'What achievements did I have?'
- 'What were my accomplishments?'

If you don't have a long list at the end of this, then you aren't letting yourself to think deep or wide enough. You want to have way more detail than what you need or will use.

Having completed this first stage, you can place a tick against that bullet list earlier of providing 'examples from a wide range of relevant tasks, responsibilities, accountabilities, skills and experience from your previous positions...'

Now that you have that list, you can then look to see where you might have repeated yourself, so you can combine points and or scale your list back a bit. For example, you might have answered under what were your duties with 'serve customers' and you might have answered under what were my responsibilities with 'to provide the customer with a positive experience'.

That is two entries under the one 'umbrella' of Customer Service as being one of your skills and experience.

Where Candidate 1 went wrong is that once they had their list, they then converted that list into Skill Summary listing on their resume, like this:

- Customer Service
- Time Management
- Industrial Cleaning

(Customer Service, Time Management and Industrial Cleaning are the skill categories.)

But we already did that earlier in the Summarised Information section; what you need to do is convert your basic list into quality Skill Statements instead.

Right Your RESUME

That is, you need to work towards demonstrating your competence for the type of work sought, by incorporating the remainder of the evidence and achievement based particulars:

- Strong, active words
- Quality descriptions of specific details
- Numbers and quantities
- Results and outcomes
- Past achievements and accomplishments
- Targeted, positive language

Because, the best skill statements use strong active verbs, provide details that (briefly and concisely) explain the 'who, what, where, when, why and how', and quantify the result which demonstrates your benefit for the potential employer.

And the good news is: I have a simple formula to help you write them!

Skill statement formula

Following a simple but powerful skill statement formula (that resume writer's use) enables you to turn a long, boring list of duties into strong skill statements that hiring managers love reading too.

That formula is:

> **Strong Active Verb + Specific Details + Results**
> **= Strong Skill Statement**

Let's discuss each part before we start putting it all together to write or right our work history listings.

Strong action words

These are 'action words' that accurately conveys the exact meaning intended with strength and conviction, and implies activeness (in movement or forward progression). For example, notice the difference between the following strong and weak action words:

Part 4
Employment HISTORY

Strong

Implemented – (the task went from not being done to completed)

Weak

Started – (means the task was started, but doesn't necessarily mean it was finished)

Strong

Won – (implies personal effort was put in)

Weak

Gained – (implies it happened, but is likely to have happened with or without your personal effort)

The key to strong action words is to consider whether an individual word sets the intention that you took action knowingly and deliberately, or whether the action occurred with or without your active involvement to bring about the result.

I have included a small alphabetised list of Action Words in the Appendix section of this book, but you could also do a search in any Search Engine, like Google, Bing or Yahoo, for the words 'Action Verbs' to find numerous sources offering greater lists of Strong Action words that you could use.

So go ahead, obtain a copy of words for resumes and then start revising each of your most important and relevant duties so that they start with strong, active verbs.

Let's now start using that formula to turn your list into strong skill statements!

Specific details

Choose a skill. Pick an appropriate Action word that best describes what you did. Let's say you wrote down:

'Supervised staff'.

Once you have chosen your strong, active verb to start your skill statement ('Supervised' is strong, and appropriate for this entry), your next task is to provide the specific details that explain the 'who, what, where, when, why and or how'.

Right Your RESUME

You do not need to explain **all** of the details (that is, all of the 'who, what, where, when, why and how'), you just need to explain the most *relevant* aspects.

We know you wrote 'staff', so that adequately explains the 'who' detail, but can you be more specific? Yes.

> **Supervised** (strong, active verb) **kitchen hand and customer service** (specific details) **staff** (the 'who').

Let's try another one:

> **Sold** (strong, active verb) **pallets** (specific detail) **of beer cartons** (the 'what').

Notice I didn't just write 'Sold beer cartons', because it doesn't adequately describe 'how' those beer cartons were sold. For instance, I could have sold beer cartons individually or by the pallet, so the word 'pallet' clarifies that I was selling multiple cartons of beer at once.

Although these skill statements are a huge improvement compared to Candidate 1's bland skill statements, we can still make these details even more interesting to hiring managers by adding numbers and quantifiable amounts.

Quantifiable amounts

Just as leaving out the word 'pallets' didn't adequately describe how beer cartons were sold, we also don't have any information yet to help hiring manager's to understand the volume level of our performance.

To do this we need to start adding *numbers* and *quantity amounts*.

For instance, one receptionist might answer ten (10) calls ***a day***, another might answer ten (10) ***an hour***, and yet another might have ten (10) phone **lines ringing all at once**! Each of those receptionists answers phone calls – but their workload (for completing just that one duty) varies greatly. I don't know about you, but if I was that last receptionist in particular, I would *want* the hiring manager to understand and appreciate just how busy my role was compared to my competition.

But, rather than telling them that '*I was busy*', it is better to **demonstrate** how busy the role was, by providing the specifics that show the volume of calls answered within a set period.

Part 4
Employment HISTORY

Numbers also carry the power, when written in numerical form rather than in word form, to jump out at readers. Because our brains see and understand the graphics faster than comprehending text, listing numbers can contribute to converting the hiring manager from skim reading to reading.

So, your next step is to add numbers to your skill statements, wherever possible.

For example

Earlier we wrote that we supervised kitchen hand and customer service staff members. So now the hiring manager would logically ask themselves, '*How many staff did you supervise?*'

Answer that question *now*, in your resume, rather than leaving it for an interview; because doing this allows the hiring manager to start imagining you in their vacancy, trying you on for possible fit (and that is a great thing!). So our earlier skill statement now becomes:

> **Supervised** (strong, active verb) **3** (quantifiable amount) **kitchen hand and customer service** (specific details) **staff members** (the 'who')

As hiring manager, I am going to see you as a good fit if your numbers closely match what will be required in our vacancy – a 'you've managed three staff members, and our position needs the person to manage three staff members'. But let's say you have less than what they are after. In this case, you've demonstrated that you have the skill, but maybe not quite at the level they are looking for. The hiring manager might decide that you are still potentially suitable – with a bit of training up. Or, that you just don't have the higher skill level that they need. Yes, your application will probably be rejected if that is the decision they reach, but you aren't going to be a perfect fit for every vacancy and at least you gave yourself a fair chance to be viewed as potentially suitable. And, you never know; if they don't get a better qualified candidate, they might reconsider your application.

If you have supervised a bit more than what they are after, then the hiring manager is probably becoming increasingly interested in you as a potential for the job, but if the level was significantly more, then they may view you as being overqualified. But, let's also remember that we are only looking at one detail in isolation, and the hiring manager is going to be weighing up from all of your history compared to other applicants.

When providing specific details think 'quantifiable', or 'proven'. A quantifiable amount is a number – in dollars, time, or rank. And any promotion, award

Right Your RESUME

or other formal recognition helps prove your strong and or exceptional performance, which demonstrates your value to potential employers.

For example

Sold (*strong, active verb*) **$50,000** (*quantifiable amount – dollars*) **worth of pallets** (*specific detail – of the 'what'*) **each month** (*time frame + implied benefit to potential employer*)

Achieved (*strong, active verb + direct achievement*) **No 1. in Sales Performance** (*quantifiable amount = rank + specific detail of Award = 'proven'*) **for January and March sales** (*time frame + specific detail*)

Promoted (*strong, active verb*) **from Sales Rep to Sales Manager to Area Sales Manager to State Sales Manager** (*specific job title details, demonstrating multiple progression*) **over a three year period** (*time frame*) (*+ the implied benefit to the potential employer is that the person is likely to continue to demonstrate strong performance and is likely to continue in their career progression*)

Results

Above all else, hiring managers like to learn about results and outcomes you gained within your previous work performance. Numbers and specifics are great, but results and outcomes help convince them of the implied benefits of high performance.

For example

Supervised (*strong, active verb*) **3** (*quantifiable amount*) **kitchen hand and customer service** (*specific details*) **staff members** (*the 'who'*) **to ensure** (*strong, active verb + goal*) **working safely while meeting food service deadlines** (*the result + implied benefit to the employer – responsibility*).

Sold (*strong, active verb*) **$50,000** (*quantifiable amount – dollars*) **worth of pallets** (*specific detail – of the 'what'*) **each month** (*time frame + implied benefit to potential employer*) **resulting in consistently exceeding monthly Sales target** (*the result + implied benefit*)

We now have:

- Strong, Active words
- Quality descriptions of specific details
- Numbers and quantities

Part 4
Employment HISTORY

- Results and outcomes
- Past achievements and accomplishments

That leaves us with:

- Targeted, positive language

I cannot reiterate strongly enough that jobseekers must sell themselves to potential employers if they stand any chance of gaining success.

Too often I have seen resumes where the jobseeker does not target the type of work they are hoping to gain, and or frame their wording so that they talk about what they **can't do**, and aspects that they **don't want**.

If you use the Skill Statement formula as described above, then your statements will naturally be positive; and if you are selective about which skills and experiences so they not only demonstrate what you did in the past but also so that it focuses on what you want to do in the future, then your skill statements are mostly likely hitting the 'targeted' element too.

But those negative elements – the 'can't' and 'don't' – do not belong in a resume. If you see them in your resume or cover letter, remove them at once, because it is a clear signal that you are taking the wrongful *'me-centred'* view instead of the *'YOUnique employer-focused'* one.

So, you now have the knowledge to work through your raw list of paid and unpaid work and development history to turn short bullet points of initial ideas into strong skill statements. Then, once you have written all these down, you can do a 'spit and polish' to ensure that you have everything just right, and move on to the final stages of editing and proofreading.

Mistakes to avoid...

Use personal achievements, not those of the company

One of the mistakes I have noticed lately occurring with greater frequency on the resumes I have assessed is that some jobseekers in their desire to ensure they have 'achievements' in their resume are listing the achievements of the company they worked for rather than their own personal achievements.

Don't make this mistake; the company you worked for isn't trying to get a job, is it? When you read the advice 'make sure your resume is achievement-based' it means your own personal achievement, not the companies (unless you were sole trader). And, as we can see by the skill statement formula, our details are now achievement based.

Be careful not to give away 'trade secret' information of former employers that could get you in trouble.

When writing your employment skill statements, although you need to anchor your competence through use of specifics, you must still take care not to expose yourself to negative consequences by ensuring you are not giving away your former employers trade secret information. Or you could find yourself in hot water. That is, trouble. Legal trouble, you'd be better off without.

Trade Secret Scenario

Let's say that for the past five years you worked for the company Griffiths Wholesale as their Sales Rep. And, you were so good at your job that the company let you handle their top three client accounts, which includes the much sought after Mercile Holdings. Every one of Griffith Wholesale's competitors would love to know who has Mercile Holdings account and would gladly love a crack at winning their business – and have a contract all prepared just in case they ever get such an opportunity.

Specifying in your resume that you managed Mercile Holdings account could cause problems for you and or Griffiths Wholesales. For starters, the company's competitors, upon receiving your application, may invite you in for an interview – not because they are considering you for the vacancy (no they can't afford to pay someone at your rate no matter how good they are), but so they can try and learn a bit more about Mercile Holdings to give them an edge at stealing away their business from Griffiths. Not only are you wasting your time and money in attending a job interview that you are never going to be offered, not only are you being tricked into providing a competitor with information, but you could have inadvertently exposed yourself to litigation by Griffiths and or Mercile for having revealed trade secret information.

The point here is that although you need to be as specific as possible in your skill statements, that doesn't mean you can throw any old specifics in there.

In the above scenario, you could still effectively demonstrate your competence by writing 'Managed the top three major accounts for the company' rather than 'Managed Mercile Holdings, Standles Inc. and Brinkles Storage'. The words 'major accounts' is still a specific detail

Part 4
Employment HISTORY

(though granted it carries less weight than naming the specific companies). If you want to provide the specifics in your resume, I suggest you obtain the companies permission to list the specific detail – maybe there is a non-disclosure clause in the contract they have with Mercile (which is why they would sue you for breaching the terms and conditions), maybe they wouldn't want competitors to find out the detail because they are in negotiations to secure contract renewal.

In this scenario above, the use of the simple term 'Key Account' or 'Major Account' would suffice. And would sufficiently protect you from unforeseen ramifications.

Showcase the range

Show your range of duties, responsibilities, accountabilities and accomplishments. Don't bloat by saying the **same thing** in **multiple ways**.

Most job roles, with the exception of perhaps production line or factory work, involves the person completing lots of different tasks rather than just the repetition of the same solo task.

Take for instance a 'Commercial Cleaner', who not only wipes down hard surfaces to keep them hygienic and clean, but might also empty out rubbish bins, vacuum and mop floors, and launder towels and surface covers like table cloths.

When you write your work and development history skill statements, you need to showcase the range of tasks you performed and ensure your highest skills are given priority over lesser skills.

Sometimes it helps to think about what you did using certain categories such as Customer Service, Technical knowledge, Communication, Time Management and Administration (to name but a few).

Would a Commercial Cleaner provide Customer Service? They might not directly serve customers as a core task, but overall the cleaner would have to work to the customers instructions and perform to a level of quality that the client would be satisfied with.

What about Technical knowledge? This could be a core part of their role, especially if they have to know how to use specialized equipment (commercial vacuum cleaners and floor polishers), or if they have to mix chemicals. All of which involves using technical knowledge and skills.

Right Your RESUME

The person, even though they mostly work alone and after office hours, would need to possess good time management skills, as they would be required to work to the time frames they set or are given, and may need to manage their cleaning schedule because they have multiple customers at multiple locations.

You could consider your tasks and skills from the following categories. You might like to use this small list as a starting point:

- Initiative
- Administration
- Communication
- Customer Focus
- Creativity
- Data and Analytics
- Financial
- Interpersonal / Self Management
- Management and Leadership
- Organisation
- Problem solving
- Decision making
- Research
- Technical Knowledge
- Training and Development
- Service Delivery
- Operational Delivery
- Business Development

The list is not comprehensive, by any standards. You should think about the industry and position and what is expected and accomplished within the role to help you with widening the range of tasks.

Be careful not to 'bloat' the resume with repetitive details, e.g. don't say the same thing in lots of different ways

The problem to avoid with writing your duties, responsibilities and key accountabilities when writing your own resume is to not 'bloat' your content with repetitive details. It is better to give more substance, show your full range

Part 4
Employment HISTORY

of duties, than to demonstrate the same task or skill in multiple ways. You know, saying the same thing, over and over; to pad the list with 'fluff' detail.

For example, with our cleaner above, it is better to address customer service, technical knowledge, communication, time management and administration rather than come up with lots of different things that they clean e.g., wipe down surfaces, polish surfaces, vacuum and mop floors.

OKay, okay, I've had my fun and will now stop!

What to exclude...

We have covered in quite depth and scope the type of information that needs to be included in the work and development history section. Now I want to cover f the details that a lot of jobseekers include in their resume which they shouldn't. The main reason is that they are simply not necessary, and to include them puts you at risk of providing additional details that enable the hiring manager to make a no decision.

Explanations

Another mistake I see frequently in resumes is the person explaining something that can be viewed as negative by the hiring manager.

Don't emphasise a negative element that is included – and really, does the negative have to even be included? Can't it be omitted, or somehow be turned into a positive?

If you do have to explain something, leave it for the job interview, and, let the hiring manager raise the issue. That doesn't mean you shouldn't think about how you will answer 'tricky' questions (which is what you are trying to do on paper, probably because you feel more confident in your explanation when it is put down on paper rather than when spoken because you can control your words on paper so your meaning is clear and less likely to be misunderstood, which you don't have as much control with spoken words).

Reasons for leaving

We all have reasons for leaving former employers. Sometime those reasons are positive ones but oftentimes, sadly, they are for negative ones.

But, that doesn't mean you add the reasons, positive or negative, into your resume. If a potential employer wants to know the reason you left a previous job, let them ask you why you left. And, when asked, you should put a positive spin on any negative experience or you will only make yourself look unsuitable to the potential employer.

If you tell the employer you left with the cranks because you didn't like the way management ran the place, that management could have been the most incompetent people around, but the hiring manager will almost always only interpret your saying this as *'This person doesn't know how to get along with people'*.

It is very rare that a *single* reason underlines our decision to find alternative employment.

Case Study

I once worked for a company in which I loved my job – I loved the people I worked alongside, I loved the work that I performed – but when we got a new Area Manager, the atmosphere suddenly changed from a place where everyone loved coming to work and happily pitched in to give each other a hand, to a place where staff were becoming miserable and self-oriented, fast.

Each week, one person was called into the Site Manager's office to have a meeting with the site manager and new Area Manager. And each week, that person came out upset and angry at having been told their performance was not good enough and that they needed to 'step up' their performance or their job was on the line.

When good, strong team members are summoned to such a meeting, and come out that fuming, upset and surprised by the formal written warning, I realised it was only a matter time before it inevitably would reach my turn to be summoned to have them say the same, unjust things. I wasn't prepared to stick around and watch our once lovely work environment completely turn into a horrible and nasty one for the sake of making the new Area Manager achieve 'increasing profits'. I justifiably felt that if I were to be summoned to that type of meeting it would be completely unwarranted. And, like most of my fellow colleagues, I was now ready to move on.

I was invited to attend a job interview and took a sneaky day off. During the interview, I was asked about why I would be happy to leave my position. I focused on the positives of the new role and what that meant for me, and at the end of truthfully telling that I would be working closer to home, be working slightly less hours and taking home slightly more

Part 4
Employment HISTORY

pay, the recruiting manager smiled and then said, 'So, it has nothing to do with your new Area Manager then?'

I agreed that the downturn in atmosphere was also an influence, but that it was a minor one as I was happy to stay in my role because although the new Area Manager was implementing changes and pushing for better performance, I could truthfully say, 'But I haven't received any written warnings, like some of the staff, so at this stage he must be happy with my performance', to which the hiring manager agreed but added bitterly, 'I'm sure he'll get to you eventually.'.

And I was offered the job because the hiring manager believed I wasn't leaving for negative reasons, and I accepted, happy to see the back of my previous job – the timing was absolutely perfect! Because the following day when I returned to work, I discovered my number was up; as I too had received an email advising me the date and time for me to meet with the manager and area manager scheduled for the following week to discuss my 'under-performance'.

My point here is you never know what the hiring manager knows about your company and situation. It just so happened in my instance, that this particular hiring manager knew of the area manager because they had both once worked for the same company, and the hiring manager knew exactly how bad the situation was about to get over at my employment because that area manager had a reputation of destroying good work environments, and overworking staff until they left in disgust (if they survived termination) – the hiring manager knew this because he was one of the ones that had left their former employer due to that area manager.

Pay rate and or salary expectations

Details of how much you were paid, and or your salary expectations for the job you are applying for should not be included on your resume.

Remember, during the application stage when you are sending out your resume, you are not already a potentially suitable candidate; you are only a candidate expressing interest in being considered for the role. You are not up to the stage of negotiating your employment conditions, so including this information is not only you jumping ahead of the process but it can be viewed as arrogant and pushy.

Your potential new employer does not need to know how much you were paid in your previous employment – not now, during the application stage. Think about it, not only can you cause a hiring manager to make a no decision

Right Your RESUME

because your previous positions were, say, $10,000 a year more than what they are offering (- are you likely to take such a significant pay cut?), but what if they were offering $10,000 more than what you had been getting (- how easy would it be for them to offer you the amount you had been receiving and save themselves from paying you the $10,000 they would have offered you had you not given them your pay details.

Pay rates and salary expectations may come into the hiring process, but usually once they have interviewed you and have decided to offer you the job, or they are still deciding between a couple of candidates and discuss pay expectations with each of the candidates to help them reach a decision.

So, no including details of your pay rate or salary expectations – it is an unnecessary detail that carries far more risk of causing a no decision and does nothing to help you gain an interview.

Capacity of employment

I discussed this at the beginning of this chapter but it is worth re-mentioning it now as we are in the what to exclude section.

Employers do not need to know the basis of your previous paid employment, so it is completely unnecessary (and even potentially damaging) to provide detail whether the position was full time, part time, on a casual basis, temporary or on a contract basis.

With the exception of full time, the rest can all 'diminish' your level of skill, knowledge and experience in that type of work or workplace task. Including the information can 'un-sell' you, which go against your aims in applying for the position.

For example, stating that you worked 10 hours per week while most full time positions fall somewhere between 37.5 hours to 42 hours per week, raises the Math that your skills and experience are only about a quarter to that of a full time employee – which sort of equates to you not believing that your length of experience is as valuable. It is you raising potential areas of concern for the hiring manager that they wouldn't otherwise have developed; and of course is also you creating a bad impression instead of a good one.

Company location

Most hiring managers aren't going to be interested in the suburb you worked in unless your application or the details are slightly unusual in

Part 4
Employment HISTORY

comparison to the average candidate. It is not that you mustn't add this detail; it is more a case of why put in information that is not absolutely necessary to help them see you as a potentially suitable option.

Having lots of lovely white space on a resume helps guide the readers eye down the page; the more the hiring manager reads, the more they are interested (or at the very least not finding things that are turning them off). As amateur document creators, we need to stop trying to fill in space, and start behaving more like professional graphic designers, by being highly selective about every single detail big and small. If it doesn't add value, or can be left out, it should be left out.

There may be some occasions when including the suburb of your former employment may be relevant, such as the potential employer needs the person to be familiar with that area, or you want to demonstrate your willingness to travel in order to fill the role. So, I'm not stating that excluding this tiny detail is a hard and fast rule; more a consideration that you need to think about and include for good, solid reason over adding any and every detail you can think of.

Right Your RESUME

Finetuning your resume...

Part 5.

Quote

FAIL =

    <u>F</u>irst
    <u>A</u>ttempt
    <u>I</u>n
    <u>L</u>earning

Unknown

Finetuning your resume

35 Consistency

One of the key indicators of a poor resume, apart from terrible formatting, is where the skill statements jump all over the place in both the person's thoughts and things like tense changes.

Before you consider your resume 'completed', review your resume content to ensure that you have consistently written strong skill statements (using the same formula), and that you have applied the same tense throughout each bullet point for that position.

36 Tense

As mentioned time and again throughout this book, you need to apply your elements consistently, and the same is true for the **tense** you use.

One technique that you can use, is to write your current position (or the last position you held, if it was recent) using **present tense.**

That is, your active verb, which starts your skill statement, uses the present tense:

Supervise 3 kitchen hand and customer service staff

Rather than using past tense:

Supervised 3 kitchen hand and customer service staff

And you consistently use present tense for *every* skill statement for that particular position.

Using present tense, on a subtle level, demonstrates that you are still employed and that your skills are current. Remember, employers like hiring known quantities over unknown quantities, so therefore will generally prefer a candidate who is still employed over one that has been out of work for any longer than a few weeks.

Then, all previous positions need to be written using **past tense**. This shows that it is in your past. And that you have good command of written communication. (If you don't, then you will need to seek help from someone who does, so your weakness in this area doesn't let you down.)

37 Wording

You also want hiring managers to see that you have created the resume your own self. Using a resume writer can sometimes be another of those double-edged swords in that the person's resume is likely to stand out in a good way, and most resumes that stand out in a positive way are oftentimes written by a resume writer rather than the person (unless the person has exceptional document creation and writing skills).

So, if you are a person who is applying for less skilled positions and struggle with spelling and grammar, although I urge you to get the help you need so that weakness is not glaringly obvious to hiring managers, do not try to use more impressive sounding words than what you would naturally write and speak in your normal everyday life.

For that reason, don't use do a 'Joey Tribani' [from the television show, Friends] who in one episode 'rewrote' his entire wedding speech for Monica and Chandler's upcoming wedding using the **synonym** feature of his word processor after recently discovering this feature and its benefit. So that although technically saying the same thing resulted in hardly anyone understanding his intended speech, and making him look foolish and ignorant in the eyes of those who knew better.

If you use simple words in everyday speech, then stay true to yourself. You are not going to impress a hiring manager by trying to make yourself seem more sophisticated than you are. That is just a trick, which hiring managers will quickly see as the lie that it is when you start speaking and such 'bigger words' don't roll off your tongue with ease.

38 Positivity

Do not include details of what you can't do, or what you don't want to do in your resume. All information provided to hiring managers needs to be positive if you want them to treat your application seriously. The words 'can't' and 'don't' etc indicate a negative mindset. Hiring managers don't want to hire negative people who can bring productivity and morale down, so avoid showing this shadow side to human nature where possible. If you have a can't or don't requirement in relation to the role, then maybe you shouldn't apply for that type of role or for that vacancy.

And for people with Depression, you should definitely seek assistance from another person (that does not suffer from Depression) with writing your resume and cover letter sentences, so that the negative side of your condition doesn't reveal itself in your application materials. (And it would be a good idea for you to undertake interview practice ahead of getting job interviews, so that any negativity doesn't come through in how you answer job interview questions also.

39 Numbers

Numbers jump off the page and capture a reader's attention when they appear as numbers rather than text because the number becomes a **visual element**, which as discussed earlier our brains process 66,000 times faster than it does text and is more appealing and interest-generating. For this reason, you should write your numbers using numbers not words.

For example

Don't write:	three
Write:	3
Don't write:	one thousand dollars
Write:	$1,000
Don't write:	five percent
Write:	5%

Also, whereas sales people are trained to 'break numbers down to their smallest possible value', as a way of encouraging prospective customers to see, understand and appreciate the affordability of a product or service, the opposite is true for jobseekers.

Take all numbers **up** to their largest possible value, so hiring managers can see, understand and appreciate your value and the implied greater benefit to their company.

For example

Instead of:	Double
Write:	200%
Instead of:	2 years
Write:	24 months
Instead of:	1 Quarter
Write:	3 months, or better still, write *26 weeks* because that number is higher

40 Priority of information

I cannot stress how important listing your skill statements in order of priority from most important to least important detail in each of your positions included can help or hinder your being considered potentially suitable for the job or not.

If your previous position title piques a hiring manager's interest, the next step is to hold on to that interest so that it builds into desire to learn more about you. When you don't prioritise the skill statement listing, you risk causing their interest to wane.

Don't bury the really important details by having them as the second or fourth item in a list. Maintain their interest by keeping the reader mentally ticking off boxes – "*Yes, we need someone with that skill*" and "*Oh, and that's good performance*" makes the lesser skills and abilities even more attractive than they otherwise would have been.

Hiring manager's will be more inclined to read the first and last few skill statements rather over the middle ones, so make sure your best skill statements are positioned at the beginning and end.

41 Get your spelling, punctuation and grammar right, and proofread before sending out!

Since I joined one of the jobseeker groups in August 2013, about once a month a (heated) debate arguing for or against the need for perfect spelling, grammar and punctuation flares up – showing just how strong people's opinions can be on the matter.

On the one hand, there is the side that strongly believes and touts *'make sure your spelling, grammar and punctuation is perfect'*, which the opposition dubs (and name calls) such believers *'the grammar police'*. On the other side are those who believe *'spelling, grammar and punctuation shouldn't matter, it is more the person's ability to do the job that matters'*, that the 'grammar police' dub (and name call) are people who are *'lazy, not serious enough about their jobsearch'*.

Every flare up, which quickly turned into a hotly-contested debate, many time which Admin ended up having to delete the entire discussion because of how nasty and personal the attacks towards people holding the opposing view could become, started off with either a jobseeker or recruiter (usually relatively new to this particular highly active Facebook group) who had observed the many 'looking for work' pitches members have posted, and the comments and enquiries jobseekers had made into employers vacancy posts and decided to *'offer a bit of advice to jobseekers'* about the need to ensure they check their spelling, punctuation and grammar before hitting the post button. And members who usually just lurked in the background competed with regular commenter's and vehemently attempted to get the opposition to see *their* (opposing) viewpoint.

Right Your RESUME

I don't wish to start (nor do I participate in those) heated debates because I respect people's right to have an opinion that differs from my own. I don't try to force people to see my point of view; so equally, I don't argue or fight other people when they express a point of view I disagree with. And frankly, I don't care about the issue deep enough to want to go into battle with others. (But I will defend myself when I am subject to personal attack.)

But I have written this book with the aim of *helping jobseekers* improve their chances of getting invitations to attend job interviews, so need to address this hotly contested issue is warranted.

For the record, I believe that it is better for jobseekers to send out a resume that adheres to the principles of good and correct spelling, grammar and punctuation for resumes, and that jobseekers who don't get it right for whatever reason (…lack of skill or laziness…) can miss out on being considered a potential candidate for the job because of not striving to make sure each element is the best it could possibly be.

But, just as there are *jobseekers* who either value or don't value the importance of good spelling, punctuation and grammar in a resume, so too are there *employers* who either value or don't value this.

Regardless of a person's personal stance on the issue, if you are a jobseekers who **doesn't** value 'getting it right' and you send your application to an employer who **does** value this, then that employer is not going to see you as being potentially suitable for their role – so your application is simply a waste of yours, and the employers, time.

If you are a jobseeker who **does** value the effect of good spelling, grammar and punctuation and the employer **doesn't** hold this fact up to the same high regard, then the fact that you have put in the additonal time and effort isn't going to negatively affect your application in the slightest – it just won't give you the competitive edge you were hoping for.

Me personally, I would rather put the extra time and effort into making my application the best it can possibly be. But, for the grammar police and their opposition, it maybe helpful to understand that a resume has slightly altered grammar rules to normal writing letters and reports.

Resume writing has its own style

For one thing, even though a resume is all about the person and strives to be YOUnique, the word 'I' is completely dropped when writing skill statements (sentences). So the person doesn't write, 'I taught children', instead

Finetuning your RESUME

they write 'Taught children'. Dropping the 'I' tightens that skill statement up.

Imagine a resume where *every* skill statement in a long bullet list started with the word 'I'. Watch how tedious this would become for the hiring manager with every applicant writing:

- I did this.
- I did that.
- I did this as well.
- I did this also.
- I did this and this.
- I did that and that.
- I did this and that.
- I did that and this.

A resume is already about a single person. All those 'I' statements make the person seem like they only think and care about them self.

(To the sound of vocal warming up):

Me, me, me, me, me, me, me.

Me, me, me, me, me, me, me.

From a READERS perspective, it is very off-putting to read the word 'I' all the time.

In real life, if we meet someone new and they talk non-stop about themselves we soon become bored by what they are talking about and uninterested in them as a person. We think to ourselves, something to the effect of, '*What a self-centred person*' – a *negative thought* in response to the *negative impression*. Writing the word 'I' on the page creates a similar negative response in a reader – and because we are sending out our resumes to **hiring managers**, we don't want *them* becoming bored by *anything* we have to say or how we say it. We don't want them forming the negative opinion that we are self-centred.

See – and feel – how less 'self-centred' those same sentences read now with just the word 'I' removed:

- Did this.
- Did that.
- Did this as well.

Right Your RESUME

- Did this also.
- Did this and this.
- Did this and that.
- Did this and that.
- Did that and this.

It reads stronger and feels more purposeful, less self-absorbed and more reader-friendly. The statements (which will each contain different points, or key messages) will become less repetitive.

So the first spelling, grammar punctuation alteration for resume writing is: drop the personal pronoun "I" from your skill statements (and avoid using too much of it in your cover letters too).

Next, is the matter of punctuating in resumes.

Punctuation in resumes

Bullet points, like those above, **do not** require a **full stop** (period). In letters and reports etc., you can change the sentence, "I went to the shops and bought, apples, pears, oranges, mangoes and peaches' into bullet list form, which looks like:

I went to the shops and bought:

- Apples
- Pears
- Oranges
- Mangoes
- Peaches

For each item in the list separated by a comma (when writing as a sentence) the item is listed in bullet form *as its own line*.

One of the purposes in using bullet points is to minimise the use of punctuation, so commas and full stops (periods) are *not needed*. (The other purpose is to make the information easier to read).

After you have created a bullet list, the equivalent of the next sentence in a paragraph becomes the start of a new paragraph, like my words '*For each item...*' above.

Finetuning your RESUME

In letter or report writing, you might be required (depending on which style convention you are following) to place a full stop at the end of 'peaches' to demonstrate the end of the bullet list. In effect, instead of writing a sentence and allowing the items to flow across the page, separated by a comma and ending in a full stop, you are instead introducing the topic and then listing each of the items in a bullet list so that the reader can see the items better.

Resume writing is its own 'art form' and does not rigidly follow *all* the rules of good grammar and punctuation.

So the second spelling, grammar and punctuation alteration for resume writing is: *no comma or full stop punctuation required in bullet lists.*

But this rule applies to ***single sentence*** skill statements.

In the above 'items purchased' list, each of the single sentence statements contained one word only (e.g. 'apples', 'pears', etc.); but single sentence statements containing multiple words should also follow the 'no punctuation required in bullet lists' rule. For example, my earlier 'did this and that' list should have no full stop or comma punctuation:

- Did this
- Did that
- Did this as well
- Did this also
- Did this and this
- Did this and that
- Did this and that
- Did that and this

Capitalising letters falls under the umbrella of 'punctuation'. And you will notice that each of the items in the list start the single sentence (multi word) skill statements with a Capitalised first word. So that is why the rule is '*no comma or full stop punctuation is required...*' rather than a '*no punctuation is required...*'

The reason is that some punctuation actually assists the reader to better understand what is written. Capitalising the first word helps the reader to ***transition*** from reading the end of the previous line to the beginning of the one below. Usually there are different letters starting off a new sentence, and our brains pick up where our eyes need to go to because it has already registered the basic *shape* of the bullet list and the Capitalised letter:

- Customer Service
- Teamwork
- Administration
- Time Management
- Supervision
- Marketing
- Sales

Now, so far we have discussed *single sentences* with *single or multiple words*, but we also have *multiple sentences* that can be turned into bulleted lists.

You won't normally find these in a resume (or, more accurately, you shouldn't!). They are great in articles and blog posts, but don't have a good place within a resume. But, when you do see multi-sentence bullet lists, as a general rule they should use *full proper* spelling, grammar and punctuation, including use of commas and full stops at the end otherwise such greater explanation lists will be hard to read and understand.

And vs. ampersand (&)

A lot of businesses replace the word '*and*' with the *ampersand* symbol (&), for example, John & Co.

In a resume section heading – for example, Licences, Tickets and Checks – you could use the short cut by listing the section as 'Licences, Tickets & Checks' instead, and that is okay as a *Style choice*. But a couple of things to keep in mind: never replace the word 'and' in a *proper sentence*, and if you do use the symbol in one section heading, then you need to do the same in any other heading that has multiple items being grouped so you are applying the style consistently.

Correct:	Licences, Tickets and Checks
(Consistent use)	Education, Training and Qualifications
Correct:	Licences, Tickets & Checks
(Consistent use)	Education, Training & Qualifications

Finetuning your RESUME

Wrong:	Licences, Tickets & Checks
(Inconsistent use)	Education, Training and Qualifications
Wrong:	Licences, Tickets and Checks
(Inconsistent use)	Education, Training & Qualifications

I prefer to use proper spelling throughout the resumes I create, and therefore use the word 'and' rather than substitute with the ampersand symbol because none of my Section Headings are longer than a single line entry, so I'm not trying to conserve space.

When I look at the section headings above, the Licences, Tickets and Checks looks cleaner and better to me than the line where I used the '&', but like I said, this one is a personal preference and other people, you included, might prefer the ampersand over the word 'and'.

Spelling

When it comes to spelling, the **normal writing rules apply**.

Use the correct spelling for names of businesses, places and items; the only time it would be appropriate to misspell a word is when the business name, the place or item carries an incorrect spelling, which on a technicality demonstrates that you have spelled the misspelled word correctly.

For example, let's say we have a business called 'Reel Estate Agent', where the word 'reel' would normally be spelled 'real', and the business is located in 'Somtown' instead of 'some town'. Perhaps this particular business is located by the ocean and deals with the buying and selling of boathouses, so chose to capitalise upon their dual roles of being a real estate agency with that of using a fishing reel to represent their specialising in boathouse sales – it would make the person who came up with the business name 'clever' and having been intentionally market savvy rather than a poor speller (though they could have just been a poor speller and it was just a lucky coincidence that their mistake serves a double purpose).

The point here is YOU shouldn't be the reason for the misspelling of a common word within your job applications.

Even people who are poor spellers are often able to see a spelling error when they come across one; they pick up on that it is spelled wrong even when they don't know what the correct spelling is.

Right Your RESUME

And readers will see that the unusual or mistake in spelling is not yours if the rest of the words on your resume are all spelled correctly.

If you aren't sure what the correct spelling or a word is, then you can use a Dictionary to try and work out what the correct spelling is, by playing around with different spelling combinations. For example, if you don't know the correct spelling for the word 'real', try sounding it out – Re Al or R Eel and look up both and read the meaning to establish which is correct.

If you are unable to work it out by using a dictionary, then perhaps try Microsoft Word (or other wordprocessing software). To do this, you can type what you think the word is supposed to spelled like, and then look for squiggly lines (in red, green or blue) underneath the word (which indicates that the program doesn't recognise that spelling, if the feature has been enabled), and perhaps use the inbuilt dictionary and Spell-check to show you possible choices to the clarify using a dictionary.

The last alternative is to type the word into Google. This is one of my favourite methods for clarifying word meanings and spelling. For example, earlier I wrote 'C'est le vie' within this book. I knew the meaning, and felt that the French phrase was appropriate for what I intended, but I wasn't sure of how it was spelled. So, I typed in Say la vie into Google, and the very first search result provided me with the correct spelling. Problem resolved quickly and easily!

Finetuning your RESUME

42. Photos, pictures and other such fancinesses

Another question that comes up from time to time is whether or not a person should include a photo of themselves on their resume.

If the type of working you will be applying for requires is creative in nature or requires advanced creative skills, such as Graphic Designers and Illustrators for example, then my answer is you are probably going to be taken more seriously for sending a resume that demonstrates your creative skill level than sending a plain-formatted resume. However, don't just go 'Woohoo' and then start sending a creative resume out to all employers; some may still prefer to receive a plain-formatted resume, and then ask you to bring a portfolio of your work with you to an interview.

For most mainstream jobs, the answer is a resounding 'No' you don't not include a photograph or other picture in your resume.

As mentioned early within this book, standing out doesn't mean do something different or gimmicky. Most employers are running professional businesses and are looking for professional individuals who will help them achieve their business goals, so doing things different to their expectations and being so different to every other candidate will achieve that you stand out to the hiring manager, but that doesn't necessarily make it a positive impression.

A graphical element, like a photograph or image can either work in your favour or do the exact opposite, and therefore you need to consider: is it relevant, is it appropriate, is it necessary, does it demonstrate you 'fitting in well?'

Including a photograph can cause the hiring manager to discriminate against you based on your *looks* rather than your skills, experiences and abilities. It might be suitable if you are applying to star in a television show or movie (because looks play a huge part in who gains a role), but we are talking about non-entertainment industry roles here – we are talking about the hospitality, retail, warehouse, administration and other mainstream employers, who have *no justifiable reason* to be hiring you based on your looks. (And most actors and television personalities apply to casting agents, film companies and television stations, and attend auditions, rather than respond to job advertisements).

Right Your RESUME

That doesn't mean you won't find the occasional job advertisement that asks for candidates to submit their photo – and when I see these, the first thing I ask myself is 'why?' What possible reason would an employer of, say, an admin role need to see a picture of the person during the application phase of the recruitment process? Employers that have ulterior motives probably: fake job advertisements by scammers wanting to steal a person's identity, sleazy employers who sexually harass young females, horrible employers who want to make sure the person isn't disabled or is older or younger than what they want (which is discriminatory to otherwise skilled and capable applicants!)

Do you need **other fanciful elements**, like coloured text or designer layouts? No. Again, for mainstream jobs, it is the candidate attempting to beat the competition by misusing the advice to 'stand out from the crowd' by interpreting that to mean 'do something different' instead of be targeted, specific and careful with the details.

Finetuning your RESUME

43 Leave out the labels

There is no need to 'label' or 'title' your resume with the words 'resume' or 'C.V.' inside the document – though using it within the document *file name* is okay. The reasons for not labelling are: firstly it wastes valuable prime resume real estate, and secondly it can create a negative impression in the reader.

As reiterated throughout this book, your goal is to generate employer interest, and when it comes time to build your electronic document to use your space well. As such, the topmost spot on the first page is the single most important space within your whole resume as it sets the reader expectation for the rest of the document; so it is a complete waste of your time and effort to gain attention if you start off with the wrong information by titling your resume with anything except your name and contact details because that is the information you want the person to remember.

Next, we must consider the impression we have on readers. It is obvious just by looking at a resume or C.V what the document or file is, because the *structure* and the *information provided* make it apparent despite the many varying styles. Stating the obvious – 'this is a resume' when it clearly is structured as one – can create a negative impression within the reader because it implies that the writer does not think the reader is smart enough to work that out without thyeir specifying what it is. Sledge-hammering again.

How would *you* feel if someone kept telling you what your name is? You'd think (and probably end up saying), '*Yeah, I know what my own name is, thank you!*' Well, it is similar thing for hiring managers who can identify a resume when they see one. It goes back to the 'Show, don't Tell' principle discussed earlier. **Show** hiring managers through structure and details that the document is a resume; ***don't tell*** them in the document itself (but included as part of the filename is okay).

Right Your RESUME

44 Saving your resume

Once you have typed up your resume you will need to save the file and give it a meaningful name so you can find it again in the future. I have a couple of quick tips for you to consider.

1. **Use a strong file name so that the hiring manager can find it on their computer, in amongst all the other resumes they receive.**

Don't call your document *resume.doc*... **please**. It might be the only resume on *your* computer but hiring managers can end up with hundreds, possibly thousands on theirs. If every applicant names and then sends in their resume with the filename *resume.doc*, how do they find yours?

And what impression are you making on the receiver when you name it *resume.doc*? The first thing a hiring manager has to do when they receive resumes with this file name is that they have to rename it so that they can tell who the resume belongs to. Which means they have to open it to find out. They are already irked at this oversight (a negative), so do you really want them to associate your name to that negative?

Next, there is a possibility, even though they weren't going to review resumes just yet, that they take a quick look at your resume. They are already irked. And if they skim read the resume and don't feel you have what they are looki8ng for, then rather than rename the file and store it in a folder so they can come back to it later, there is a chance they could decide your application isn't strong enough and will delete it immediately.

Eliminate this potential problem immediately. Name your resume file something meaningful to the employer, like *yourname.doc* (at a minimum). I personally like to *date* my resumes with the month that I currently am in when I applied for the role, so that the impression the employers gain when they receive it is that it is a fresh and current document (rather than a stale one, which I was happy for them to assume because it also equates to making me a freshly available candidate rather than one that has been looking for some time.)

For example

CharMesan_July 2014.doc

Finetuning your RESUME

If you are applying for more than one type of role, you could also distinguish between your different job roles you are applying for – to make it easy for yourself to send the right resume – by taking a similar approach with naming your file.

For example

    CharMesan_CaseManager_July2014.doc

2. **Have a dedicated Folder on your computer hard drive / storage device.**

There is nothing worse than not remembering, for whatever reason, *where* your resume is on your hard drive or storage device when you want to send off an application quickly.

Having a dedicated Folder on your hard drive or storage device makes it easier for you when it comes to applying for a job using a Job Board like Seek or My Career. I personally don't keep a copy of my resume on those sites for two (2) reasons. Firstly, because I jobsearch using my own computer and found that when I did hold such an account with these popular job boards I immediately started receiving high volumes of spam job emails. And secondly, I found it easier to send a tailored resume to the potential employer, and it is just as easy to choose the 'Browse computer' option and attach the file from a folder on the computer hard drive or storage device.

I created a dedicated Folder on my hard drive titled **Job Applications**, and have a sub-folder titled **Resumes**. In that folder I have yet another sub-folder titled **Previous versions**, so that I always keep a copy of older versions – which is useful for when I want to go back and re-add a section or particular skill statement that I had cut out of my current version (because it was irrelevant for the job I applied to but is relevant again for this next application).

I also keep a copy of *every* cover letter I send (even though I personally use the 'Write a cover letter now' option rather than having a generic letter), which makes it easier for me to work out which cover letter sent got fastest results and which didn't. That way, I can base the wording of my current application on the cover letters that I know worked well.

Right Your RESUME

Finetuning your RESUME

Appendix

Part 6.

Right Your RESUME

45 Action words

Achieved	Consolidated	Eliminated	Increased
Adapted	Constructed	Empathised	Influenced
Addressed	Consulted	Energised	Informed
Administered	Contracted	Enforced	Initiated
Advised	Contributed	Established	Inspired
Analysed	Controlled	Estimated	Instituted
Anticipated	Coordinated	Evaluated	Instructed
Appraised	Counselled	Examined	Integrated
Arbitrated	Created	Expanded	Interpreted
Arranged	Decided	Experimented	Interviewed
Assembled	Decreased	Explained	Introduced
Assessed	Defined	Extracted	Invented
Attained	Delegated	Filed	Inventoried
Audited	Designed	Financed	Investigated
Budgeted	Detected	Fixed	Involved
Built	Determined	Formulated	Judged
Calculated	Developed	Founded	Learned
Charted	Diagnosed	Gathered	Lectured
Checked	Directed	Generated	Led
Clarified	Discovered	Guided	Listened
Classified	Dispensed	Handled	Made
Coached	Displayed	Hauled	Maintained
Collected	Disproved	Headed	Managed
Communicated	Dissected	Helped	Manipulated
Compiled	Distributed	Hypothesised	Mediated
Completed	Doubled	Identified	Mentored
Composed	Drafted	Illustrated	Modelled
Computed	Dramatised	Implemented	Monitored
Conducted	Drew	Improved	Motivated
Conserved	Edited	Improvised	Multiplied

Finetuning your RESUME

Action words

Navigated	Purchased	Sensed	Trained
Negotiated	Questioned	Separated	Transcribed
Observed	Raised	Served	Transferred
Obtained	Realised	Set up	Translated
Offered	Reasoned	Shaped	Travelled
Opened	Received	Shared	Tripled
Operated	Recommended	Showed	Uncovered
Ordered	Reconciled	Simplified	Unified
Organised	Recruited	Sketched	Upgraded
Oversaw	Reduced	Sold	Used
Painted	Referred	Solved	Widened
Perceived	Rehabilitated	Spoke	Won
Performed	Related	Stimulated	Wrote
Persuaded	Remembered	Streamlined	
Piloted	Repaired	Strengthened	
Planned	Reported	Structured	
Played	Represented	Studied	
Predicted	Researched	Succeeded	
Prepared	Resolved	Summarised	
Prescribed	Responded	Supervised	
Presented	Restored	Supplied	
Processed	Retrieved	Supported	
Produced	Reviewed	Surveyed	
Programmed	Revised	Symbolised	
Projected	Revitalised	Systematised	
Promoted	Risked	Talked	
Proposed	Saved	Taught	
Protected	Scheduled	Team-built	
Provided	Screened	Tended	
Publicised	Selected	Tested	

Right Your RESUME

Quote

"The key is not to prioritise what is on your schedule, but to schedule your priorities."
Stephen R. Covey

Thank you

The last thing I want to tell you before I conclude this book is this simple advice:

Everyone is employable. Including YOU.

I hope you have found this book of great assistance, and that you now feel well equipped to carry forward with jobsearching and that your resume indeed stands out and impresses the hiring manager – so you have barely any competition and nail the job interview. I sincerely wish you all the best in gaining the type of work you seek and that you gain it quickly and easily.

If after you have created your resume you still have any doubts about whether the document you have created will hit the right mark as intended, then please visit my blog and arrange for me to do a Resume Assessment. Which, as a thank you for purchasing Right Your Resume: Fix or Create your Resume Content so you Stand Out and Impress the Hiring Manager, I'm happy to offer you at a 50% discount off the normal price – when you provide copy of original Receipt or relevant Proof of Purchase.

Char Mesan

Right Your RESUME

Connect with Char

Blogs

Right Your RESUME

To contact the author, access bonus content and to subscribe to future resume and jobsearch publications, visit:

> http://rightyourresume.blogspot.com

Char Mesan resumes & job training

To read articles and access Char Mesan resume and jobsearch services, visit:

> http://charmesanjobtraining.blogspot.com.au

Social media

You can find and connect with Char Mesan on social media:

- rightyourresume@gmail.com
- www.facebook.com/pages/Char-Mesan/134466020048932
- @CharMeJST
- +CharMesan
- http://www.pinterest.com/charmesan/

Finetuning your RESUME

Available now for purchase and instant download at:

http://charmesanjobtraining.blogspot.com.au

This resume content builder template has all the sections and dedicated space so you can easily fill in the form as you work on creating your resume content. The template, which you print out, also provides you with a neat and tidy visual structure which you could replicate when building your electronic version.

Leave a review

If you found the information in *Right Your Resume* helpful, please support the author by leaving a review at the retailer's site where you purchased the book from and or provide direct feedback to Char via Char Mesan's Right Your Resume blog found at:

> http://rightyourresume.blogspot.com

Bonus information

Any **Bonus information** relating to the contents of this book will be available at Right Your Resume blog.

www.ingramcontent.com/pod-product-compliance
Lightning Source LLC
LaVergne TN
LVHW061213060426
835507LV00016B/1905